D0147786

In Labor's Cause

In Labor's Cause

Main Themes on the History of the American Worker

David Brody

New York   Oxford
OXFORD UNIVERSITY PRESS
1993

Oxford University Press

Oxford   New York   Toronto
Delhi   Bombay   Calcutta   Madras   Karachi
Petaling Jaya   Singapore   Hong Kong   Tokyo
Nairobi   Dar es Salaam   Cape Town
Melbourne   Auckland   Madrid
and associated companies in
Berlin   Ibadan

Copyright © 1993 by Oxford University Press, Inc.

Published by Oxford University Press, Inc.
200 Madison Avenue, New York, NY 10016

Oxford is a registered trademark of Oxford University Press

All rights reserved. No part of this publication may be reproduced,
stored in a retrieval system, or transmitted, in any form or by any means,
electronic, mechanical, photocopying, recording, or otherwise,
without the prior permission of Oxford University Press.

Library of Congress Cataloging-in-Publication Data
Brody, David, 1930–
In labor's cause : main themes on the history
of the American worker / David Brody.
p. cm.   Includes bibliographical references.
ISBN 0-19-506790-8
ISBN 0-19-506791-6 (pbk.)
1. Trade-unions—United States—History.
2. Labor movement—United States—History.
  I. Title.
HD6508.B81125   1993
331.88'0973—dc20   92–42134

9 8 7 6 5 4 3 2 1

Printed in the United States of America
on acid-free paper

For Paul Goodman

Preface

The novella is a minor but useful literary form for the author who has too much to say to fit into a short story but not enough to fill up a novel. The essays in this collection are the historian's counterpart to the novella, negotiating a middle ground somewhere between the narrowly defined topic of the research article and the book-length treatment of a subject. Each essay starts with a question that under other circumstances might have led to a book but here is considered more briefly and without the authority granted by lengthy immersion in the sources. The limitations of such an enterprise are, of course, evident. But consider the advantages: for the historian, the opportunity to range widely and learn new things—self-education, so to speak, at the profession's expense; and for the reader, historical fare rich enough to feed but not exhaust the intellectual appetite. It is to such a reader that this collection of essays is addressed and, in particular, to students in upper-division courses and seminars who, beyond the text, want a more sustained—perhaps more stimulating—exploration of some of the main themes in American labor history.

So let me describe what this collection contains and suggest how it might best be read. The opening essay, like all the others, starts with a question: why, from 1791 onward, did American workers begin to demand a ten-hour day? Or, to give the issue its larger meaning, how did a modern time calculus implant itself in the consciousness of American workers? The answer to that question serves as a prism through which we can see how working people experienced the industrial revolution as it took hold in the early decades of the nineteenth century.

From this starting point, the next three chapters advance labor's story in long chronological leaps up to the present. Each of these chapters is thematic. Chapter 2 deals with labor politics. Chapter 3, actually composed of three separately written essays, explores ideology, career leadership, and ethnicity as shaping influences on the American labor movement. Chapter 4 is a case study of how one union, the Mine Workers, over the course of a century struggled to master the powerful economic forces dominating its industry.

We are inclined, in the classes we teach, to cut history up into manageable chronological pieces. These three essays opt for the longer view, tracing their themes from origins to the present in hopes of capturing the central tendencies and connections that give coherence to historical development. In my view, that's not a bad way to study the past, even though it makes for some awkwardness in matching reading assignments to class lectures. In fact, chapters 2 (on politics) and 4 (on the coal miners) are divided into sections that can be assigned separately, although I hope students will be encouraged to read them straight through as well; while the three essays comprising chapter 3 can be read where they have optimum relevance in a course (the ideology segment can be linked to the crisis over the Knights of Labor in the 1880s, for example, or the union leadership segment to the discussion of the AFL and pure-and-simple unionism).

Chapters 5 and 6 revert back to the style of the opening chapter, treating in greater detail consequential issues rooted in specific time periods. Chapter 5 deals with World War II, starting with the question of why so great a national crisis should have had so modest an impact on labor/state/capital relations in the United States. Chapter 6, entitled "Workplace Contractualism," refers to the formalized system of work rules and grievance procedures governing labor-management relations on the shop floor under industrial unionism. This distinctive system of workplace representation has come under severe criticism in recent years, from the Left for disempowering rank-and-file workers, and from the Right for promoting adversarial and inflexible workplace relations injurious to American "competitiveness." Those being the charges, the chapter poses a question of historical causation: Was workplace contractualism the result of compelling and inescapable forces or a contingent event that might, under slightly different circumstances, have gone in another direction? My discussion should say something to the reader about the nature of historical argument as well as about an issue at the heart of the crisis of American labor today.

The essays in this book were written at different times in bursts of enthusiasm, triggered mostly by invitations to attend a conference or to contribute to a scholarly collection. From this kind of irregular creation a book can only be imperfectly fashioned. For one thing, major topics—topics, in particular, like gender, which have become major—are bound to be left out or treated only tangentially. Moreover, because the writing occurred over a period of years, what is offered cannot uniformly pretend to be at the cutting edge of scholarship. Given the industry of scholarly production now prodigiously at work, in fact, even very current publications are quickly no longer the last word. For those essays written during the past few years, I have tried to cite later research that seemed especially pertinent. But other essays go back in time. The essay on ethnicity, for example, appeared in 1980. Since then, the study of working-class ethnicity has leapt forward, and I initially contemplated a substantial revision to incorporate recent scholarship, but then thought better of it, in the end only adding a couple of paragraphs taking account of the renewed surge of immigration in recent years. The essay seemed to have an integrity of its own and resisted being patched up. And so, I discovered, did the other essays of somewhat ancient vintage; at least they enjoy the coherence arising from a particular time and perspective. Historical writing ages, but not like automobiles, which depreciate the minute the next model comes along. My hope is that the imperfections of this book are outweighed by the singleness of voice with which the individual essays are written and by the unifying perspective they offer on some of the main themes in the history of American workers.

The first draft of "Time and Work During Early American Industrialism" was written while I held a Guggenheim fellowship for 1983–84. A year as CULMA professor at Wayne State University in 1988–89 offered the time to rework and complete chapters 4 and 6. For permission to reprint various selections, I would like to thank *Labor History*, Charles Scribner's Sons, *Dissent*, Berg Publishers, the Free Press, Harvard University Press, the Ohio State University Press, and the Woodrow Wilson International Center for Scholars.

Kensington, Calif.   D.B.
May 1993

Contents

In Labor's Cause

1

Time and Work During Early American Industrialism

"They will work from six to six—how absurd!" So remarked the *Federal Gazette* in 1791 on the occasion of a strike by Philadelphia's journeymen carpenters. Theirs was the first collective demand for the ten-hour day, 6 a.m. to 6 p.m., with two hours off for breakfast and dinner, for which there is a record in American history.[1] When Boston carpenters revived that demand nearly thirty-five years later in 1825, the master carpenters were no less put off. It was a matter of "surprize and regret" that the journeymen "entered into a combination for the purpose of altering the time of commencing and terminating their daily labor, from that which has been customary from time immemorial. . . ." The employers of the master carpenters likewise deplored the effort "to curtail the usual number of working hours" as "a departure from the salutary and steady usages which have prevailed in this city, and all New England, from time immemorial. . . ."[2]

Jacksonian Americans took it as an article of faith that life was better for workers in the United States than in England. But the ten-hour day, as it happens, had been an accomplished fact for English workers for a century and more. Around 1720, the English building trades had gone on to a six-to-six schedule (with two hours off for meals), followed by most other artisan and industrial trades after the middle of the eighteenth century.[3]

England did have a ten-hour movement. But it was directed primarily

From *Labor History*, 30 (Winter 1989), 5–46. Reprinted with permission.

against the cotton mills, which, from the time they had first started up in 1770s, had operated on a far longer work schedule. But this was taken as an anomoly. It was, one witness told the Select Committee of 1816, "a system of oppression . . . contrary to the usual and acknowledged hours of daily labour in England."[4] The long day in English textile mills generated protest, argues economic historian M. A. Bienefeld, because it violated an established norm. In America, the perspective on the ten-hour day was entirely otherwise: the demand seemed radical, and came up against "usages . . . from time immemorial."

In resisting a shorter workday, the master carpenters did not fail to make familiar calculations—ten hours would mean "lessening the amount of labor each day in a very considerable degree." The reduction would, like a wage increase, raise costs. But employers did not treat the ten-hour issue as they did a wage demand. Nor did the workers. They spoke, almost invariably, of the "Ten Hour System." And when Boston carpenters resumed the ten-hour struggle in 1835, the New York General Trades' Union praised their efforts as an action "relative to a revolution in their system of labor."[5] We would do well to take them at their word.

What prevailing notions of work time could have prompted the *Federal Gazette* to dismiss a demand for ten hours as "absurd"? The place to begin is before those pioneering Philadelphia house carpenters first raised that claim in 1791, back a generation earlier before gathering economic forces began to inculcate the notion that the workday ought to begin at 6 a.m. and end at 6 p.m.

Although overwhelmingly agrarian, the eighteenth-century American economy contained a substantial artisanal sector. Household manufacturing was widely practiced, but even the remotest rural community had some need of artisans—blacksmiths, wheelwrights, carpenters, itinerant shoemakers and weavers who "put the finishing hand" to family rough work. In more developed farm regions, artisans comprised up to 10 percent of the rural population. Scattered across the countryside, exploiting accessible resources and waterpower, were extractive and processing enterprises of many kinds. Along forty miles of the Brandywine River in Delaware in the 1760s, sawmills, papermills, powder works, and flour mills occupied 130 improved mill seats. There were also artisan villages in more settled areas. Eastern Massachusetts seemed to La Rochefoucauld to resemble "in every respect true European industry. In every village the streets along the road are lined with shops. Cabinetmakers, shoemakers, saddlers, coachmakers and tanners are very numerous.''[6] Urban artisans constituted over a third of the gainfully employed in Boston, plying ninety-six crafts in 1790 by Kulikoff's count.[7] In the more dynamic economies of Philadelphia and New York, close to half the labor force was engaged in artisan production, probably even higher in the booming inland town of Lancaster, Pennsylvania.

What characterized this traditional artisan economy was, above all, *industriousness*. After the American Revolution, the British government set up a claims board to compensate for the losses sustained by Loyalists who had fled the colonies. The board records testify vividly to self-advancement—to the ownership of shops, land, houses—by mustered-out soldiers, indentured servants and apprentices, poor artisans who had settled in America during the pre-Revolutionary decades. The case histories are not statistically significant—as claimants, they were a self-selected lot, not to speak of being given to some natural exaggeration—but their example (as well as their testimony) does lend credence to Crèvecœur's belief that the immigrant could expect to "procure an easy decent maintenance by his industry."[8]

For artisans, there is systematic evidence sustaining Crèvecœur's view. We know, for example, that entry into the masters' ranks was open and swift. In 1756 among Philadelphia journeyman cordwainers and tailors, 38 percent became masters within a decade. We have fuller evidence of accumulating wealth within the artisan ranks. Although there was a hierarchy among crafts, within each craft wealth-holding spread up the scale, with some representation at the upper end by such trades as silversmithing, printing, and carpentry. Of Philadelphia artisans in four crafts who died between 1700 and 1745, one in six left personal wealth of £300 or more, while three out of five left enough (over £100) to be counted of middling wealth.[9] Such achievements bespoke lifetimes of unstinting labor, visible testimony to what a Virginia writer boasted of as "the certain rewards of industry."[10]

The rewards of industry were not, in truth, certain for urban masters. They could not escape the risks of a volatile market economy. The effect was to sharpen the edge of rational calculation. Consider, for example, the credit problems in an economy that was money poor and lacking in banking institutions. The artisan generally laid in supplies on credit, and likewise extended credit to his customers. His soundness depended not on himself, but on those with whom he did business (and they in turn on others). At any moment, his loans might become un-collectible or his debts called in. In these circumstances, real property acted as a stabilizer, a kind of reserve that might be drawn on in case of need (or opportunity). According to a statistical analysis of real estate transactions in Boston from 1692 to 1779, it was the artisans who turned out to be the most active group.[11] Nor were their dealings a way of salting away earnings: they were constantly more active in borrowing on their property than in lending to others.

The confined market for their goods and services likewise prompted masters to diversify beyond artisan production. Urban craftsmen commonly retailed many other items than those of their own handicraft, and they were occasionally inclined to take flyers in other directions, as, for example, when Ben Franklin's partner David Hall sent a consignment of flour to Lisbon. If he found "that it will answer," Hall expected "most probably [to] enlarge my Business in that Way."[12] Traditional norms of artisan production were unlikely to fare well in the face of this kind of sharp thinking.

We should be careful not to ascribe to artisan proprietors a modern mentality that they did not possess. In the mid-eighteenth century, Philadelphia printers had not yet mastered basic accounting principles. Domestic and business records were intermingled, capital and depreciation costs were ignored, and the profit-and-loss balance sheet left unreckoned.[13] The medieval notion of the just price still existed and was enforced by the assize of bread and by other public regulations. Within the craft trades, a corporate sense survived, and artisans as a group shared a strong social identity. It was true that entrepreneurial craftsmen sometimes drifted beyond the handicraft realm, and that their sons moved at a faster rate into the merchant class. Of Boston merchants in 1789, a quarter traced their origins to artisan fathers.[14] But such ambition was not especially inculcated within the artisan ranks. A 1779 broadside by the tanners and shoemakers of Philadelphia asserted: "Proud of that rank, we aspired no higher." They also recognized that such aspiration was beyond their grasp: "No person of . . . these trades, however industrious and attentive to his business, however frugal in his manner of living, has been able to raise a fortune rapidly, and the far greater part of us have been contented to live decently without acquiring wealth."[15]

The pursuit of a competency gave reason enough for industrious work. But the market forces that penetrated the traditional artisan world in-

tensified the incentives, and not only among those responsive to entrepreneurial opportunities. Small masters were ill equipped to cope with
the hazards of the colonial economy. There is evidence of an increasingly uneven distribution of wealth in the seaboard cities during the
eighteenth century, of declining real wealth for the bottom half of
Boston's gainfully employed (although not for this group in the more
dynamic Philadelphia economy), and everywhere a rising incidence of
urban poverty.[16] If the book sellers of Philadelphia are representative,
small shops suffered a high turnover rate.[17] In hard times, the only
answer was greater effort, as evidenced by the sad complaint of one
failing New York artisan who found "it beyond my ability to support
my Family with my utmost Industry—I am growing every Day more
and more behind hand, tho' my Family can scarcely appear with De-
cency, or have necessaries to subsist."[18]

What of the larger number of artisans settled in the countryside? In
a penetrating article, James Henretta has made the case for a premodern
mentalité in colonial rural society. Lacking access to markets, farmers
produced primarily for family subsistence and, to the extent that goods
and services were needed, exchange took place through bartering, with
little money ever changing hands. The basis for exchange was reciprocal
need, governed by "use-value" rather than market price and set within
a communal web of cooperative relations based on kin and neighbor-
liness. In such a precommercial rural order, there was not much purpose
in accumulation beyond comfortable self-sufficiency, and hence not a
high value placed on industriousness. This was, Henretta remarks, the
cause of much colonial concern. The easy rural life was productive of
an "abundance of *Idleness* with us, and a manifest defect of Industry
thro' the Country."[19]

In less favored regions, as in much of New England, the contrary
might equally have held true. Where land was infertile and the size of
farms reduced over several generations of settlement, only intensive
effort sufficed to wrest a living from the soil. Nor is it clear that rural
exchange, even within self-sufficient communities, was on a significantly different basis than commercial exchange. Accounts were always
reckoned in money terms, carefully recorded, and, although often carried for years between exchanging parties, ultimately settled. In a productive system in which the demand for extra hands and specialized
skills was irregular but vital, moreover, labor constituted the most important item of exchange. A principal economic asset of middle-aged

Massachusetts farmers, indeed, was the exchange value of the labor of their sons—and was the key to generating the surplus for settling estate portions on them.[20] There are, finally, open questions about the extent to which colonial farmers were in fact outside a market economy.[21] Entrepreneurial values are certainly suggested by the degree to which early American industrialism sprang up within the interstices of the rural economy.[22]

Even accepting Henretta's characterization of a precommercial agrarian economy (as at least partly true), we have to differentiate rural artisans from their farming neighbors. Artisans were very largely what Crèvecœur called "half-farmers." The surviving accounts of eighteenth-century Yankee shoemakers indicate that nearly all were engaged in farming and stock raising.[23] But artisans were a more mobile group. In a trade like gravestone carving, we know that rural artisans ranged far afield as demand necessitated, and, from a study of the designs, that they probably formed a craft network that covered New England.[24] Even in a thoroughly subsistence region (such as the western portions of Virginia and the Carolinas in the 1760s), nonmonetary exchange would have operated differently for the artisan than for farmers, for he would have been engaging in a much greater number of exchanges.

Rural artisans, too, would have had some incentive for accumulating beyond subsistence needs, especially the younger sons of farmers put out to trades for lack of sufficient family acreage. In 1765 of seventy landless artisans in Chester County, Pennsylvania, 55–60 percent were landowners twenty years later. This shades over into more entrepreneurial activity. Of the fifteen Yankee account books mentioned above, ten detail lines of business, in addition to shoemaking, that range from half a dozen other crafts to storekeeping to gristmill operation.[25] And there were, finally, rural artisans who broke entirely from the surrounding subsistence economy. In Pawtucket, Rhode Island, for example, available water power attracted the iron-making Jenckes family and (as the eighteenth century progressed) a variety of other artisan producers. The battle that blew up after 1760 over the damming of Pawtucket Falls sharply delineated the contrast between the farmers (who would be deprived of migrating fish) and the entrepreneurial artisans (who wanted a better regulated power source).[26]

Country or town, the incentives for industriousness apply only to those expecting to profit from their labor. And this brings me to certain key characteristics of the colonial artisanal economy. The first can be put bluntly: the artisan labor force was substantially a labor force of masters. Lacking any effective guild regulation (save that achieved in the licensed trades), the master was simply an artisan who had managed to set up for himself. The term *master*, in fact, meant any self-employed artisan. A variety of evidence suggests the ease of entry into the ranks of master. The scale of artisan activity was small, in the countryside and in the cities. Compared to the London trade, colonial printing for example was distinctly minor league. Benjamin Franklin's shop, the largest in Philadelphia, contained three presses, while London shops averaged four, and a really large English operator like John Watts, who had once employed Franklin, had a staff of upward of fifty journeymen. By contrast, remarks Stephen Botein, "the ordinary colonial printing shop could not be expected to maintain more than one family. . . . "[27]

Colonial tax lists, wills, and other quantifiable evidence do not consistently distinguish between masters and journeymen—itself indicative of the indistinctness of the categories. A recent study, based on refined identifying techniques, concludes that half or more of the taxable cordwainers and tailors in Philadelphia functioned as masters on the eve of the Revolution.[28] In the Philadelphia printing trade, likewise, master printers made up roughly half the total number of printers listed in the tax rates.[29] A comparison of the membership of the two masters' companies in Philadelphia with all the carpenters on the city tax lists yields essentially the same results—44 percent were company members.[30]

Not all forms of artisan production lent themselves to small-scale enterprise. Self-employment was often translated into subcontracting systems. This was true, for example, of shipbuilding. The yard owner acted in effect as the master contractor, letting out portions of the ship under construction to shipwrights, joiners, caulkers, sailmakers, blacksmiths. They might be paid by the day or by the job, but they were contract workers, not employees, and they might be engaged simultaneously by several different yards. Subcontracting was likewise used in the building of St. Paul's Church in Philadelphia in 1761. The master carpenter who had taken the contract hired four other masters to do portions of the work, and, for work he actually did, credited himself in the books along with the other master workmen.[31]

In the port cities, finally, municipal regulation of public services elevated much of the needed manual work into respectable forms of self-employment. Cartmen and porters were licensed tradesmen, granted a highly prized privilege in exchange for close regulation. Although their fees and hours were prescribed (and sometimes even their work stations), they were self-employed. In New York City, in fact, cartmen were specifically prohibited from being in the hire of others or from selling shares in their enterprises.[32] Nothing perhaps better exemplifies the early American penchant for self-employment than the extent to which it reached the settled unskilled population of the colonial cities.

To the degree that self-employment prevailed, to that degree did the incentives for industriousness spread through the artisan economy. Self-employment was a condition fostered by the rapidity of colonial settlement and economic growth. Hence the warning of one North Carolinian that anyone hoping to hire help in his neck of the woods "will have a bad time on't, . . . everyone having business enoo' of his own."

This economic truth was powerfully underscored by the message of the colonial work ethic. The prospect of "quick profit" would do more "to reduce a People to a habit of Prudence and Industry than is possible to be effected by Whip, or Hunger or by all the penal Laws, that can be Invented for the Suppressing of Idleness." It was a fixed conviction that men were "Laborious and Industrious while [they] work for themselves." The obverse was equally true: those who labored for the advantage of others became "mere Negroes [and] grow lazy and careless."[33] There was, in truth, undisguised contempt for those who settled for such work, as sailors, "like froward Children not knowing how to judge for themselves," "concerned only for the present . . . incapable of thinking of, or inattentive to, future welfare."[34] An ironic conclusion arose from this grim distinction: if a man could not employ himself, he did not deserve to be free—as indeed sailors were not once they went shipboard.

The seagoing colonial economy could not do without sailors. Nor could iron be made without men to carry out the brutal work around the primitive blast furnaces and forges. Processing industries of all kinds required hands. In varying degrees, so did the artisan trades. A tailor or shoemaker might work efficiently by himself, but not a printer or silversmith, still less the operator of a rope works. And in every trade, a prospering enterprise could grow in only one way—by finding more hands.

Nantucket whalers hit on one solution to this problem: they lured the local Indians into debt, then transformed them into forced labor in an early American version of peonage.[35] Such invention was not ordinarily required. Entrance into the colonial labor force largely occurred via some form of bondage. Africans came as slaves. About half of all European immigrants up to 1775 arrived as bound servants, mainly financing their passage by contracting out as indentured servants.[36] Children of both sexes, from the middling ranks downward, entered the labor market through apprenticeship. All these streams of bound workers were seized on and adapted to the needs of colonial masters eager for hands.

African slaves, imported mainly for field work in the southern colonies, began to replace white servants as artisans on the plantations and increasingly did the same in Charlestown and other southern towns. Less appreciated until recently has been the extent to which slaves were drawn into the Middle Atlantic artisan economy. Slaves made up 30 percent of New York City's laboring population in 1746. Philadelphia, a major entry point for immigrants, relied on indentured servants in roughly the same proportion until the outbreak of the Seven Years' War forced a switch to slaves. Bound workers made up nearly half the labor force of Philadelphia's handicraft economy in the pre-Revolutionary years.

Those from England must have come almost wholly from what Bernard Bailyn has called the "metropolitan" stream originating in the heavily populated Thames Valley and represented typically by

> an inpecunious young artisan or craftsman who has served all or some part of his apprenticeship, . . . has found employment irregular or nonexistent, and, without prospects, still unmarried and without family encumbrances, has decided to head out to the colonies alone [and] has assumed a burden of debt for his transportation, to be paid off by four years of bonded labor.

The artisan economy relied heavily on his skills. In urban shops, servants and slaves performed a wide range of tasks, including the most demanding of craft jobs. Not even the rigidities normally associated with bound labor fully applied: an active market developed for the hiring out of servants and slaves, even apprentices, on a day basis in the Middle Atlantic port cities.[37]

This reliance on bound workers constitutes the second structural basis for the industrious artisanal economy. Where workers are unfree, work standards are by definition the exclusive domain of their employers. And, beyond the lawful rights of the master, the artisan economy conferred on him other ingenious advantages for disciplining bound workers. For one thing, artisan masters were not absentee owners, but workers themselves, constantly present and beyond being hoodwinked by foot-dragging servants. Furthermore, the artisan trades were household enterprises. Home and shop were physically joined, and joined also in the minds of the participants. The bound workers were taken in, in effect, as members of the household and subject, like family members, to paternal discipline. (In Puritan discourses, in fact, disobedient servants were always treated as a *family* problem.)

In a more attenuated way, the same logic applies to journeymen. They were free workers, of course, and at liberty to accept and terminate employment at will. In practice, however, the journeyman fell into a condition that Gary B. Nash has called "economic clientage."[38] If unmarried, he joined the master's household, received "diet" as well as a money wage, and was treated as a household member. For practical purposes, he was, like the bound worker, expected to conform to the work standard of the master. While the master worked, so did the journeyman, and he probably was expected not to absent himself without the master's permission.

At this juncture, what I am arguing moves on to disputed ground. As historians have been discovering, even the extreme subordination of serfdom and slavery does not render the unfree wholly powerless. Marcus Rediker's recent book on eighteenth-century Anglo-American sailors compellingly demonstrates the degree to which that labor force, notwithstanding the legal constraints of shipboard service, developed an autonomous work culture of resistance.[39] In a fragmentary way, there is much to suggest something like that process in the artisan economy, for example, in the complaints about lazy and incompetent journeymen, in the alarm over rebellious servants and apprentices, and in the high incidence (estimated at 5 percent of the indentured-servant population) of runaways.[40]

Still, there are several fault lines that can be discerned—first, between those in coerced bondage (slaves, convict servants, poor-law apprentices) and those in voluntary bondage; second, as regards the promise of advancement, between the expectant and the hopeless and/or indifferent; and, cutting across those lines, between those subject to household discipline and those (e.g., sailors, iron-plantation servants) subject to gang discipline. For the artisan economy, the balance clearly falls on the one side, not wholly, but sufficient for purposes of asserting the work standards of industrious masters.[41]

No social process sweeps clean. Still, the compulsions for indus-triousness ran exceedingly strong through the American craft economy, operating directly on the self-employed and, through their power over everyone else, penetrating down into the entire labor system. We pro-ceed now to translate the notion of industrious work, insofar as evidence and inference permit, into the actual dimensions of work time in prein-dustrial America.

"Hours of labor were inordinately long," writes Carl Bridenbaugh in *The Colonial Craftsman*. "Twelve to sixteen hours a day—from sunrise to sunset—were commonly [the colonial worker's] lot."[42] Bridenbaugh states this matter-of-factly, without citation, as if dealing with an evident truth. There is scattered supporting evidence in the secondary literature, but no study of hours comparable to Bienefeld's for England. The conclusive evidence is that inferred from the ten-hour demand—that six to six would shorten the work day. A further inference might be added—that the workday was not fixed but, as in the household and on the farm, was as long as there was work to be done and strength to do it.

What of regularity over the work week? In England, E. P. Thompson writes, "the work pattern was one of alternate bouts of intense labour and of idleness. . . ."[43] Under the regime of Saint Monday, workers exchanged free time after the weekend for harder effort later in the week. English social historians seem in agreement with Thompson that Saint Monday prevailed "wherever men were in control of their own working lives." And in the colonies? The leading modern historian of the colonial city, Gary Nash, writes in *The Urban Crucible:* "One of the English holidays that did not persist in the American port towns was 'St. Monday' [which] fell victim to the belief that opportunities were greater and that men, by the steady application of their skills, could raise themselves above the ruck."[44] We have no comparably authoritative statement about rural artisans. But, insofar as the work incentives of urban artisans applied to them, so would Nash's conclu-sion, and, insofar as they shared the work rhythms of the farmer, that too would have militated against a cyclical work week pattern. The surviving account books of Yankee shoemakers record no such pattern (although much variety in the tasks undertaken from day to day).[45] Silence serves perhaps as the best evidence—the apparent absence of Saint Monday references in which the English records abound.

A holiday calendar did begin to cut into the colonial working week.

Days set aside for civic duties increasingly took on a holiday air. Election days became an occasion for tavern-gathering, training day turned from serious militia exercises to target shooting and feasting. By the early eighteenth century, Boston was celebrating royal birthdays, British military victories, and Pope's Day (Guy Fawkes' Day) with fireworks, parades, and feasting—"frolicks . . . especially among People of the lower or Middling Class."[46]

Yet the sum of colonial holiday-making was substantially sparser than in England. For one thing, English holiday traditions did not travel well. Parish festivals or wakes, for example, were deeply rooted, originating beyond memory in the patron saint's day of the early church and evolving into a local, mainly secular event that could have no meaning anywhere else.[47] Moreover, New England adhered with much greater fidelity to the Puritan mandate against "all Festival dayes, vulgarly called Holy dayes, having no Warrant in the Word of God. . . . "[48] There was no counterpart in New England, and not much in the middle colonies, for the celebrations of a week or more that took place in rural England from the Restoration onward at Christmas, Easter, and Whitsun. In his recent study of seventeenth-century Springfield, Stephen Innes notes "the conspicuous absence of the countless English feast days. . . . "[49] For a rural Massachusetts shoemaker like James Weston in the 1790s, breaks in the year, aside from Sundays (and frequent funerals), consisted of Thanksgiving, Fast Day in the spring, training day, and election day[50]—not much competition for the holiday making of the English rural artisan.

We come finally to the elusive matter of how artisans worked over the course of the day. Was theirs a habit of hard and steady application? Or did they, as British social historians hold for English artisans, work irregularly, with "no great sense of conflict between labour and 'passing the time of day'?"[51] On both sides of the Atlantic, the technologies were traditional, and identically permissive. In most trades, tasks could be picked up and put aside at will. The artisan had many reasons to leave the bench—to serve a customer, pick up materials, collect an outstanding bill. Bad weather, shortages of materials, lack of orders militated against steady work habits. Among rural artisans, farming added all manner of extra duties. And, of course, everywhere household and craft activity flowed together.

Then there is the question of rum. The price plummeted after 1700: a gallon could be got for two shillings in 1738. "At that low price," remarks W. J. Rorabaugh, "a common laborer could afford to get drunk every day." Annual alcoholic consumption reached 6.6 gallons per adult (fifteen and over) in 1770 and was probably 10 gallons or more for male adults. Liquor was widely available by the quart in stores and dram shops—118 held licenses in Philadelphia in 1752—and formed a part of the staple diet of artisans and most other colonists. Thus the sardonic ditty of Samuel Sewell:

> There's scarce a Tradesman in the Land,
> That when from Work is come,
> But takes a touch, (perhaps too much)
> of *Brandy* or of *Rum*.

How much did he consume while in the shop? Liquor was commonly believed to be nutritious and health giving, a restorative for the weary workman. Ought its consumption to be taken as a sign of irregular and casual work habits? Rorabaugh observes that "Americans who took their spirits in frequent and comparatively small doses did not become intoxicated," and that, according to experts, such drinking inculcated "a tolerance to alcohol's intoxicating effects."[52]

Outside diversions also affected the day's work. By far the most important was the tavern. Town and country, this was the primary social center for colonists of every occupation. Traveling through New England in 1761, it seemed to the disapproving John Adams as if "every other house [had] a sign of entertainment before it. . . . If you sit the evening, you will find the house full of people, drinking drams, flip, toddy, carousing, swearing." The port towns were well stocked with taverns: in Boston the number of licensed premises stood at 155 in 1732. Some catered particularly to artisans of one craft. Did artisans repair regularly during the day to their favorite alehouse to read the papers, hear the news, play backgammon? City life offered a host of other possibilities. A Brookline tavern announced "a Bear, and a Number of Turkeys set up as a Mark next Thursday Beforenoon," or it might be a horserace or cockfight. Artisans might be drawn from the shop to see "a very strange & Wonderful Creature called a Sea Lion," some other exotic animal on display, or a band of acrobats. A few days after John Childs announced his plans "to fly off of Dr. Cutler's Church," the Boston *Gazette* reported that "as the performances led many People from their Business, he is forbid flying any more in the Town."[53]

If temptations were ever-present, so were the compulsions against casual work. In the Puritan ethic, man's nature was plainly intended (so said a Boston minister) "for an exact and regular, constant Course of Action," just as "the *Wheels* of a *Clock* or *Watch* when set in order and wound up, are manifestly designed by the *Artificer* for *Motion*."[54] The funeral sermon on the death of the Boston silversmith John Coney in 1712 granted in full measure the honor accruing to a life of constant application:

> He was a rare Example of Industry, a great Redeemer of his Time, taking care to spend not only his Days, but his Hours well, and giving Diligence in his Business. . . . He was excellently talented for the Employment assigned, and Took a peculiar Delight therein. . . . He was a Humble Man.[55]

Colonial America was certainly into the age when, in E. P. Thompson's felicitous phrase, time "is not passed but spent." If Pawtucket farmers lacked clocks,[56] such was much less likely to be true of artisans. And they could, in any case, mark out the hours by the town clock.[57] To what purpose was admirably spelled out in *Poor Richard's Almanack* (January 1751):

> Since our Time is reduced to a Standard, and the Bullion of the Day minted out into Hours, the Industrious know how to employ every Piece of Time to a real Advantage in their different Professions: And he that is prodigal of his Hours, is, in effect, a Squanderer of Money.

To bring Franklin's nice abstraction down to grim reality, we cannot do better than to quote the obligation undertaken by the carpenter Benjamin Buckler when he contracted to work for George Washington in 1771: "[T]hat is to say, he shall be *constant and diligent* at his business from day break till dark: and if the weather is such that he cannot work out of Doors or is unfit for him to do so that he shall in these cases keep himself *closely employed* in making of shoes for the said George Washington or at any other business he may be set about." And since he was also to supervise several slave carpenters, "the said Benjamin Buckler doth oblige himself to use his utmost endeavours *to hurry and drive them on* to the performance of so much work as they ought to render. . . ."[58]

The colonial economy fostered leisurely occupations. The tempo of mercantile life differed from that of the productive trades. Business proceeded with excruciating slowness and uncertainty. It could take up to two months to turn around a ship in port, three months or more to receive an answer from London, maybe much longer to learn whether a cargo sent out had been sold profitably or gone down in a storm. In the meantime, there was not much to do. The leading Boston merchant Thomas Hancock transacted an average of three credit sales a day between 1755 and 1771; a group of merchants whose account books survive sent an average of four to six letters out a week; and much time was left for social and political affairs.[59] The physician John C. Warren, recalling mercantile life in Boston in the late eighteenth century, remarked that "time was not very important to most men at that period," and they spent much of it "occupied in eating, drinking and card playing." The lesser merchants "were condemned to small business, which did not fill up their vacant hours."[60]

The question of work time sometimes rubbed into the political line of conflict between artisans and merchants. Thus, in the wake of the impressment riots in Boston in 1741, "Amicus Patriae" castigated "Some of Figure and Interest [who] live at Ease upon the Produce" of the lower ranks.[61] Merchants turned the time issue to their own advantage when, as in New York City in 1786, artisans sought political representation from their own ranks. "Two Shoes" wrote: "Let the mechanics tarry at home and follow their different employments, as I think they will not be able to do both at once." "Censor" doubted the capacity "of the laborious mechanic, whose whole study and progress in life has been to secure a maintenance for himself and family . . . to frame laws for a large and commercial community."[62]

Edward P. Thompson has rightly observed that "a community in which task-orientation is common appears to show least demarcation between 'work' and 'life.' "[63] That cuts two ways, however—"life" may intrude on "work," but "work" may also seize "life," and so it did in the colonial artisan economy. At least that was the conviction of the paragon of the artisan work ethic when he retired from his craft in 1748. Benjamin Franklin gave his printing business entirely over to his partner David Hall and thereby "secur'd Leisure during the rest of my Life, for Philosophical Studies and Amusements. . . . " It was Franklin's "hope soon to be quite a Master of my own Time."[64] The phrase was precisely the same as that used by ten-hour advocates in later years. Franklin, of course, retired comfortably to a life of science and public service on the income from his investments. Journeymen carpenters could only hope to secure from the ten-hour day a bit of their "own Time."

Like Benjamin Franklin, the Jacksonian workingman yearned for more out of life than unremitting labor. Beyond that shared human need, however, they parted company. For the wage-earning artisan, escape into early retirement was no solution. But what was practicable—a shorter workday—required a fundamental break from Franklin's assumptions about work. For these had not been framed in terms of hours. How long the artisan labored was only the by-product of other work decisions. The wage worker had first to discover that time was part of the employment transaction. And there was, as it happened, much in the way industrialism came to America that conspired to delay that discovery.

The colonial artisan economy, which I have held constant for purposes of analysis, was in fact highly unstable and always in flux. An inherent tension existed between marketplace calculations and dependent-mutualist labor relations. If, for example, apprenticeship served primarily as a source of cheap labor, was it not altogether likely that master-apprentice mutuality would gradually be transformed into an economically defined contractual relationship? According to Ian Quimby's study, precisely such a change occurred in eighteenth-century Philadelphia.[65] Or consider the growing uncertainties over how to employ journeymen. After mid-century, Philadelphia master carpenters were prepared to hire them on a long-term basis at a lower wage rate (and absorb the costs of underemployment) or at a higher rate on a strictly daily basis (with the unemployment risks transferred to the journeyman).[66] The second option became increasingly attractive from the 1760s onward, partly because of the volatility of the economy during the Revolutionary years, partly because of an easing of the labor scarcity in the port cities. Much more remarkable was the declining reliance on bound workers, evidently as the result of a sharp reversal in the relative costs of bound and free labor. By the end of the eighteenth century, slaves and servants had virtually disappeared from the artisan economies of the port cities. They had been replaced by a journeyman wage-labor force.[67]

The advent of free-market labor occurred within the framework of traditional artisan production. Work processes remained undisturbed and so did the local-market orientation. This was true of the building trades and of the many kinds of artisans—shoemakers, tailors, silver-smiths—who produced goods on a custom or retail basis. Only the mutualist relationship of master and worker was ruptured. The effects were manifold—separating households from shops, masters' neighbor-hoods from workers' (at least in Philadelphia and Baltimore), and, in the shop, the masters from manual labor. Journeymen swiftly found interests distinctly different from those of the masters. Nothing better revealed this discovery than the emergence of journeyman societies, going back in some forms to the 1760s, and fully mature and self-conscious as trade-union bodies by the 1790s. By then, Philadelphia printers, carpenters, shoemakers, cabinet and chair-makers, and hatters were organized and regularly in contention against the master crafts-men. Labor strife became so endemic in New York City after the turn of the century as to prompt public advertisements deploring "the in-creasing evils . . . of the disputes between the masters and Journeyman Mechanics."[68]

In at least three ways, past artisanal experience militated against making work time an issue comparable in importance to wages. First: the force of custom. When the transition to wage labor came, the indeterminate schedule of the artisan household gave way to a more definite workday, but this was set by what had been the *norm* until then. The workday was dawn to dusk for outdoor workers; for the shop crafts it was by the early nineteenth century generally until 8 p.m. by candlelight during the winter months, until dusk the rest of the year.[69] Whatever the standard, it had behind it the weight of long usage, going back (as the Boston master carpenters insisted) to "time immemorial."

Second: the wage-labor system injected a greater element of economic insecurity into the lives of journeymen. Trade disruptions caused re-peated cycles of unemployment in the port cities during the last third of the eighteenth century. And, in the best of times, winter as always cut short the supply of artisan materials and kept outdoor workers at home. Unemployment was much harder on the growing numbers of unskilled laborers in the port cities, but it was by no means easy on the artisans—in 1772 some form of poor relief was required by 17 percent of Philadelphia's shoemakers, 13 percent of the tailors, and 9 percent in the building trades.[70] Later on, workers would come to see shorter hours as an answer to unemployment but initially the new experience of job insecurity probably served to distract attention from the question of work time.

Finally: a bit of self-employment was grafted on to wage labor in many traditional trades. This happened wherever the product could be reckoned by the piece. The term for piecework recalled independent enterprise: the journeyman was paid a "price" for his output. Hence the early form that collective bargaining took. The journeyman unions did not seek contracts. They issued "bills of prices" which all members were expected to abide by.[71] They thereby preserved the notion that they were paid not for their time, but a price for the product they produced.

In those fields where the reorganization of production took the form of domestic manufacture, self-employment was much more of a reality. The merchant-manufacturer owned the materials on which outworkers worked, and he marketed the products they made. These arrangements constituted, needless to say, fundamental irreversible losses of control for the artisan. But the artisan retained what must have seemed to him the essentials of independence. He owned his tools; he worked on his own premises; he was subject to no man's oversight; he set his own pace and schedule. He received, more truly than the hired journeyman, a "price" for his work. And it was the price over which he bargained: the time was his own.

The direction for outwork prices was unrelentingly downward. Most disastrously affected were the hand-loom weavers once they came up against the competition of the power loom.[72] The New York General Trades' Union voiced its "strong indignation" at the news from Philadelphia in 1835 of further cuts in "the already too much reduced prices the journeymen receive for their labor . . . being about one dollar for fourteen hours close application to their toil."[73] For anyone passing through Philadelphia's weaving neighborhoods, one observer wrote, "the sound of these looms may be heard at all hours—in garrets, cellars, and out-houses, as well as in the weavers' apartments."[74]

Shoemaking was likewise subject, although not so dramatically, to price pressures. Battling in intensely competitive markets, merchant-manufacturers began to subdivide the work—first, by establishing central shops for the cutting operations, then by transferring out the less skilled tasks of binding, that is, the sewing of the uppers. The shoemaker, although in his own shop, became increasingly a specialist doing the repetitive, if demanding, work of lasting and bottoming the shoes. As the illusion of self-employment was thus stripped from them, Lynn shoemakers could finally not deny that they labored under "slaving conditions." Shoemakers were "compelled to work every day, and some of them twelve to sixteen hours in each day that they may be enabled to discharge that highest of all other obligations that they are under, the maintenance of their families."[75]

The first unions in Lynn were formed in 1830, the first hesitant strike over prices came in 1835; during the 1840s, there were more unions, larger strikes, cooperative stores, a labor press and labor politics; and, culminating this process, the great shoemakers' strike of 1860 engaging the entire New England industry. Yet the Lynn shoemakers never (so far as extensive recent study of them reveals) linked up with the national ten-hour movement—and this notwithstanding the clearest recognition that their long hours were a consequence of the exploitative systems under which they then worked.[76] Shoemakers and other outworkers may have been caught up in the toils of industrial capitalism, but work time remained, as in the days of colonial artisanship, their own.[77]

In other ways, too, the putting-out system reached back to the older artisanal order. The primary unit of production was not the individual worker, but the small shop. In Lynn, shoemakers worked in "ten-footers" with helpers and family members. In New York City, some journeymen tailors undertook outwork in family shops. In Philadelphia, some shoemakers and binders were employed by "garret bosses." Hand-loom weaving was mostly done at home, but "in some cases a manufacturer, as he may be termed, has ten or twelve looms in a wooden building attached to his dwelling, and employs journeymen weavers— the employed in some instances boarding and lodging in the same house as their employer." More commonly, this was the case in the specialized trades of carpet and lace weaving. Beyond the putting-out industries, of course, small-shop production was extensive. In Newark, a third or more of the jewelers, trunkmakers, and leathermakers in 1840 listed as householders operated their own shops.[78] In the small-shop trades, one surmises that work time was predicated on much the same terms as in colonial artisan households, that is, by the acceptance by the subordinate members of the work schedule of the master.

Women had always, as household members, played a role in eighteenth-century artisan production (occasionally, when widowed, as master artisans). The putting-out system served as one entry point into female wage labor. In rural areas, women wove cloth, made buttons, and braided palm-leaf hats. Much of this was on top of household chores, done, so the *McLane Report* noted, "in scant time, when they have nothing else to do." But outwork led also to full-time wage-earning status. Where a division of labor occurred, the diluted portion became defined as women's work, and always (as an observer remarked of the New York vest and pantaloon business as early as 1817) "at from 25 to 50 per cent cheaper than if men were employed." Binding in the New England shoe industry was entirely taken over by women.

A similar innovation brought an entirely new industry into being in the form of New York City's ready-made men's clothing trade. Inside shops cut the standardized garments, outside shops sewed them. The outworkers were almost entirely women, drawn into the labor force for the skills that were part of the equipment of every respectable nineteenth-century woman. An enormous industry by mid-century, the New York men's clothing trade employed in 1860 over seventeen thousand women, most of whom worked at home. Their work schedules were fixed by the same economics that governed Lynn shoemakers and Philadelphia weavers—that is to say, they worked "day and night."[79] But the context was not artisanal; it was the expectation of endless toil that was the eternal lot of women in the family.

That was partly why country girls were attracted to the Lowell cotton mills, remarked Lucy Larcom, a one time Lowell girl herself: "The feeling that at this new work the few hours they had of every-day leisure were entirely their own was a great satisfaction to them."[80] By physically concentrating production, the factory ruptured the age-old inter-mingling of life and work—as the Lowell girls filed out the factory gates, the day became "entirely their own." But the impact, ultimately vast, did not overnight change the way people thought about work time. Customary notions were adapted, evidently without reflection, to the early factory.

Samuel Slater began America's first successful spinning mill in late 1790. His labor force consisted of a handful of the children of local Pawtucket artisans and farmers, supplemented after a few years by pauper apprentices. By 1800, Slater was relying mostly on entire fam-ilies—the children as mill hands, the fathers outside as carpenters, teamsters, and farm laborers.[81] The family system became the norm in the mills that sprung up in ever-growing numbers along the rivers and streams of rural America. Surviving labor contracts specify in detail the wages for the children, the duties and day rates for the father, the rental terms for the tenement, the charges for wood and cow pasturage. They are silent on the length of the workday, however, as if this matter was understood and beyond requiring specification.

The family system, Barbara Tucker has argued, was a concession to traditional ways, a means of recruiting a factory labor force without endangering family patriarchy and solidarity.[82] But if the central values were thus conserved, so was the household conception of work time. Within the family, the labor of children had never been subject to any time measure, so why should it be in the mill? And likewise with the household head: as a day laborer, his industrial employment was of an entirely familiar kind. From the first, Slater seems to have run his mills from dawn to dusk in summer months, and (from some undated time well before the 1820s) until 8 p.m. in winter.

The factory mode of production that began with Slater's rudimentary yarn-spinning mill remained in the early years deeply linked to the world of customary time. That machinery might replace hand labor represented something revolutionary, to be sure. And the Boston Manufacturing Company (1813) soon built in Waltham, Massachusetts, an integrated textile mill that showed the country a fully realized example of modern mass production. But no other industries were able to emulate the Waltham-Lowell model; it remained sui generis for another half century. Nor was sustained mechanization central to the early development of the factory system. In industrializing Massachusetts, firms grew larger between 1820 and 1850, and economies of scale were realized, but fixed capital (tools and machinery) per worker remained static during this early period.[83] Outside of textiles, in fact, industrial production got started with no technological breakthrough comparable to the Arkwright water frame or power loom, and, as with shoe manufacture, sometimes without even the benefit of factory organization.

Recent scholarship has stressed the evolutionary character of the early factory system, and particularly its ties to the prefactory economy. In rural settings, incipient industrial capitalists succeeded not only because they occupied strategic places in the preindustrial economy but because they mobilized local resources and skillfully adapted existing modes of production. "Factories were rarely created out of nothing," writes Christopher Clark of the economic transformation of the upper Connecticut Valley between 1800 and 1860. Factories "usually developed out of other forms of organization," frequently involving "a long period of close interaction between capital and household labour," mainly through reliance on outwork production.[84]

In the cities, not even water-powered machinery served initially to mark off the factory as a distinctive system of production. The Philadelphia textile industry took the form of what Philip Scranton has called "proprietary capitalism," with a large number of privately held, mostly small firms, a mobile highly skilled labor force, and a diversified flexible mode of operation that relied on every combination of factory, outwork, and artisanal production. Sean Wilentz describes a manufacturing sector in New York City "of almost baffling diversity . . . a metropolitan labyrinth of factories and tiny artisan establishments, central workrooms and outworkers' cellars, luxury firms and sweat-work strapping shops." In industrializing Newark across the harbor, the factory system evolved after 1820 in slow, sometimes imperceptible stages out of shop and outwork production, with little division of labor and no steam-driven machinery until the 1840s.[85]

In this transitional world, Slater's adaptation of customary time to the factory was everywhere replicated. Only rarely can one capture the actual moment of choice, as, for example, when the Philadelphia Guardians of the Poor opened a hand-operated textile factory in 1807 as a program of poor relief. Their rules specified a work schedule of sunrise to 8 p.m. in winter, half an hour before sunset in summer.[86] "Sun to sun," with candlelight until 8 p.m. during the fall and winter months, became the standard for mill workers in textiles—including those in the Waltham-Lowell mills—and in other kinds of factories as they began to appear. "An average through the year of twelve hours, is everywhere understood as factory hours," responded a textile master to the query of George S. White in 1827. Excepting tanning, paper-making, iron-making (where processing technologies dictated the work routine), the factory norm was twelve hours on average over the year.[87]

To ask about the length of the workday, of course, meant to elicit responses in terms of hours, but a defined number of hours was not the basis on which the first factory workers had hired on. Thus an employee of William Almond's cotton factory in Philadelphia explained the work schedule in 1837:

> There are no fixed hours—no set time of working at our mill—but we work from the time we can see, in the morning, until the light is insufficient to see in the evening. In the early part of the winter season, we

begin to work at daylight, and continue until eight and a half o'clock at night; when the days get shorter, we are called up before day, to breakfast, and go to work at daylight. . . .

Remarked another Philadelphia worker whose years in the textile industry went back to 1812, "The number of hours required was a custom at the time." It was "customary to require more hours in long days to make up for loss at other seasons, so as to produce an average of seventy-two hours per week for the year." He "never knew of any desire expressed relative to hours; the hours were understood. . . ."[88]

For the first generation of factory workers, the novel elements were real enough. Machine tending in textile mills was an entirely new experience, and so largely was the close, noisy atmosphere and the sense of being in a "crowd" of fellow operatives.[89] But the mitigating influences ran very strongly. Rural industry was linked in many ways to the surrounding countryside. The system of payment, with accounts built up over lengthy periods and mostly settled (as one labor contract at the Scoville Manufacturing Company put it) by "taking what trade he may want for his family use from our store," paralleled the traditional exchange relationships that existed among farmers, artisans, and hired hands in the precommercial rural economy.[90] Workers did not immediately lose their agrarian ties and moved regularly out of the mills during harvest time or at the call of family responsibility. This was true even of Lowell, where a quarter of the labor force left or arrived at the Hamilton mill in a five-week period during the summer of 1836, and was entirely the norm for country mills such as those around Hadley and Northampton.

The factory did not necessarily demand more intensive work than the farm or the artisan shop. Country mills operated irregularly even in good times—materials were often in short supply, key workers absent, machinery broke down, the mill pond froze in winter and fell too low in summer. In the Lowell mills, which ran much more steadily, the work pace in the early years was what Thomas Dublin has characterized as "leisurely," so much so as to permit women to leave the mill on errands while friends doubled up on their throstles and looms.[91]

The notion of an industrial discipline itself was slow to take hold. "If idle people who have no business in the factory be allowed to go every place through the house they will very much interrupt the workmen," noted the clerk of a newly opened woolen mill in Hagerstown, Maryland. And when the management posted a notice fixing the starting time and requesting "all hands . . . to attend regularly," the workers took it down, "saying (so the clerk recorded), that advertising them thus publicly was considered by them disgraceful to all hands in the Factory. . . . "[92] In his diaries, one country-mill agent, N. B. Gordon, accepted laconically the lack of punctuality and irregular attendance of his workers. He did "enter [his] dissent" against election day (May 26, 1830), "being one spent in a useless & worse than useless manner"; nevertheless Gordon "could not peaceably work the mill as all hands seemed determined to have the whole day."[93]

After closely studying the upper Connecticut Valley's emerging factory system in the first half of the 1800s Christopher Clark concludes: "Capitalist manufacturing demanded new forms of work-discipline, but there was no sudden or simple process by which these were established." He found that "many old habits connected with work continued to be followed."[94] And so, in the first phase, did acceptance of the customary workday of the prefactory world.

For many industrial workers, it was even possible to retain the sense of independence that underlay traditional notions of work time. Skilled workers producing measurable output were almost always paid on a piece-rate basis. Such workers might well perceive the factory at first as merely a new setting in which they turned out goods for a "price," and the time, as with the artisan or outworker, remained their own. At one Maryland woolen mill, the agent was obliged to instruct the weavers and other piece workers that they were subject to the same regulations as the day workers.[95] In the federal armories, the skilled workers literally did control their own time. "No regular hours were established," reported a board of inquiry for the Springfield armory in 1841. "Every mechanic, working by the piece, is permitted to go to his work any hour he chooses, and to leave off at his pleasure."[96] In the *McLane Report*, the query about hours commonly elicited no response except: "Work by the piece," or by tonnage. In iron mills, puddlers continued for many decades to set their own schedules, with "no stipulated number of hours. . . . Our men simply turn out so much weight in iron per day."[97] The same was true of blowers producing window glass and of coal miners working on a tonnage basis.

Only where work was truly autonomous, however, did workers retain so much control over their time. The logic of the factory ran strongly toward coordinated operations—whether because of a common power source, the division of labor, or, in the simplest case, the desire to create a disciplined work force—and this, among other things, called for a common starting and stopping time. "No large private manufactory, nor any operations requiring numerous workmen, can be properly conducted without certain regulations and fixed hours for work," insisted the government inspectors of the federal armories in 1841. In every private firm they had visited, "the hours of labor are fixed by regulation, and are observed by those who work by the piece as well as those who work by the day."[98] It was long past due that the federal armories, whose operations by 1841 involved considerable division of labor and some machine processing as well, join the mainstream of American factory practice.

> The pretext that *because men work by the piece,* they should be allowed to run the machinery when they please and be absent whenever it suits their whim, finds no favor at private workshops nor can it be allowed where the work of one man depends on that done by another, for carrying on and keeping up all branches to a proper standard.[99]

At Harpers Ferry, the armorers walked out in protest against the new time regulations, but to no avail. The imperatives of factory operation seemed to compel a common starting and stopping time.

A new time calculus was taking hold. The federal armorers, piece workers, had established a group production norm regulating the time they put in over the month. "At the end," complained armory managers, "their pay was generally the same in amount as if no absence had occurred." The output limitation, so the managers felt, kept the piece rates artificially high. The managers might have responded by cutting the rates and forcing the armorers either to increase their hours or to accept reduced earnings. That remained the approved cost-cutting method in outwork and in other forms of autonomous labor. But no longer in factory production. To require a full day's work would attack the armorers' power at its source; it would "lay bare their secret practices (frauds—for I can use no better term)." Regular hours would enable "the master of the Shop [to keep] a time account showing the time *actually spent in labor*" and hence to know "what is the *fair price* to be paid for piece work!!!"[100] Not as price for production, but as compensation for time, was how factory managers came to conceive of piece rates. This marked an opening phase in the nineteenth-century managerial offensive against workers' control. And it rested centrally on the notion of time as a measured commodity in the employment transaction.

The application to piecework was still novel in 1841, but time valuation had long since begun its corrosive work on the customary workday. Consider, for example, Samuel Ridley's attempt to explain the hours of labor at his Pennsylvania cotton mill in 1837:

> I have made a calculation, and, as near as I can ascertain, when we run and do full work, we average sixty-nine hours a week the year round. If we were paying by the hour, we would call seventy-two hours the week; but we seldom run that time. Seventy-two hours are calculated to be a week's work. We make no longer time in summer than in winter; it depends on the length of days. In the summer, our mill starts at five in the morning; stops half an hour for breakfast, three-quarters for dinner; and we stop, I believe, at seven; but I can't say positively whether we stop at seven or half-past seven—but I believe at seven; and on Saturday, we stop at four o'clock. In winter, we aim at seventy-two hours the week; and our only difference is in beginning and ending the work each day. In winter, we run till half-past eight, unless we stop at supper; if we stop at supper, we stop half an hour. We have generally stopped for supper, at our factory. We commence in winter, as soon as we can see.[101]

Here clearly is a man in transit between customary and industrial time. He can conceive of paying workers by the hour, but it is not yet his practice to do so. He has a notion of a standard work week of seventy-two hours, "but we seldom run that time." He is likewise abandoning the notion of a natural workday fixed by the rising and setting of the sun. He wants a standard, twelve-hour day all year round, but in winter work still commences "as soon as we can see." For all his uncertainty, Riddle has passed a crucial threshold: he knows that work time is a measurable commodity.

The factory bell was the instrument of this knowledge. Thus the mill agent N. B. Gordon habitually rang the bell at variable times well before dawn in the fall and winter of 1830—"Dark morning Bell," he calls this practice in one diary entry.[102] It remains unclear whether or not such creeping tactics had gradually transformed 8 p.m. into the customary winter closing hour. We do know it was not fully accepted in parts of southern New England as late as 1831. Spurred by the example of the Taunton, Massachusetts, workers, Providence operatives refused any longer to work "by candle light" and henceforth would not labor

"after the *usual* hours of employment and daylight have expired."[103]
The eight o'clock closing in turn gave rise to the more insidious practice
of slowing the clock, which had become so notorious by the early 1830s
that labor reformers could speak scornfully of two kinds of time—
"*factory time*" and "true *Solar* time." A few years earlier, the citizens
of Pawtucket, in public acknowledgement of the problem, raised a
subscription for a town clock as a remedy to "the vexatious confusion
occasioned by the difference of time in the ringing of the factory
bells."[104]

The reality was, a Manayunk manufacturer testified before a Pennsylvania Senate committee in 1837, that "the additional labor of one
hour in establishments, where from one to five hundred hands are employed, is an important item, and offers great temptations to the employer to over-work his hands." And this, remarked a mill
superintendent, "operates to the loss of those proprietors who impose
the shortest hours of labor. . . . [It gave] one manufacturer . . . an advantage over another." Under the pressure of market competition, the
very notion of a customary day began to unravel. So "want[ing] in
uniformity" had the hours of labor become in the Manayunk mills by
1837, a witness claimed, that families contracting to work in mills "do
not know what they have bargained for; they do not know how many
hours make a working day, or how many a week."[105]

The first known strike of textile workers, which occurred in Pawtucket
in 1824, was touched off by a reduction in "the time allowed at the
several meals" in the town mills.[106] And we can be sure that every
infraction of the customary day was noted and resented. But if exploitation cannot be hidden from workers, they do not necessarily grasp its
underlying logic. The Pawtucket strikers were conservatives. They were
bent on defending the customary work day. That was generally true of
the new breed in the factories. Another more traditional group of workers
first saw the futility of defending customary time, and fashioned a
response that met time exploitation on its own terms.

Philadelphia carpenters made the first known demand for the ten-hour
day in 1791. At every stage in the ten-hour movement, from its revival
in the mid-1820s to its transformation into a national cause a decade
later, carpenters stood at the forefront. Why the carpenters?

Among the traditional trades, first of all, they experienced most completely the labor-market revolution that began in the last third of the

eighteenth century. Functions became sharply differentiated. No longer laboring artisans in 1791, Philadelphia master carpenters spent their time "procuring materials, superintending the workmen, and giving directions." They had grown steadily wealthier over the course of the eighteenth century, as evidenced by the estates they left. Their rising status was reflected in the activities of the Carpenters' Company. In the early 1770s, the Company erected the noble Carpenters' Hall (which still stands); and during the 1780s its leaders became a predominant force in municipal politics. The journeyman labor force meanwhile grew apace. In the jury lists for three New York wards in 1819, journeymen carpenters outnumbered masters better than four to one—much the largest proportion of any major artisan group. An age breakdown of those jury lists reveals nearly a third of the journeymen carpenters over forty, two-thirds over thirty. Increasingly, the journeymen were becoming a permanent wage labor force. As class lines hardened within the building trades, so did the journeymen's sense of exploitation. They were becoming "mere slaves to inhuman, insatiable and unpitying avarice."[107]

For carpenters, work time peculiarly defined the lines of conflict. In an artisanal economy, craftsmen of all kinds figured prices on a fee-for-service basis. Silversmiths, for example, normally worked up metal owned by the customer, charging a fee per ounce plus some differential based on the intricacy of the task. Other artisans calculated on a similar basis whenever they worked on customers' materials, and, for practical purposes, even when they produced bespoke work: while there might be a markup on the cost of materials, the price was essentially determined by their labor. Only as the market changed and artisans began to produce for future sales—a fundamental shift—did a new calculus of profit, not labor, become the measure of earnings. Carpentry differed from other artisan trades in two ways. First, it mostly did not evolve from fee-for-service into production-for-sale. Second, carpenters provided a particularly complex service, that is, they built houses.

How was the contracting price to be set? Back in 1681, the great London architect Christopher Wren had laid out the options: by the day, which was the choice of carpenters who "are Lazy"; "by Great" (i.e., a total bid), which would encourage poor workmanship if too low a price had been set; or "by Measure," in which the carpenter received in effect a piece rate for his work. This last was favored by Wren, and by the master carpenters of Philadelphia. It was primarily for the purpose of "mensuration," in fact, that the Carpenters' Company had been set up in 1724—that is, to devise a standard method of measuring and valuing work and to make available the services of impartial "measurers" to figure house prices for members and customers. What was being reckoned, of course, was the *time* for each job, or, in the Company's words, "the labour required in the performance."[108]

As a work force of hired journeymen emerged, theirs was the labor being measured. And this brings us to the nub of the problem: what was to be the journeyman's relation to the masters' system of mensuration? In the 1791 dispute, the Philadelphia masters had supplied a traditional, precapitalist answer. The going wage for journeymen working by the day was five shillings, but this might move "higher or lower in proportion to the prices at which the masters have engaged their work. Those Journeymen who have chosen piece work, have generally received four-fifths of the price at which the work has been undertaken. . . . " The masters took the remainder as "but a moderate and reasonable compensation" for providing supervision, tools, and work space.[109] Assuming that the proportions (presumably at a ratio of four to one) were deemed equitable, this arrangement allowed for no expropriation of surplus labor value, since both masters and workers were compensated according to the accepted standards assigned their contributions.

But, in fact, it was precisely against the breakdown of this traditional system that their employees were protesting. In 1786, the Company's mensuration guide had been fundamentally revamped. The original, simple system of measuring "by the square" had worked well enough when "houses were plain and simple, the different parts nearly the same labour." It had become inadequate, however, as Philadelphia construction had grown more elaborate and richly detailed. The Carpenters' Company therefore adopted a new method that "set a price on every particular part, according to the mode of finishing, either by the square, yard or foot." The details were set down in forty-four closely printed pages in the Company's new *Rule Book* (1786). So complex a measuring system would not accommodate piece-rate payment to workers, unless—inadmissible notion—they were taken into the confidence of the master and became, in effect, partners. Although in 1791 Philadelphia masters claimed that journeymen could choose to be paid by a piece rate, this was clearly becoming unfeasible: journeymen carpenters everywhere would be paid by the day. Moreover, the complexity of the measuring system prevented journeymen from estimating the piece-rate value of their labor. Nor would the masters give them (or anyone else, including Thomas Jefferson) access to the *Rule Book*. It was a closely held document, immediately retrieved at a member's death and available to no one outside the Company.

The journeymen carpenters were thereby excluded from the central calculation of their trade. This was a crucial weakness, and they knew it. "Many of us would prefer working piece-work if we could know the price that would be paid on our work; but we cannot know it in consequence of the employers' book of prices being secret: that it is unjust we have learned to our cost."[110] The injustice derived from the opportunities for exploitation now in the hands of the master carpenter. He bought their labor by the day and sold it (at a price unknown to the journeyman) by the piece. The crux of the issue was a very specific disjuncture: the journeymen abided by the traditional notion of work time—a customary day, in this case dawn-to-dusk—while the master measured their labor by a modern time/money calculus.[111]

One practice, universally experienced in the building trades, brought the conflict sharply into focus. "Many employers have been in the habit of employing hands only during the long days of summer, discharging them as soon as the days become short." Winter weather was sometimes bad, true. And there was some wage differential: in 1835, Philadelphia carpenters received $1.25 a day from April 1 to November 1, $1.12½ a day in winter. The complaint nevertheless held. The masters concentrated their work on the seasons when they got the most out of the workday. It was to remedy this practice, in fact, that from 1791 onward the journeymen specifically demanded the ten-hour day. Six-to-six the year round would deprive the masters of the advantage they found in the seasonally variable workday.

Contained within ten hours was a challenge to the entire exploitative system that had taken shape in the building trades. On calling for the ten-hour day in 1832, the Boston ship carpenters gave assurances that they stood ready to handle any additional rush of work. But in that event, employers would have "to pay for each and every hour over and above ten, an extra compensation in proportion to our day's work."[112] This was a notion grasped by the very first exponents of the ten-hour day. The Philadelphia carpenters of 1791 took as their "*main* object . . . to have it a matter entirely at *our* option, whether we will begin our work before, or continue at it after, six in the morning, and the same hour in the evening. If we labour early and late, as has been the case heretofore, we shall expect compensation *extraordinary* for the time each day's work exceeds the hours before mentioned."[113] Although language was slow to change—journeymen were still paid by the day well past the 1830s—the reality had instantly been altered: ten hours meant employment by *units of time*. Thus did the journeymen answer the master's monopoly on the measurement of their work. If they were excluded from that central calculation, journeymen would assert a different measure of value. They would be paid by units of time. And, to close the circle of protection, the New York ship carpenters in 1831 petitioned the Common Council for a bell for the shipbuilding district "of sufficient size to be heard and give notice at the various hours," so that they would have "a correct standard for the different hour of commencing and letting off work."[114]

We are witnessing a remarkable shift in industrial consciousness. Other workers, of course, shared the experience of the carpenters. The New York bookbinder John Bradford, for example, wrote a poem for his mates to the tune "Yankee Doodle," which he entitled "A Song for the Tenth of March: The Night on Which Journeymen Mechanics Cease Working by Candlelight" (1813). While the song does not question the customary workday, lasting until 8 p.m. in winter and until sundown the rest of the year, there is this stanza about the coming daylight season:

> Though if at night at work we stay,
> You know as well as can be,
> For each hour we'll get the pay,
> Yankee Doodle Dandy.[115]

Such thoughts must have been occurring to other journeymen, as for example, New York printers who in 1809 were paid a piece rate for composition work, but 15.5 cents an hour for setting columns and taking down presses, and to a growing laboring population that began to see, in one way or another, that their employers were measuring the workday in hours.[116] Once the carpenters raised the ten-hour standard, moreover, other workers flocked to it.

Factory workers were the laggards, and only partly because of their collective weakness. In the midst of the ten-hour struggles in Philadelphia in 1835, only the Manayunk mill operatives struck for a shorter day rather than ten hours. They settled for an earlier closing time, thereby improving their working conditions but not making the crucial

step to a time calculation for their labor.[117] Pieceworkers in factories
brought up the rear. Only in 1842 did the Lowell power-loom weavers,
who had struck twice in the 1830s over money, begin to espouse the
ten-hour day, and they did so as much because of the intensification of
work they were experiencing as from their discovery, after repeated
rate cuts, that piecework meant not pay for production but only a different and more mischievous form of time compensation.

In the case of the carpenters, the insight into the nature of time
exploitation was peculiarly precise. It derived directly from the particular characteristics of work in the building trades. Major changes were
in the offing—the balloon frame, standardized building materials, large-
scale construction for sale—that would sweep the carpenters into the
industrializing mainstream. But skill dilution and speed-up had not yet
caught up with them. Certainly carpenters claimed to work hard—and
beyond what "a man of common constitution" ought "to perform [for]
more than ten hours faithful labour in one day"—but not *harder* than
in the past.[118] If some transformation was under way, it consisted not
in how journeymen carpenters worked, but in what might be termed a
rise in their level of popular intelligence. Journeymen observed their
calculating masters, and became themselves calculating. Thus this response to the Philadelphia masters' claim over how much time would
be lost under the ten-hour day:

> They say we are depriving them of a fifth part of the usual time of
> working, it is a miscalculation: in the longest day in summer there are
> but 15 hours sun, and deducting 2 hours for meals, leaves 13 hours for
> work; in the shortest day there is but 9 hours sun, and of course 8 hours
> work averaging 10½ throughout the year, now we propose to work 10
> hours during the summer, and as long as we can see in the winter, taking
> only one hour for dinner, and we can accomplish nearly 9 hours work
> in this manner in the shortest day. The average is 9½ hours; thus their
> loss would be but about one 12th part of the time, and we maintain not
> any in the work.[119]

The Jacksonian labor leader John Ferral spoke of "the ten hour
system" as "our bloodless revolution." This referred, in the first instance, to its impact on the employer-worker relationship. If customary
notions of work time were lapsing, ten hours signified the invocation
of new rules of the game. By asserting that change, workers were also
asserting their equality in that relationship. They ought "not to be
governed by the will and pleasure of an unprincipled and unfeeling

employer.'' But thoughts more fundamental had been set in motion. ''The God of the Universe has given us time, health and strength,'' pronounced the Boston carpenters in their Ten-Hour Circular. ''We utterly deny the right of any man to dictate to us how much of it we shall sell.''[120]

Time had become a divisible commodity. ''To the man whose dependence is solely on his labor,'' said ''Regulus,'' ''time is everything; and he cannot be too careful of it, or of the rate of compensation for which he gives it.''[121] Some of it workers expended in the commerce of the labor transaction. The part they retained held a different kind of value. The industrial revolution was in full swing. Workers had to make their place in the emerging social order. In that quest, time became a precious commodity. So, as the Ten-Hour Circular argued, workers were ''contending for . . . the Natural Right to dispose of our own time in such quantities as we deem and believe to be most conducive to our own happiness, and the welfare of all those engaged in Manual Labor.''

Notes

1. *Federal Gazette,* May 11, 1791; Ian M. G. Quimby, ''The Cordwainers' Protest,'' *Winterthur Portfolio,* III (1967), 90–91; John R. Commons et al., *History of Labor in the United States* (4 vols., New York, 1918–35), I, 69–71. There is an ambiguous reference to a 1785 dispute in the New York building trades ''concerning a day's work'' in *New York Packet* (Jan. 20, 1785), cited in David Roediger, '' 'Liberty of Leisure': Colonial Realities, Revolutionary Citizenship and the Beginnings of the American Artisanal Movement for the Shorter Working Day,'' paper presented at the Third International Conference of the Centre de Recherches sur l'Histoire des Etats-Unis, Paris, June 1987, n. 23.

2. *Columbian Centinel,* April 20, 23, 1825, in John R. Commons et al., *A Documentary History of American Industrial Society* (11 vols., Cleveland, 1910–11, reprinted New York, 1958), VI, 76, 79 (hereafter cited as DH). The master carpenters of Philadelphia had similarly protested that the ten-hour demand violated ''the custom of Journeymen Carpenters, as well as other mechanics, to work from sunrise to sunset throughout the year. . . . '' *Federal Gazette,* May 17, 1791. New York carpenters seem to have been the first to break from a sunrise-to-sunset schedule. For an 1805 broadside by master carpenters and masons that refers to fixed starting and stopping times for the four seasons of the year, see Howard R. Rock, *Artisans of the New Republic: The Tradesmen of New York City in the Age of Jefferson* (New York, 1979), 250–52. A ten-hour day evidently had come into effect by the 1820s. Sean Wilentz, *Chants Democratic: New York City and The Rise of the American Working Class, 1788–1850* (New York, 1984), 190–91.

3. M.A. Bienefeld, *Working Hours in British Industry: An Economic History* (London, 1972), chs. 1, 2. The Philadelphia journeymen carpenters were acutely aware of

this fact. One of their arguments for the ten-hour day was that it already was "the universally prevailing custom of Great-Britain, together with the general usage of the other parts of Europe. . . . " *Dunlap's American Daily Advertiser,* May 11, 1791.

4. Quoted in Bienefeld, *Working Hours,* 40.

5. *Columbian Centinel,* April 20, 1825, in DH, VI, 76; *National Trades' Union,* Aug. 1, 1835, in DH, V, 252–53.

6. Quoted in Victor S. Clark, *History of Manufactures in the United States, 1607–1860* (Washington, D.C., 1916), 186.

7. See the tables in Gary B. Nash et al., "Labor in the Era of the American Revolution: An Exchange," *Labor History,* 24 (1983), 435; Gary B. Nash, *The Urban Crucible: Social Change, Political Consciousness, and the Origins of the American Revolution* (Cambridge, Mass., 1979), App., 387–91; Allen Kulikoff, "The Progress of Inequality in Revolutionary Boston," *William and Mary Quarterly,* 3d ser., 28 (1971), 378, 411–12.

8. Catherine S. Crary, "The Humble Immigrant and the American Dream: Some Case Histories, 1746–1776," *Mississippi Valley Historical Review,* 46 (1959), 46–66, Crèvecœur quoted p. 66.

9. Nash, *Urban Crucible,* Table 5, App., 397–98.

10. Jonathan Boucher, quoted in Crary, "The Humble Immigrant," 48.

11. G. B. Warden, "The Distribution of Property in Boston, 1692–1775," *Perspectives in American History,* 10 (1976), 81–130.

12. Hall quoted in Stephen Botein, " 'Meer Mechanics' and an Open Press; The Business and Political Strategies of Colonial American Printers," *Perspectives in American History,* 9 (1975), 145.

13. Peter J. Parker, "The Philadelphia Printer: A Study of an Eighteenth-Century Businessman," *Business History Review,* 40 (1966), 24–26.

14. Jackson T. Main, *The Social Structure of Revolutionary America* (Princeton, N.J., 1965), 191.

15. Quoted in Gary B. Nash, "Artisans and Politics in Eighteenth-Century Philadelphia," in Nash, *Race, Class, and Politics: Essays on American Colonial and Revolutionary Society* (Urbana, Ill., 1986), 246–47.

16. See, e.g., Gary B. Nash, "Urban Wealth and Poverty in Prerevolutionary America," in Nash, *Race, Nationality, and Politics,* 173–210.

17. Parker, "Philadelphia Printer," 25.

18. Quoted in Nash, *Urban Crucible,* 256.

19. James Henretta, "Families and Farms: Mentalité in Pre-Industrial America," *William and Mary Quarterly,* 3d ser., 35 (1978), 3–32; also, Michael Merrill, "Cash is Good to Eat: Self-Sufficiency and Exchange in the Rural Economy of the United States," *Radical History Review,* 4 (Winter 1977), 42–71; Robert E. Mutch, "Yeoman and Merchant in Pre-Industrial America: Eighteenth-Century Massachusetts as a Case Study," *Societas,* 7 (1977), 279–302. The quotation is in J. E. Crowley, *This Sheba, Self: The Conceptualization of Economic Life in 18th-Century America* (Baltimore, 1974), 82.

20. Fred Anderson, *A People's Army: Massachusetts Soldiers and Society in the Seven Years' War* (Chapel Hill, 1984), 28–39; Philip J. Greven, *Four Generations: Population, Land and Family in Colonial Andover, Massachusetts* (Ithaca, N.Y. 1970).

21. See, e.g., Winifred B. Rothenberg, "The Market and Massachusetts Farmers, 1750–1855," *Journal of Economic History*, 41 (1981), 283–314; Carole Shammas, "How Self-Sufficient Was Early America?" *Journal of Interdisciplinary History*, 13 (1982), 247–72; Paul G. E. Clemens, "Household Economy and Market Economy in the Urban Countryside of Eighteenth-Century America," unpublished paper.

22. See, e.g., Christopher Clark, "Household Economy, Market Exchange and the Rise of Capitalism in the Connecticut Valley, 1800–1860," *Social History* (1979), 170–89; Gregory H. Nobles, "Commerce and Community: A Case Study of the Rural Broom-making Business in Antebellum Massachusetts," *Journal of the Early Republic*, 4 (1984), 288–308; Alexander J. Field, "Sectoral Shift in Antebellum Massachusetts: A Reconsideration," *Explorations in Economic History*, 15 (1978), 146–71.

23. John P. Hall, "The Gentle Craft: A Narrative of Yankee Shoemakers" (Ph.D. diss., Columbia Univ., 1954), 62.

24. James Deetz, *In Small Things Forgotten: The Archaeology of Early America* (New York, 1977).

25. Main, *Social Structure*, 182; Stephanie G. Wolf, *Urban Village: Population . . . in Germantown, Pennsylvania, 1683–1800* (Princeton, 1976), 308–9; Hall, "The Gentle Craft," 62.

26. Gary B. Kulik, "Dams, Fish and Farmers: The Defense of Public Rights in Eighteenth-Century Rhode Island," in Herbert G. Gutman and Donald H. Bell, eds., *The New England Working Class and the New Labor History* (Urbana, Ill., 1987), 187–213. For the work ethic of one such entrepreneurial artisan who became a Worcester iron manufacturer, see *Autobiography and Memorials of Ichabod Washburn* (Boston, 1878).

27. Botein, " 'Meer Mechanics,' " 134, 143. On the plight of French journeymen printers, see Robert Darnton, *The Great Cat Massacre* (New York, 1984) 79–82.

28. Billie G. Smith, "The Material Lives of Laboring Philadelphians, 1750 to 1800," *William and Mary Quarterly*, 3d ser., 38 (1981), 197, 200.

29. Calculated from Botein, " 'Meer Mechanics,' " 152, and Nash, *Urban Crucible*, 390.

30. Roger W. Moss, "Master Builders: A History of the Colonial Philadelphia Building Trades" (Ph.D. diss., Univ. of Delaware, 1972), 135.

31. Joseph A. Goldenberg, *Shipbuilding in Colonial America* (Charlottesville, 1976), 68–71; Simeon J. Crowther, "A Note on the Economic Position of the White Oaks," *William and Mary Quarterly*, 3d ser., 29 (1972), 134–36; William H. Woodwell, "The Woodwell Shipyard, 1759–1852," *Bulletin of the Business Historical Society*, 21 (1947), 58–74; Moss, "Master Builders," 152–53.

32. Rock, *Artisans of the New Republic*, 207; Graham R. Hodges, *New York City Cartmen, 1667–1850* (New York, 1986), chs. 3, 4.

33. Quotations in Crowley, *This Sheba*, 92, 93, 100.

34. Quoted in Jesse Lemisch, "Jack Tar in the Streets: Seamen in the Politics of Revolutionary America," *William and Mary Quarterly*, 3d ser., 25 (1968), 372.

35. Daniel Vickers, "The First Whalemen of Nantucket," *William and Mary Quarterly*, 3d ser., 40 (1983), 560–83.

36. Richard S. Dunn, "Servants and Slaves: The Recruitment and Employment of Labor," Jack P. Greene and J. R. Pole, eds., *Colonial British America: Essays in the New History of the Early Modern Era* (Baltimore, 1984), 159.

37. David Galenson, *White Servitude in Colonial America: An Economic Analysis* (New York, 1981), ch. 8; Nash, *Urban Crucible,* 106–8; Nash, "Slaves and Slaveowners in Colonial Philadelphia," *William and Mary Quarterly,* 3d ser., 30 (1973), 223–56; Sharon V. Salinger, "Artisans, Journeymen, and the Transformation of Labor in Late 18th-Century Philadelphia," *William and Mary Quarterly,* 3d ser., 40 (1983), 67; Bernard Bailyn, "The Peopling of British North America: An Introduction," *Perspectives in American History* (n.s., 1985), 7–11, 46–49 (quotation on p. 9); Charles G. Steffen, *The Mechanics of Baltimore* (Urbana, Ill., 1984), ch. 2; W. J. Rorabaugh, *The Craft Apprentice* (New York, 1986), chs. 1, 2.

38. Nash, *Urban Crucible,* 258.

39. Marcus Rediker, *Between the Devil and the Deep Blue Sea: Merchant Seamen, Pirates, and the Anglo-American Maritime World* (New York, 1987).

40. On the problems of disciplining servants and slaves, see Richard B. Morris, *Government and Labor in Early America* (New York, 1946), 424–49; Lawrence W. Towner, "A Fondness For Freedom: Servant Protest in Puritan Society," *William and Mary Quarterly,* 3rd ser., 19 (1962), 214–15; Samuel McKee, *Labor in Colonial New York* (New York, 1935), 116–18. The estimate of runaways is in Bailyn, "Peopling of British North America," 49.

41. It is worth noting that Richard B. Morris's detailed survey of legal actions brought by aggrieved servants includes only one involving work time, in which (among other complaints) a master was accused of requiring work on Sunday (Morris, *Government and Labor,* 481).

42. Carl Bridenbaugh, *The Colonial Craftsman* (New York, 1950), 138.

43. E. P. Thompson, "Time, Work-Discipline, and Industrial Capitalism," *Past and Present,* no. 38 (Dec. 1968), 73 ff. The following discussion takes as a point of reference Thompson's seminal essay, which has since its appearance in 1968 defined our thinking about the relationship of work time to industrialism.

44. Nash, *Urban Crucible,* 12. On England, see especially Douglas A. Reid, "The Decline of Saint Monday, 1766–1876," *Past and Present,* no. 71 (May 1976), 76–101.

45. Hall, "The Gentle Craft," chs. 4, 5.

46. Quoted in Carl Bridenbaugh, *Cities in the Wilderness* (New York, 1938), 437.

47. Robert W. Malcomson, *Popular Recreations in English Society, 1700–1850* (Cambridge, Eng., 1973), ch. 2. For an example of the hold of village wakes on English workers, see Neil McKendrick, "Josiah Wedgewood and Factory Discipline," *The Historical Journal,* 4 (1961), 46.

48. Quoted in Bienefeld, *Working Hours,* 18. The Puritan assault on festival days was of course linked to strict observance of the Sabbath, which tolerated neither work nor play on the Lord's Day. Winton Solberg, *Redeem the Time: The Puritan Sabbath in Early America* (Cambridge, Mass., 1977), 45 ff., and for Sunday observance in the colonies, ch. 3.

49. Stephen Innes, *Labor in a New Land: Economy and Society in Seventeenth Century Springfield* (Princeton, 1983), 75.

50. Hall, "The Gentle Craft," 110–11.

51. Thompson, "Time, Work-Discipline, and Industrial Capitalism," 60.

52. W. J. Rorabaugh, *The Alcoholic Republic* (New York, 1979), 26, 29, 33 (Sewell

quotation), 149, 333; Sarah Francis McMahon, " 'A Comfortable Subsistence': A History of Diet in New England, 1630–1850" (Ph.D. diss., Brandeis Univ., 1982), 64–68. For accounts of "footing" by new men in printing shops and "jeffing" at breaktimes, see Milton W. Hamilton, *The Country Printer* (2d ed.: Port Washington, N.Y., 1964), 40–41; Rollo Silver, *The American Printer* (Charlottesville, 1967), 8–9. Both, however, are referring to the early nineteenth century.

53. Quotations in Foster R. Dulles, *America Learns to Play: A History of Popular Recreation, 1607–1940* (New York, 1940), 36, 37, 40, 42.

54. Quoted in Crowley, *This Sheba*, 57.

55. Quoted in Bridenbaugh, *Craftsman*, 129.

56. Gary B. Kulik, "The Beginning of the Industrial Revolution in America, Pawtucket, 1672–1829" (Ph.D. diss., Brown Univ. 1980), 45–46.

57. See, e.g., the notice by "Bob Chizel" in the New York *Weekly Journal* (Jan. 7, 1733), reprinted in Rita S. Gottesman, ed., *The Arts and Crafts in New York: Advertisements and News Items from New York City Newspapers, 1726–1776* (New York, 1936), 191–92.

58. The contract (Feb. 25, 1771) is printed in Morris, *Government and Labor*, 220–21 (my italics).

59. Arthur H. Cole, "The Tempo of Mercantile Life in Colonial America," *Business History Review*, 33 (1959), 277–99.

60. Quoted in Paul Faler, *Mechanics and Manufacturers in the Early Industrial Revolution: Lynn, Massachusetts, 1780–1860* (Albany, N.Y., 1981), 106–7.

61. Nash, *Urban Crucible*, 223.

62. Quotations in Staughton Lynd, "The American Revolution and the Common Man: Farm Tenants and Artisans in New York Politics, 1777–1788" (Ph.D. diss., Columbia Univ. 1962), 242; also, Roediger, " 'Liberty of Leisure,' " 8–9.

63. "Time, Work-Discipline, and Industrial Capitalism," 60. For an example of extreme time discipline and industriousness in a society in which work and life were not demarcated, see Thomas C. Smith, "Peasant Time and Factory Time in Japan," *Past and Present*, no. 111 (May 1986), 165–97; for alternative lines of argument that emphasize malnutrition and underemployment, see Edmund S. Morgan, "The Labor Problem at Jamestown, 1607–18," *American Historical Review*, 76 (1971), 595–611, and, for a critique of Thompson that stresses the variability of work time reckoning, Richard Whipp, " 'A Time to Every Purpose': An Essay on Time and Work," in Patrick Joyce, ed., *The Historical Meaning of Work* (Cambridge, Eng., 1987), 216–23.

64. Quoted in Botein, " 'Meer Mechanics,' " 159.

65. Ian Quimby, "Apprenticeship in Colonial Philadelphia" (M.A. essay, Univ. Delaware, 1961), discussed in Salinger, "Journeymen," 68–69.

66. Nash, *Urban Crucible*, 259–60; Moss, "Master Builders," 143–46.

67. Salinger, "Journeymen," 68–69; Salinger, "Colonial Labor in Transition: The Decline of Indentured Servitude in Late 18th Century Philadelphia," *Labor History*, 22 (1981), 180, 182 (tables 3, 4). Baltimore, whose economy boomed between 1790 and 1820, followed a somewhat different pattern. Shipyards and other larger-scale enterprises employed slaves, small-shop crafts relied on poor-relief apprentices, but these bound workers functioned within a larger free-labor market and were regarded primarily as cheap competition for journeymen workers. Charles G. Steffen, "Changes

in Artisan Production in Baltimore, 1790–1820," *William and Mary Quarterly,* 3d ser., 36 (1979), 101–17.

68. Quoted in Rock, *Artisans of the New Republic,* 264.

69. The after-dark, wintertime schedule for inside workers seems to have been made possible by the shift from tallow candles to the much superior spermaceti candle. John E. Crowley, "Artificial Illumination in Early America and the Definition of Domestic Space and Time," paper delivered at the Third International Conference of the Centre de Recherches sur l'Histoire des Etats-Unis, Paris, June 1987.

70. Nash, *Urban Crucible,* 325.

71. See, e.g., DH, IV, 117; also, Rock, *Artisans of the New Republic,* 24–49.

72. For weaving prices in Philadelphia, see Richard A. McLeod, "The Philadelphia Artisan, 1828–1850," (Ph.D. diss., Univ. of Missouri, 1971), 151–52.

73. DH, V, 275.

74. Quoted in McLeod, "Philadelphia Artisan," 35.

75. Faler, *Mechanics and Manufacturers,* 22–23, 77 ff., and, for quotations, 172, 213.

76. Neither Faler, nor Alan Dawley, *Class and Community: The Industrial Revolution in Lynn* (Cambridge, Mass., 1976), nor Mary H. Blewett, *Men, Women, and Work: Class, Gender, and Protest in the New England Shoe Industry, 1780–1910* (Urbana, Ill., 1988) makes any reference to the ten-hour movement.

77. See, e.g., the observations of Edwin T. Freedley (1857) about Philadelphia hand-loom weavers, quoted in Bruce Laurie, *Working People of Philadelphia, 1800–1850* (Philadelphia, 1980), 25.

78. Christine Stansell, "The Origins of the Sweatshop: Women and Early Industrialization in New York City," in M. H. Frisch and D. J. Walkowitz, eds., *Working-Class America: Essays on Labor, Community, and American Society* (Urbana, Ill., 1983), 92–93; McLeod, "Philadelphia Artisan," quotation, 35, also 37–38; Susan B. Hirsch, *Roots of the American Working Class: The Industrialization of Crafts in Newark, 1800–1860* (Philadelphia, 1978), 79.

79. Thomas Dublin, "Women and Outwork in a Nineteenth-Century New-England Town, Fitzwilliam, N.H., 1830–1850," in Steven Hahn and Jonathan Prude, eds., *The Countryside in the Age of Capitalist Transformation* (Chapel Hill, N.C., 1985), 51–70: Blewett, *Men, Women, and Work,* chs., 1–3; quotations in Egal Feldman, "New York's Men's Clothing Trade, 1800 to 1861" (Ph.D. diss., Univ. of Pennsylvania, 1959), 192, 215; Hirsch, *Roots of the American Working Class* 26 (table 6), 28 (table 7); Stansell, "Origins of the Sweatshop," 90–91.

80. Quoted in Nancy Cott, *Bonds of Womanhood: Women's Sphere in New England, 1780–1835* (New Haven, Conn., 1978), 49.

81. See, e.g., the contracts of the Pomfret Manufacturing Company, printed in Gary Kulik et al., eds., *The New England Mill Village, 1790–1860* (Cambridge, Mass., 1982), 437–50.

82. Barbara Tucker, *Samuel Slater and the Origins of the American Textile Industry, 1790–1860* (Ithaca, N.Y., 1984).

83. Kenneth L. Sokoloff, "Industrialization and the Growth of the Manufacturing Sector in the Northeast, 1820 to 1850" (Ph.D. diss., Harvard Univ., 1982), ch. 1.

84. Christopher F. Clark, "Household, Market and Capital: The Process of Economic

Change in the Connecticut Valley of Massachusetts, 1800–1860'' (Ph.D. diss., Harvard Univ., 1982), 240. See also, e.g., Edward S. Cooke, "Rural Artisanal Culture: The Preindustrial Joiners of Newtown and Woodbury, Connecticut, 1760–1820'' (Ph.D. diss., Boston Univ., 1984), ch. 3; Jonathan Prude, "Town-Factory Conflicts in Antebellum Rural Masachusetts,'' in Hahn and Prude, eds., *The Countryside,* 71–102; and the citations in note 23.

85. Philip Scranton, *Proprietary Capitalism: The Textile Manufacture at Philadelphia* (New York, 1983), ch. 1 and passim; Wilentz, *Chants Democratic,* 107, and ch. 3, passim; Hirsch, *Roots of the American Working Class,* ch. 2.

86. Cynthia J. Shelton, *The Mills of Manayunk: Industrialization and Social Conflict in the Philadelphia Region, 1787–1837* (Baltimore, 1986), 41.

87. M. B. to George S. White, Dec. 26, 1827, in White, *Memoir of Samuel Slater* (1836), reprinted in Kulik et al., *New England Mill Village,* 362–63; *Documents Relative to the Manufactures in the United States* [H.R. Doc. 308; the *McLane Report*] (Washington, D.C. 1833), passim. On work schedules in one processing industry, see Judith A. McCaw, *Most Wonderful Machine: Mechanization and Social Change in Berkshire Paper Making, 1801–1885* (Princeton, N.J., 1987), 54–55.

88. "Testimony of Witnesses, accompanying the Report of the Committee of the Senate, appointed to investigate the subject of the Employment of Children in Manufactories,'' *Journal of the Senate of the Commonwealth of Pennsylvania* (1837–38), II, 282–83, 286, 294.

89. Clark, "Household, Market and Capital,'' 314–15.

90. Quoted in Theodore F. Marburg, "Aspects of Labor Administration in the Early Nineteenth Century,'' *Bulletin of the Business Historical Society,* 15 (Feb. 1941), 6.

91. N. B. Gordon Diary, in Kulik et al., *New England Mill Village,* 283–307; Tucker, *Samuel Slater,* 161–62; Thomas Dublin, *Women at Work: The Transformation of Work and Community in Lowell, Massachusetts, 1826–1860* (New York, 1979), 72–73, 109.

92. Clerk's Reports, July 14, Dec. 26, 1814, Antietam Woolen Manufacturing Company MS, Hagley Museum and Library, Wilmington, Del. (Courtesy of Brian Gratton).

93. Gordon Diary (May 26, 1830 entry), in Kulik et al., *New England Mill Village,* 298–99.

94. Clark, "Household, Market and Capital,'' 320–21.

95. Clerk's Report, July 18, 1814, Antietam Woolen Manufacturing Company MS.

96. Quoted in Felicia J. Deyrup, *Arms Makers of the Connecticut Valley, 1789–1870* (Northampton, Mass., 1948), 162–63.

97. John Jarrett, quoted in Francis G. Couvares, *The Remaking of Pittsburgh: Class and Culture in an Industrializing City, 1877–1919* (Albany, N.Y., 1984), 13–14. See also, e.g., the testimony of Thomas Lawton, the manager of an Ohio ironworks, in *Journal of the Senate of Pennsylvania* (1837–38), II, 335.

98. Deyrup, *Arms Makers of the Connecticut Valley,* 163; quoted in Merritt Roe Smith, *Harpers Ferry Armory and the New Technology* (Ithaca, N.Y., 1977), 272.

99. Quoted in Smith, *Harpers Ferry Armory,* 274 (italics in original).

100. Quoted in Smith, *Harpers Ferry Armory,* 274 (italics in original). For an example of an employer who did try to break the stint by cutting rates, see the statement of Samuel W. Collins to his workers (1846), printed in Henrietta M. Larson, "An Early Industrial

Capitalist's Labor Policy and Management,'' *Bulletin of the Business Historical Society,* 18 (Nov. 1944), 137–41.

101. *Journal of the Senate of Pennsylvania* (1837–38), II, 299.

102. Gordon Diary (Oct. 9, 1830 entry), in Kulik et al., *New England Mill Village,* 304.

103. Quoted in Gary J. Kornblith, ''From Artisan to Businessman: Master Mechanics in New England, 1789–1850'' (Ph.D. diss., Princeton Univ., 1983), 503–4 (my italics).

104. ''Resolution of the New England Association of Farmers, Mechanics and Other Workingmen,'' in *The Free Inquirer,* June 14, 1832, reprinted in Kulick et al., *New England Mill Village,* 497–98; *Pawtucket Chronicle,* Oct. 18, 1828, reprinted in Kulik et al., *New England Mill Village,* 266.

105. *Journal of the Senate of Pennsylvania* (1837–38), II, 292, 307, 327.

106. Kulik, ''The Beginning of the Industrial Revolution,'' 360 ff., 372.

107. *Federal Gazette,* May 17, 1791; Rock, *Artisans of the New Republic,* 266 (table 10.1); Nash, *Urban Crucible,* 397 (table 5); Moss, ''Master Builders,'' 184–85.

108. Charles E. Peterson, ''Introduction,'' facsimile edition of *The Carpenters' Company 1786 Rule Book* (Philadelphia, 1971), x-xii, xiv; *Rule Book,* vi.

109. *Federal Gazette,* May 17, 1791.

110. *Pennsylvanian,* March 21, 1836, in DH, VI, 56.

111. For an egregious example, in which Boston ship carpenters charged that employers paid nothing if bad weather halted work during the day—on the principle that ''we never pay hours''—see *Independent Chronicle and Boston Patriot,* May 23, 1832, in DH, VI, 84. The shipyard owners, for their part, considered ''sunrise to sunset, allowing two hours for meals . . . one good, old-fashioned day's work. . . . '' George E. McNeill, ed., *The Labor Movement: The Problem of Today* (New York, 1888), 340.

112. DH, VI, 85.

113. *Dunlap's American Daily Advertiser,* May 11, 1791. See also, e.g., the constitution (1832) of the New England Association of Farmers, Mechanics, and Other Workingmen, quoted in Kornblith, ''From Artisan to Businessman,'' 506.

114. Quoted in Wilentz, *Chants Democratic,* 137.

115. Quoted in Rock, *Artisans of the New Republic,* 301.

116. Rock, 249; Henry P. Rosemont, ''Benjamin Franklin and the Philadelphia Typographical Strikers of 1786,'' *Labor History,* 22 (1981), 406–407. Clark, ''Household, Market and Capital,'' 324–325, found an instance of an Amherst, Massachusetts, carriage manufacturer who was paying by the hour in 1835.

117. See, e.g. the strike summary, App. B, in William A. Sullivan, *The Industrial Worker in Pennsylvania, 1800–1840* (Harrisburg, Penn., 1955), 221–27.

118. DH, V, 80.

119. DH, V, 82.

120. The Ten-Hour Circular is reprinted in DH, VI, 94–99.

121. ''On a Reduction of the Hours of Labour,'' *New England Artisan,* June 21, 1834.

2

The Course of American Labor Politics

Trade unionism is everywhere, in Selig Perlman's term, job-conscious. It is, by definition, the collective effort by workers to advance their job interests. That trade unionism is an economic activity does not, however, place it outside of politics. The precise relationship of any national movement to its political system turns on two primary determinants. One might be called instrumental, the employment of political means for trade-union ends; and the second, sacrificial, the expenditure of trade-union energies for larger purposes (generally associated, to be sure, with ultimate working-class interests). If a politico-economic scale of trade unionism based on those measures was constructed, the American movement would occupy one extreme. At the other (leaving aside movements that are instruments of the state) would come the highly political Indian and Latin American movements; then the French and Italian movements, which have bargaining functions but whose strikes and other activities are closely tied to political objectives; next the Northern European movements, which in varying degrees participate in national incomes policies and rely on state welfare systems, and invariably have formal ties to labor or socialist parties. Even the Canadian movement, despite strong institutional and ideological links to the United States, has moved toward the Northern European model since the 1930s. In

Reprinted with permission of Charles Scribner's Sons, an imprint of Macmillan Publishing Company, from *Encyclopedia of American Political History,* Jack P. Greene, Editor-in-Chief, Vol. II, pp. 709–27. Copyright © 1984 by Charles Scribner's Sons.

1961 the Canadian Labour Congress helped found and affiliated itself with the New Democratic party.

No trade-union movement stands wholly outside of politics, and in the United States the relationship to the political system has evolved and deepened during the twentieth century. This development has not moved the American movement out of its end place on the world scale of trade unionism. American trade unionism remains today the child of a history that located organized labor at the margin of the political system.

Independent Labor Politics: The First Impulse

In the summer of 1827, the journeymen societies of Philadelphia formed the Mechanics' Union of Trade Associations. Although local unions of individual trades went back to the 1790s and even earlier, this was the first effort at citywide organization and properly marks the start of the American labor movement. Prompted initially by the desire to support a carpenters' strike for ten hours, the Mechanics' Union of Trade Associations shifted its attention within a few months to politics. The amended bylaws called for the nomination of "such individuals as shall pledge themselves . . . to support and advance . . . the interests and enlightenment of the working classes." After a slow start in 1828, the resulting Workingmen's party scored a considerable success in both the city and state-assembly races in 1829. That year, a workingmen's party sprang up in New York City, and the movement swiftly spread across the country. Often fragmentary and derived mainly from the contemporary labor press, the evidence suggests that workingmen's parties, under a variety of names, existed in as many as fifteen states. Although this political activity was mostly local in scope, some state and regional activity did occur in this first surge of labor politics in the early 1830s.

Workers had not been absent from American politics in the past. Laboring men of all ranks had figured in the mob activity characteristic of eighteenth-century politics. Mechanics had participated, in a more or less organized way, in the drive for independence after 1773 and again in the movement for a strong federal union during the 1780s. And they were a visible element, mainly in the Jeffersonian camp, in the first American party system that emerged during the next decade.

In the deferential politics of these early years, however, workers accepted the lead of their betters. They mobilized for objectives—independence, the Constitution, Jeffersonian republicanism—that surmounted class lines. The self-interested goals that they pursued were attached to specific crafts and represented concerns defined by the master mechanics. The workingmen's parties thus marked a sharp break with the past. For the first time, artisans entered politics as an independent force and for the express purpose of "promot[ing] the interests and support[ing] the claims of the Working People."

Jacksonian artisans were heir to two intertwined ideological traditions. The economic one derived from the Ricardian labor theory of value. "Wealth," asserted William Heighton, the cordwainer who had founded the Philadelphia Workingmen's party, "is the *sole* and *exclusive* product of LABOUR." The civic counterpart, rooted in the ideals of the American Revolution, was "equal rights," with its vision of a harmonious republican society of equal, independent, and virtuous citizens. Counter to this artisan republicanism ran transforming economic changes that increasingly pitted employers against workers, subjected labor standards to market pressures, and raised up a new moneyed class. The effect was to create, as the workingmen saw it,

> two distinct classes, the rich and the poor; the oppressor and the oppressed; those that live by their own labor, and they that live by the labour of others . . . ; the one seeking to introduce and perpetuate among us invidious and artificial distinctions, unnatural and unjust inequalities, while the other party declares that all men are created free and equal, enjoying a perfect uniformity of rights and privileges.

That the artisans' response should have taken political form was partly dictated by the nature of the perceived problems. These had their sources, according to the workingmen, primarily in "injudicious and partial legislation," in laws made "for the benefit of the rich and the oppression of the poor." A process of political mobilization was also under way. "Systems of oppression" would triumph in America, pronounced George Warner of the New York Workingmen's party, only if "tradesmen, craftsmen, and the industrial working classes consider themselves of TOO LITTLE CONSEQUENCE to the body politic." They had, in fact, been of little consequence in the recent past; voter turnout had been at record lows between 1816 and 1828. During those years, however, a remarkable extension of the suffrage had occurred. Voting barriers, it was true, had never fully excluded laboring men; during the 1790s as many as half held some voting rights in New York City. But as property qualifications for white adult males disappeared, so probably did the inhibiting notion that politics was the proper concern of the privileged ranks of American society. The resumption of two-party conflict raised political temperatures but also revived traditional suspicions of party domination. Antipartyism was, indeed, a main article of the workingmen's rhetoric: "So long as the people will be satisfied with the sound of a name, such as Federalist or Democrat; so long [will they be] the slaves of corrupt office hunters and designing politicians." Workingmen should "throw off the trammels of party spirit, and unite under the banner of equal rights."

The surge of independent political activity was a new event, and not one limited to the workingmen. The Anti-Masonic parties, which appeared on the scene at the same time, represented a somewhat different constituency but were venting very much the same kind of popular reaction against the alien forces of modernism. Both movements pitted the people against an enemy "at war with the rights and interests of republican America."

Institutionally, the workingmen's parties were very fragile. They lacked funds, seasoned leaders, precedents to follow. The class lines on which they were built, moreover, were still quite indistinct. Although much debated by historians, it now seems clear that the main impulse came from journeymen workers and their unions. But it is true also that, in varying degrees, employers and professionals as professed "workingmen" did participate and that penetration by outside interests was an easy matter. Everywhere, the workingmen's parties proved highly vulnerable to the machinations of the established parties. In Boston, the Workingmen's party was the out-and-out creation of the National Republicans. Such utopian reformers as Thomas Skidmore, Frances Wright, and Robert Dale Owen also found the workingmen's parties to be fertile ground for the peddling of their various nostrums. The workingmen's parties lived scarcely an average of two years, and by the mid-1830s this first surge of American labor politics had entirely disappeared.

The underlying causes, however, were not transitory—an abiding sense of grievance against nascent industrial capitalism, an equal-rights ideology rooted in artisan experience and community life, and political means readily accessible for expressing popular protest. For the next half century, the political impulses first manifested in the workingmen's parties would repeatedly take hold of the American labor movement.

The Preemptive Political Order

Never again, however, would labor enjoy so open a political field as during that initial foray in the early Jacksonian period. Until then, the reach of American politics had extended only intermittently down into the laboring population. Enlivening party competition had been absent from most states, even after contested national elections revived in 1828. Nor did party operation, closely held by insiders, allow for much popular participation. And the party system lacked legitimacy; at best it was tolerated as a necessary evil that lent some order to representative government. All this changed dramatically during the 1830s.

Both Democrats and Whigs developed national structures that were capable of waging strong campaigns in virtually every state. (The average gap between the parties in state votes for president shrank from 36 percent in 1828 to 11 percent in 1836.) Cadres of party workers were intensively recruited, and, especially through the introduction of the convention, party affairs democratized. Party leadership, on the other hand, became more professional, at once highly effective at ruling the organization and skilled at the business of campaigning. The election of 1840 was an authentic political milestone. William Henry Harrison was transformed into "the Cincinnatus of America" and the aristocratic Whigs into the party of the log cabin. Voters turned out in record numbers. The participation rate had been 26.9 percent in 1824, 55.4 percent in 1832, 80.2 percent in 1840. The rituals of campaigning, the fury of electoral battle, the symbolic meaning of party loyalty—these amounted to a preempting political culture that acted powerfully on American working people.

The invasion of labor's political terrain thrust much deeper. The mass parties emerged at a time of rising ethnocultural tensions. A new wave of revivalism swept the country during the 1830s, unleashing a crusade for moral regeneration and, with it, a zealous attack on alien elements within American society. The country, declared the Michigan Baptist convention of 1850, was threatened by "the tide of immigration . . . beating incessantly upon our shores." Popery stalked the nation "with superabundant means to prosecute its work. It is grafting its ugly scions upon every branch, and growing with . . . the Tree of Liberty.'' The antagonisms thus set in motion penetrated deep into the nation's political life. For one thing, evangelical Christians saw the state as a proper instrument of social control. Many of their objectives—temperance, Sabbath keeping, the defense of the public schools against Catholic influences—demanded political solutions. Nor could the encompassing political culture, in any case, be insulated from the rising tide of ethnocultural passions. Party affiliation intertwined with ethnic and religious identity. On this point, if on no other, the quantitative evidence seems entirely conclusive. The Democratic party attracted the Irish, the Germans, and the Catholics; the Whig party, evangelical Christians, both native-born and British. Other groups tended to split more evenly between the two parties. But for those swept up in ethnocultural conflict, religious and ethnic identity served as the primary determinants of party affiliation.

These ethnocultural forces, cutting across class lines as they did, profoundly affected the political behavior of workers. The evangelicals among them were bonded more closely to their employers, not only by the ties of religious conviction but also by a shared commitment to sobriety, the work ethic, and self-advancement. On the other hand, Protestant worker was set against Catholic worker. During bloody Philadelphia riots in 1844, native artisans laid waste Irish working-class Kensington in a battle sparked by Catholic opposition to Bible reading in the public schools.

The nativist impulse carried Protestant workers to some degree beyond the orbit of the business-dominated Whig party. The Know-Nothing movement, when it sprang up in the early 1850s, drew heavily on labor support, and it included considerable working-class representation among its candidates. In Massachusetts, the Know-Nothings championed labor legislation (including the ten-hour day) and political reforms (including the secret ballot) aimed at the Whig elite. This by no means signified working-class solidarity, however. The Know-Nothings fervently championed a host of anti-Catholic and antiforeign measures, including the disbanding of Irish militia companies, dismissal of aliens from public jobs, and deportation of paupers. By serving as a key element in the emergent Republican party, the Know-Nothings transmitted—if indeed they did not intensify—the ethnocultural strain in the party politics of the second half of the nineteenth century. The primacy of those ties, and the working-class divisiveness that they revealed, spoke powerfully against the logic of a workingmen's party.

The mass parties, finally, readily absorbed labor's political impulses. They were, first of all, highly accessible. In Pittsburgh during the 1840s, fully a quarter of the secondary leadership of both parties was drawn from the city's wage earners (mainly artisans and skilled workers). Both parties, too, pitched their rhetoric to the economic concerns of working people. The Whigs stressed class harmony: public policies that fostered business prosperity would redound to the benefit of workers. The Whig program, countered the Democrats, was class legislation. Protective tariffs gave "bounties to particular interests to the detriment of the great industrial classes of the Country . . . and sought to aggrandize the few at the expense of the many." Less wedded to the established business community, the Democrats were probably faster afoot in making class appeals. Labor defection to the Loco-Foco (Equal Rights) party in New York in 1836–37 prompted Tammany Hall to move aggressively to repair the damage. It accepted Loco-Foco candidates, approved Martin Van Buren's independent treasury scheme, and "adopted a Declaration of Rights essentially the same as ours." At the time, remarked John R. Commons, a pioneer scholar of the subject, Tammany "began its modern career of organizing the labour vote." In an act of great symbolic importance, the Van Buren administration introduced the ten-hour day for federal workers in 1840. It was, on the other hand, the Whig-dominated Supreme Court of Massachusetts that handed down the landmark *Commonwealth* v. *Hunt* decision (1842) establishing the legality of trade unionism. A large, native-born industrial population had some bearing on the relative progressivism of Massachusetts Whiggery. Between them, in any case, Whigs and Democrats managed for two decades to absorb the political energies emanating from a growing working class.

The sectional crisis of the 1850s cruelly tested this particular capacity of the mass parties. As a new two-party system emerged from the ruins of the old, racism became magnified in the appeal to the workingman. The Republicans stressed what he stood to lose in the extension of slavery into the territories: the central issue was "whether the West should become the homes of white Freemen or colored slavery." Republican victory, answered the Democrats, would mean abolition "and bring the Negroes into the Northern States to take the place of white laborers." The Democratic party believed "that the white laboring masses should never be subjected to ruinous competition with the almost countless hordes of cheap and needy negro laborers." There was this added dividend to the Democrats: immigrant workers, always at the receiving end of nativist hostility, now had in the black man a suitable target on whom to discharge their own rage.

The prize for inventiveness, however, went to the Republicans. Although they inherited most of the Whig vote, the dispersal of the elite stratum made for a certain leveling within the emergent Republican party. There was, too, a strong labor component to the Know-Nothings who flowed into Republicanism. Perhaps most important, the assault on the Slave Power cast "free labor" in a fresh light. Slavery was "a system which degrades labor, enriching a few aristocrats at the expense of labor." The issue, proclaimed Detroit Republicans in 1856, "is between ARISTOCRATS AND SLAVEOWNERS! and the Free Working Men of the Union." No major party ever so closely identified itself with the cause of labor as did the Republicans in their bid to become a mass party. "To make labor honorable is the object and aim of the Republican party," asserted a gubernatorial candidate in Illinois in 1860. To a remarkable degree, too, these sentiments echoed the claims of labor radicals themselves. In 1859, Lincoln said that "labor is prior to, and independent of capital"; according to William Evarts, speaking in 1856, labor is "the source of all our wealth, of all our progress, of all our dignity and value." Spoken by others, these words might have signified a workingmen's party in the making; here they served, on the contrary, to undo any such possibility. By this brilliant appeal to labor, the Republicans were manifesting the cooptive genius of an emergent mass party.

Subsequent Republican history exposed the unyielding limits on the range of that appeal. Contemporaneous with the rise of Republicanism, and to some degree stimulated by its equal-rights ideology, a major labor-reform movement sprang up. The resulting National Labor Union (NLU), which was formed in 1866, advanced strong legislative demands, foremost among them the eight-hour day. Like the ten-hour movement before the Civil War, the call for shorter hours expressed the anxieties of an embattled native-born working class: more leisure would make for self-improvement and better citizenship. For the eight-hour day, however, the reform rationale went deeper. With increasing leisure, the principal theorist, Ira Steward, argued, workers would incessantly raise their demands on employers and eventually so undercut the profitability of the wage system as to lead to the cooperative commonwealth. The theory did not much trouble Republicans, but the cost of the eight-hour day did. Try as they might, the Republicans could not evade the issue, and inevitably the Republican party came down on the side of its business wing.

This was the breaking point that every mass party sought desperately, but not always successfully, to avoid. The labor reformers broke from the Republicans, allied with the Democrats in Connecticut, and elsewhere launched labor parties. In 1872, the NLU formed the National Labor Reform party. Industrial strife likewise frequently exposed the underlying realities within the political order. In Lynn, Massachusetts, the great shoemakers' strike of 1860 prompted the embittered local labor movement to launch a workingmen's party that briefly took control of the city government. The strike wave of 1877, crushed by state and federal troops, sparked independent action across the country, much of which flowed into the Greenback-Labor campaign of 1878–80. The high point for this kind of protest labor politics probably occurred under the ascendancy of the Knights of Labor during the mid-1880s. Workingmen's tickets have been counted in at least 189 cities and towns nationwide during that turbulent time. The duplicity of the major parties was a recurring lesson for labor during the nineteenth century. "Our rights demand protection at our own hands," insisted one Lynn shoemaker in 1845. "It would be folly in us to expect aid from any other source; past experience kills all hope of help from the rich and powerful."

To act independently, on the other hand, was to incur no less great a risk. Labor's forays into third-party politics invariably failed, petering out on election day in a handful of votes or, occasionally in industrial towns, winning once and then disappearing into one of the major parties. There was, in the end, no denying the futility of these ventures. In Europe, labor movements battled for the franchise and access to the political arena. In America, labor faced an altogether different form of exclusion, involving not the right to participate, but the room to participate.

Labor Reform, Trade Unionism, and Socialism

For half a century and more, the emerging labor movement struggled to come to terms with this unyielding political reality. Why not simply abandon the political field? That easy course attracted even the infant trade unions. "No Party, political or religious questions shall at any time be agitated in, or acted upon by this Union," stated the constitution of the General Trades' Union of Philadelphia. Founded in 1833, this was the city's second central labor body, successor to the lamented Mechanics' Union of Trade Associations, which had spawned the first Workingmen's party in 1828 and then expired. The lesson was not lost on the revived Philadelphia movement: "The Trades' Union never will be political, because its members have learned from experience, that the introduction of Politics into their Societies has thwarted every effort to ameliorate their Conditions." That conviction became firmly implanted in the trade unions as they took root in nineteenth-century industry. They aggressively asserted their job-conscious functions and equally their insulation from partisan politics. Few trade unionists would have taken issue with the assertion in 1872 of the secretary of the Bricklayers' International Union that "the only way we can be successful with our local and national unions is by excluding politics from them."

The labor reformers had a harder time of it. They turned, as Samuel Gompers remarked, "instinctively to political activity for reform." But many of them also came to see the hazards of partisan politics. The NLU, for example, took this course with evident reluctance. At the first convention in 1866, a labor party carried only by a narrow margin—and then only in principle. The actual creation of a national party took place when the NLU was nearly dead, more as a symbolic gesture than as a serious venture into politics. One alternative, much favored by the land reformers who dominated the movement in the 1840s and early 1850s, was to lobby legislators of the major parties in a way that prefigured the nonpartisanship of the later trade union movement. By so doing, the Industrial Congress of 1851 hoped to "eschew partyism of every description." That same desire attracted labor reformers to nonpolitical solutions, above all, to cooperation. In practice, however, producer cooperatives did rely on the state for enabling legal mechanisms and, much more important, for currency reform that would break the grip of "banks and money lenders" on the economy. It was this second need that rendered greenbackism so crucial to the labor reformers from the late 1860s onward. There was, it seemed, no way to the cooperative commonwealth except through politics.

This truth the Knights of Labor explicitly accepted. "All the evils that labor rests under," admitted its first national leader, Uriah Stephens, "are matters of law and [are] to be removed by legislation." On the other hand: "Our order *is not a political one* [and] can never be." From the moment it emerged nationally in 1878, the Knights wrestled with this dilemma. Leaders could run for office as individuals, and many of them, including Grand Master Workman Terence V. Powderly, did. Considerable lobbying was undertaken, including the successful campaign for a contract labor law in 1885. District and local assemblies were permitted to take up politics, but only after the close of formal business and with no power to bind individual members. For itself, the national order could only come up with "education," so that members would learn "to depend upon thorough organization, cooperation and political action, and, through these, the abolishment of the wage system." Translation of political education into action, however, the Knights of Labor stubbornly resisted. The most it hoped for was that its teachings would "give birth to political parties and issues." Only when it was nearly finished in the late 1880s did the Noble Order, like the NLU before it, commit itself to independent labor politics.

By then, the Knights' irresolution had already precipitated a crisis within the American labor movement. Until the 1880s, a fragile balance had been maintained between labor reform and trade unionism. These were not independent phenomena but, on the contrary, rooted as one within the nation's working-class communities. Both drew on the same constituencies and, indeed, largely on the same leadership. William Sylvis, simultaneously head of the Iron Molders' Union and the NLU, found nothing contradictory about trade unionism and labor reform: the first tended to the worker's immediate needs, the second to his higher hopes. These differing functions, however, demanded strict institutional separation. The Knights violated this cardinal rule of functional differentiation. They did so, at bottom, because they lacked confidence in their capacity—in the political means available to them—for carrying out their labor-reform mission. Their great surge during the 1880s came when the Knights began to assume trade-union functions. Their labor-reform orientation was extremely beneficial in one way: it enabled them to organize on an industrial rather than a craft basis. But there was no denying that the Knights had violated the traditional division of functions within the labor movement. When they concluded that the order would not retreat, the threatened national trade unions moved in late 1886 to form the American Federation of Labor (AFL).

Initiated in defense of the old order, the new federation was actually inaugurating the modern age of American organized labor. William Sylvis had once expected that labor reform (greenbackism in this case) would "do away with the necessity of trade-unions entirely." Such a self-immolating notion was utterly alien to the next generation of trade union leaders. In setting up the AFL, they were asserting the supremacy—soon, indeed, the monopoly—of trade unionism as the expression of the collective will of the American working class. In part, this claim stemmed from an undeniable reality. As industrialism matured, trade unionism gained the ascendancy, while labor reform faltered and began to die. The Knights of Labor marked, in fact, the end of the line. Ever more confident, increasingly effective as functioning organizations, the trade unions demanded center stage.

For this claim, there now existed a compelling doctrinal justification. Marxian socialism, firmly implanted by the 1870s on the American radical scene (especially in the German-speaking sector), exerted a powerful influence on such founders of the AFL as Samuel Gompers, Adolph Strasser, and J. P. McDonnell. From furious debates within the First International, they learned above all else that trade unionism was the indispensable instrument—and premature politics a primary obstacle—in preparing the working class for revolution. Beyond thrusting trade unionism to the center of the labor movement, this Marxist formulation provided ideological underpinnings to the antipolitical stance long since enunciated by American trade unionism. The founders of the AFL elevated this animus into the explicit doctrine of "pure-and-simple" unionism—only by self-organization along occupational lines, only by a concentration on job-conscious goals, would the worker be "furnished with the weapons which shall secure his industrial emancipation."

The clarifying influence of Marxism went in the contrary direction as well, however. The political socialists, no less than those in the economist wing, were invested with a sure sense of direction. Prevailing over the trade union advocates, they captured the socialist movement and committed it to independent politics. It was not only fear of America's preempting political culture that had immobilized the labor reformers. They had, as David Montgomery has remarked, "no conception of an active role for the machinery of state. The sole function they attributed to government was that of enacting just and general laws applying impartially to all citizens. Within the framework of these laws, social development would take care of itself." For the socialists, the stakes of politics were very much higher, for they saw it as a system of power. Through politics, they proposed to organize the working class, seize the state, and, through its powers, overturn capitalism. Never mind that the Socialist Labor party (SLP) utterly lacked the popular base on which the labor-reform parties had been able to draw. The confidence in political action more than compensated for the bleakness of the immediate electoral prospect. From the inception of the SLP in 1877 onward, the socialist movement would continuously have in the field an alternative to the major parties.

It took the better part of a decade to sort out the precise relationship between trade unionism and socialism. Born during an infectious wave of labor politics, the AFL actually endorsed independent efforts at its founding convention. Gompers himself had led New York labor in support of Henry George's mayoralty campaign on the United Labor party ticket earlier in 1886. Beyond the need for caution in the uncertain formative period, there was the underlying ideological agreement that AFL leaders still shared with the political socialists. The differences, Gompers often remarked, were over means, not ends; and, he conceded, "when the economic movement has sufficiently developed so as to produce a unity of thought on all essentials, that a political Labor Movement will be the result."

The AFL moved in two decisive steps to close this early vulnerability to socialist claims. First came the rejection of the New York Central Labor Federation in 1890 on the ground that among its affiliates was an SLP branch: only trade unions could participate in a trade-union movement. The invocation of this basic rule answered the SLP demand that, as a workers' party, it stood in a special relationship to the AFL. When it came to representation, no distinctions could be drawn among political parties—all had to stand outside. The dramatic rise of the Populist party completed this process of political disengagement. Midwestern socialists, envisioning a grand farmer-labor alliance, introduced a political program in 1893 that, among other planks, endorsed, first, independent political action and, second, "collective ownership by the people of the means of production and distribution." By rejecting both (in a hard-fought campaign that cost Gompers a year of the presidency), the AFL formally renounced independent politics and formally put aside revolutionary ends. It had completed the task of disentangling itself from socialist politics.

That outcome the socialists could not accept. Without the support of a flourishing trade-union movement, they could not expect to prevail in electoral politics. On this point, the European experience seemed definitive. When the dogmatic Daniel DeLeon gained the leadership in the early 1890s, the SLP abandoned its efforts within the AFL and, after giving up on the expiring Knights of Labor, launched its own trade-union movement in 1895. The Socialist Trade and Labor Alliance, a loyal instrument certainly, failed dismally as a rival to the AFL. A second effort, more broadly sponsored, likewise came to grief. Founded in 1905, the Industrial Workers of the World (IWW) developed into a considerable movement, but along lines that confounded its politically oriented creators. As it took hold among the most exploited of western workers, the IWW became militantly syndicalist, contemptuous of the ballot box, and committed to a workers' revolution through direct action and the general strike.

Dissatisfaction with DeLeon's dual-union tactics had, more than any other issue, sparked the creation of the Socialist Party of America in 1901. Fast outdistancing the increasingly sectarian SLP, the new Socialist party explicitly acknowledged the AFL to be the legitimate trade-union movement and consequently also accepted the task of pulling the AFL into its orbit. The very dictum by which the AFL had asserted its independence of partisan politics—that trade-union membership could entail no political test—meant that no obstacle could be placed against the radicalization of the membership. Nor did the AFL, under its basic institutional rule of "trade autonomy," have any authority to interfere in the internal affairs of the affiliated national unions, including their political practices. This access to the trade-union movement the Socialist party vigorously exploited; as much as 40 percent of the delegate vote supported socialist resolutions at AFL conventions in the pre–World War I era.

The genius of pure-and-simple unionism was in permitting this penetration while rendering it ineffectual. Only in part was this because the socialists never gained a majority within the AFL. Had they done so, the rule of trade autonomy would have prevented dictation to the national unions. Beyond this was a basic imperative of trade unionism: even in the national unions led by socialists, trade-union concerns took precedence over socialist principles. The ultimate weakness of trade-union socialists was that they were obliged, in practice, to act like any other unionists.

"The working people are pressing forward," Gompers told the U.S.

Commission on Industrial Relations in 1914, "pressing forward, making their claims and presenting those claims with whatever power they have . . . to secure a larger, and constantly larger share of the products." At bottom, this confidence in self-organization, in the efficacy of labor's economic power, was the driving force that kept socialist politics at bay. Whether that confidence would hold, however, remained something of an open question in the first decades of the twentieth century. The trade-union movement operated in an unrelentingly hostile environment, beset by open-shop employers and injunction-wielding courts. That struggle took, in the end, a highly ironic turn. Philosophically antistatist, job-conscious unionism prevailed ultimately through its reliance on the state.

Trade Unionism and the State

In a famous debate in 1914, Gompers asked the socialist leader Morris Hillquit how the freedom of workers would be preserved under socialism. Did Hillquit "have no apprehension that under the democratic management of socialism, the administrators could or or would attempt to exploit the workers under them?" Gompers's question stemmed from a voluntaristic ideology gradually crystallizing within the AFL leadership that sundered the remaining principled ties to socialism. Insofar as any vestigial radicalism survived, it envisioned a syndicalist society, not state socialism. At its most dogmatic, voluntarism became a blanket argument against welfare legislation: "Any surrendering of a right . . . to the state means certain control by the state and no one can tell how far reaching that may be." Even so doctrinaire an assertion left some room for flexibility—a balance always had to be struck between the dangers and benefits of state action. But however variable in practice, voluntarism did express the general bent of conservative trade unionism toward the state. The less the state intervened, the better; and, as a concomitant, the less labor's need for involvement in politics.

Trade unions had never supposed that they could function strictly in the economic sphere. Its opposition to workingmen's parties, the General Trades Union of Philadelphia had asserted in 1834, did not mean "an entire renunciation of everything having a political bearing; for it is generally conceded, that many of the subjects upon which we are to act, are political in their nature." Some—like a mechanics' lien law, the abolition of prison contract labor, the creation of state bureaus of labor statistics—clearly fell beyond the immediate relationship with employers. Others complemented the efforts of individual trades—apprenticeship and licensing regulation, Sunday closing for clerks' unions, union labor on municipal work for the building trades, state mine inspection and railway safety laws. As leaders of the Cigarmakers' Union, Strasser and Gompers waged a five-year campaign to prohibit tenement cigar manufacturing in New York beginning in 1878. From the 1880s onward, immigration regulation became a primary objective in congressional lobbying.

A structure gradually evolved to sustain this political activity. The city central bodies, first launched by the local unions for defensive purposes, increasingly served as their political voice in municipal affairs and, in later years, often as a powerful force in city machine politics. During the 1860s, beginning in New York, state federations began to do lobbying work in state capitals. The Federation of Organized Trades and Labor Unions (FOTLU), predecessor of the AFL, was formed in 1881 specifically to act as labor's legislative representative in Washington. Although charged with added responsibilities, the AFL was, like the FOTLU, designated the political arm of the national movement. Starting with the existing city centrals and state federations, the AFL developed a comprehensive network paralleling the country's political structure. Unlike the affiliated national trade unions, the city centrals and state federations were directly subordinate to the AFL (although, in practice, the AFL was hard put to exercise its authority over them). Nor were they conceded much voice in federation policy. They held only one vote each at AFL conventions, while national-union representation was on a generous per capita basis. At every level, AFL included, labor's political units were severely circumscribed. Their share of the dues flowing into the trade unions was tiny, and compliance with their political decisions was strictly voluntary. This distribution of power and resources quite precisely reflected the low standing of political action within the trade-union movement.

From the 1890s onward, that estimate came under increasing pressure. The Homestead strike of 1892, the Pullman boycott of 1894, and the violent suppression of the Western Federation of Miners revealed the class nature of the state. An idealistic Eugene V. Debs might have been confounded (and set on a course to socialism), but hardly the class-conscious founders of the AFL. They had favored voluntarism precisely in the hopes of keeping coercive state power at bay. Those hopes proved ill-founded. Between 1897 and 1904, union membership multiplied almost fivefold to over two million. As collective bargaining spread, open-shop employers mounted a furious counterattack and enlisted the courts in their cause. Injunctions and, to a lesser degree, antitrust suits had a devastating effect on labor's economic weapons. In Chicago, a court order literally brought to a halt the peaceful strike by the conservative printers' union for an eight-hour day in 1906. The Chicago injunction, which Gompers considered the final straw, evoked from him the cry of "judicial usurpation and anarchy." It "violated every fundamental right of citizenship" and could be answered only in the political arena.

Hitherto confined to lobbying activities, the AFL after 1906 began to direct its efforts at the electoral process. Although some campaigning and fund-raising might have been undertaken, the primary thrust was informational in nature—party platforms compared, voting records carefully assembled, data disseminated to all affiliates. In principle, this intensified activity was strictly nonpartisan; parties and candidates were judged on the basis of their records. In practice, party differences initiated a marked drift to the Democrats. So hostile was its reception by the Republicans in 1908, and so distasteful their presidential nominee, William Howard Taft, "the Injunction Standard Bearer," that the AFL endorsed the Democratic ticket (while denying any abandonment of nonpartisanship). In 1914 these efforts yielded a modest return when the Wilson administration accepted amendments in the Clayton Act that seemed to grant labor immunity from antitrust suits. Perhaps a clearer indication of labor's growing influence was the legislation pushed through Congress in advance of the 1916 election: the Seamen's Act (1915), a federal workmen's-compensation law (1916), a federal child-labor law (1916), and the Adamson eight-hour law for railway workers (1916).

If defense was the primary motive of the AFL, closer to the grass roots the trade-union movement was activated much more by the positive benefits that the state could offer to working people. Largely indifferent to the dogma of voluntarism, the city centrals and state federations enlisted in the reform movements that swept across the country from the 1890s onward. In this, they were not so different from the urban political machines. Neither of them was an innovator in social and political reform—that was the task of middle-class progressives—but both learned fast and became in the end sustaining elements in what historians have designated as "urban liberalism." When the New York

State Factory Investigating Committee was set up in the aftermath of the Triangle fire of 1911, both Tammany and union leaders took part and were instrumental in putting through a model program of labor reform—fifty-six measures in all—covering fire hazards, unsafe machines, homework, regulation of hours and wages for women and children, and much else. Across the country, labor movements battled for such protections and, largely because they saw them as means of breaking the resistance of the vested interests, for such political reforms as the initiative, the referendum, and the direct primary.

To some degree, labor progressivism within the states infected the AFL leadership. Gompers himself served on the Triangle committee; and if he dragged his feet, accept its recommendations he did. But the divergence became more marked as well. Except for workmen's compensation for industrial accidents, the AFL adamantly held to the conviction that protective legislation for adult male workers was "at variance with our concept of voluntary institutions and of freedom for individuals." Such dogma was lost on the state movements. The Illinois Federation of Labor wanted the eight-hour day "any way we can get it." Until the New Deal, the struggle for social reform went on mostly within the states and—the official voluntarism of the AFL notwithstanding—almost always with the support of organized labor.

The Progressive Era thus saw a marked, if uneven, expansion of labor politics. The legislative agenda lengthened. Participation intensified. The effectiveness of the nonpartisan approach, in fact, became an argument against a third party. "Suppose in 1912 we had had a labor party in existence," Gompers later remarked. The AFL then would have lost its bargaining power with the major parties. Only by being nonpartisan could organized labor extract the kind of legislative gains that had been won under the Wilson administration. Such an argument, of course, cut both ways. If the criterion was effectiveness (and not principled voluntarism), why not a third party if nonpartisanship should fail labor's needs? Precisely that question arose after World War I.

The Postwar Crisis

World War I stirred up the labor movement. Union membership, almost stagnant since 1904, surged. For the first time, organization penetrated the advanced mass-production sector. Between 1914 and 1920, the movement doubled in size. A new militancy accompanied this growth, awakened partly by labor's sense of power, partly by war-borne ideas of "industrial democracy" and "reconstruction." Always bastions of conservatism, the railroad brotherhoods opposed the restoration of the roads to private ownership; they advocated instead the Plumb plan for tripartite control by labor, management, and government. The mine workers demanded mine nationalization and the six-hour day. The Chicago Federation of Labor, a center of wartime militancy, led the way toward third-party politics. In December 1918, the Labor party of Cook County adopted a platform, "Labor's Fourteen Points," that became the programmatic basis for the postwar independent third-party movement. Included were demands for public ownership of the nation's utilities and resources and "democratic management" of industry. During 1918–19, labor parties sprang up in more than forty cities, and a national structure began to take shape.

A new configuration of American radical politics was emerging during this period. The Socialist party, dominant for nearly twenty years, was shattered, a victim partly of wartime repression, partly of a disastrous split in early 1919. The expelled Leninist groups formed the basis of the communist movement that would surface in 1921 as the Workers' party. Other dissidents on the right gravitated, often as key leaders, to non-Marxian labor politics. The weakened Socialist party, which had always opposed coalitions, began in the early 1920s to conceive for itself the role of Britain's Independent Labour party in the making of an American Labor party. Despite the fracturing on the extreme left with the rise of communism, in the center the chances for coalitional activity became better than ever before.

The second key event was the political revival in agriculture. In 1915, North Dakota wheat farmers had launched the Nonpartisan League (NPL) on a platform of state-run enterprises. Successful in the 1916 elections, the NPL began aggressively to sow its particular brand of independent politics across the West—the seizure of a major party through the primary. This development mattered enormously to labor-party advocates. From the Populist era and before, farmer-labor unity had figured centrally in American radicalism, partly on the practical ground of mutual electoral interest, partly on the ideological ground that both farmers and laborers were equally subject as producers to capitalist exploitation. They were, as Senator Lynn Frazier of North Dakota said, "in the same boat." Wherever the NPL spread in the

West, it supported labor's causes and linked up with local labor movements. Only in Minnesota was organized labor consequential enough to meet the NPL on equal terms. Here the partners moved, after failing with the nonpartisan tactic in the Republican primary of 1918, to form the Minnesota Farmer-Labor party. The groundwork was being laid, notwithstanding a fiasco in the national elections of 1920, for the most serious challenge to the two-party system in the twentieth century.

Labor's bright hopes faded fast after World War I. Employers went on the offensive to restore the open shop in the steel and other mass-production industries. In the unprecedented strike wave that broke out in 1919, the power of government came down heavily on capital's side. The Esch-Cummins Transportation Act (1920) not only returned the railroads to their owners but also saddled the unions with a hostile Railway Labor Board with extensive authority over the terms of work. When the shop crafts finally walked out in 1922, the operators crushed the strike with the active assistance of the Labor Board and a sweeping injunction initiated by the Harding administration. Worst of all was a series of Draconian decisions handed down by the courts. The use of injunctions was upheld and broadened, picketing rights were severely limited, the *Duplex* decision (1921) nullified the immunities that the AFL thought it had achieved under the Clayton Act, and, to cap all this, in the *Coronado* decision (1922) unions as entities became liable for damages. The concerted attack on trade unionism, an AFL emergency conference declared in 1921, was opening ''the road to autocracy, unfreedom, and chaos.''

The crisis of the early 1920s shifted the balance sharply in the direction of political action. The angry railway unions, both independent brotherhoods and AFL shop crafts, led the way. In February 1922, they set up the Conference for Progressive Political Action (CPPA). The participating unions, including needle trades and miners, represented roughly half the trade-union membership in the country. The NPL, the Socialist party, local farmer and labor parties, and a miscellany of progressive organizations joined in. The trade unions dominated, however. Overcoming strong sentiment for a third party, the CPPA opted instead for an aggressive and flexible brand of nonpartisanship. State and local branches would push progressive candidates in the primaries of the major parties. If this failed, independent tickets could be run. The CPPA tactic differed in kind from the self-denying nonpartisanship of the AFL. The CPPA proposed to choose its friends, not simply to reward them. By this entry into the party process, the CPPA was implicitly setting its sights on the seizure of political power. So strong were the forces running in this direction as to carry over into the pure-and-simple sanctum of the AFL. While steering clear of the CPPA, the executive council of the AFL likewise directed city centrals and state federations to take part in primaries and, where both party slates "are unfriendly to our cause," to enter labor candidates in the field.

The 1922 elections yielded a considerable return on farmer-labor efforts. Of sixteen CPPA gubernatorial candidates, twelve won. In Minnesota, the Farmer-Labor party captured the state legislature, half the congressional delegation, one Senate seat in 1922, the other in 1923. These successes precipitated a crisis over the third-party issue. The Chicago group, led by John Fitzpatrick, split off from the CPPA and launched an abortive national labor party in March 1923; the Minnesota Farmer-Laborites likewise failed the next year. Within the CPPA, the appeal of an independent party remained much alive also. The Labour party victory in Britain was hailed by the CPPA in early 1924 as evidence that workers "may come into peaceful control of their government whenever they have the intelligence to do so." Still, while lifting the ban against independent parties by its affiliates, the CPPA hewed to the line laid down in 1922.

The CPPA might well have projected its nonpartisan approach nationally had a candidate been found within the major parties. The man the CPPA wanted was the Democrat William G. McAdoo, much admired by the railway unions for his part in the wartime railroad program. McAdoo's involvement in the Teapot Dome scandal ended that hope in 1923. The one available figure of truly national stature was the veteran Wisconsin Progressive Robert M. LaFollette. The CPPA fielded an independent ticket (the Montana Democrat Burton K. Wheeler was LaFollette's running mate), but not one based on a new national party. An opening was thereby given to the AFL to embrace an activist brand of labor politics without having to repudiate formally its nonpartisan doctrine. With nothing to hope for from either major party ("both parties have flouted the desires of labor [and are] in a condition of moral bankruptcy"), the AFL endorsed the Progressive ticket. Never would modern trade unionism come closer to surmounting its political marginality than during the onset of the 1924 presidential campaign.

Nor would radical politics ever again make so determined an effort to accommodate the American electoral system. The parliamentary system, even without proportional representation, is far more congenial to third parties. Discipline on party issues, demanded by the reliance of the cabinet on a house majority, gives parliamentary parties less capacity for containing dissident elements. Within a parliamentary house, too, even a very minor party has standing and, in close divisions, considerable bargaining power. And on election day there is not the disheartening prospect of throwing away votes on hopeless candidates for executive office. A farmer-labor crisis very like that in the United States thus gave rise in Canada to the Cooperative Commonwealth Federation, which by 1933 had become the second party in the two westernmost provinces. For the NPL below the border in North Dakota, it had seemed more practical to push its candidates within the Republican party, especially after the primary had democratized the nominating process. That logic appealed on a larger scale to the CPPA. Its decision to field a national ticket in 1924 reflected in some measure the persistent hold of independent politics on the radical mind. (Thus LaFollette, on accepting the CPPA nomination, spoke hopefully of a vote large enough to justify "a new political party.") But the LaFollette candidacy was even more a response to the complex and extensive political structure. At a time when no presidential candidate could be put across in the major parties, LaFollette was a means of staking out a national claim, of giving the Progressives an identity that surmounted forty-eight state jurisdictions.

LaFollette ran strongly, and not only among rural voters. He won nearly 17 percent of the popular vote, 20 percent outside the South. He carried Wisconsin and ran second in nine western states. The two largest, California and Minnesota, had substantial industrial populations, as did Wisconsin. In the major industrial states, moreover, the Progressive ticket came within hailing distance of the Democrats—to within half the Democratic vote in New York and Massachusetts, three-fourths or better in Illinois, Michigan, Ohio, and Pennsylvania. In Pittsburgh, where the Democratic organization was nearly moribund, LaFollette took 36 percent of the vote. The immigrant, working-class support he got formed the basis for Roosevelt's victory in Pittsburgh in 1932. Allan Lichtman, in a quantitative analysis of national voting behavior, likewise finds no "sharp break between the electoral base of Robert M. LaFollette's brand of protest politics and the electoral base of the New Deal."

As a staging operation against the two-party system, the Progressive campaign succeeded. But it was a victory that the labor movement at once rejected. The CPPA met only once after the election and disbanded. Neither contemporaries nor historians have been short on explanations for this sudden collapse of labor politics. Internal problems certainly contributed—persistent divisions over the third-party issue, the disruptive role of the Communists, the loyalty of key labor leaders to the major parties (Daniel Tobin to the Democrats, John L. Lewis and William L. Hutcheson to the Republicans). Other explanations refer to the conservative climate of the 1920s and the declining strength of organized labor. It may even be that the significance of the Progressive vote was not clearly grasped at the time. None of these explanations can account for the decisiveness of labor's rejection of independent political action. Never again would the trade-union movement make the kind of bid for political power that it had mounted during the early 1920s, not in the throes of the Great Depression, not even after the triumph of industrial unionism.

The New Deal Settlement

Even before the 1924 election, the Republican administration had begun to back away from the postwar antilabor reaction. The key figure was Herbert Hoover in the Commerce Department. He prodded President Harding into interceding with the steel industry to end the twelve-hour day in 1923. He rescued the industrywide coal agreement in the Central Competitive field (Ohio, Illinois, Indiana, Pennsylvania) in 1924. During the campaign, Coolidge began to speak of amending the hated Transportation Act of 1920, and behind the scenes Hoover was already pressing for negotiations between carriers and unions for new railway labor legislation. These conciliatory steps help account for the trade union drift away from the Progressive ticket even before the election. Thereafter, the machinery of party accommodation began to hum once more. In 1926, the passage of the Railway Labor Act ended the discontent of the railroad unions. In the 1928 campaign, party behavior improved vastly over 1924, both in the choice of presidential candidates and in the platforms adopted. Prospects for injunction relief now brightened, opening the way for the passage of the landmark Norris-LaGuardia Anti-Injunction Act in 1932. An essential premise of traditional labor politics had been restored: the receptivity of the two-party system to labor's interests.

However, it was not only aberrant party behavior that had spurred the farmer-labor radicalism of the early 1920s. On the agricultural side, indeed, Congress had been highly responsive to the demands of the American Farm Bureau Federation. The intractable fact, both for agriculture and labor, was that they faced difficulties not susceptible to conventional solutions. The farm-bloc legislation of 1921–23, wide-ranging as it was, could not rescue farmers from disastrously low crop prices. Nor did corporate industry need public allies to crush the trade unions; its enormous resources were fully up to that task. Only by the active enlistment of the state could labor and agriculture hope to meet the systemic problems that had emerged after World War I.

For agriculture, wartime experience brought forth an answer to the farm crisis—a federal price-support system. First broached in 1921, the equality-for-agriculture plan gained popularity during the second half of 1923 and emerged in 1924 as the McNary-Haugen farm relief bill. These developments promptly deflated the agrarian protest movement and set off a decade-long lobbying campaign that ended triumphantly with the passage of the Agricultural Adjustment Act (1933). World War I likewise provided an answer to labor's crisis—public protection of the right to organize. The trade unions, however, were somewhat slower to accept this kind of formal, ongoing state intervention in the labor-management arena. Within the craft-dominated AFL, for one thing, the imperative to organize the unorganized abated. During the Coolidge-Hoover years, too, hopes persisted that open-shop industry might yet be brought around to the voluntary acceptance of collective bargaining. Even so, from World War I onward the notion of state intervention was implanted in trade-union calculations. Protection of organizing rights was granted to the railway unions in the Railway Labor Act, and it was a central feature of the coal stabilization bill that the beleaguered United Mine Workers began to advocate after the collapse of the Jacksonville agreement in 1927.

Only with the advent of the New Deal, however, did the constraints of trade-union voluntarism come fully undone. Three years of catastrophic depression had already eroded the historic opposition to protective labor legislation. In 1932, the AFL came out for unemployment insurance and the Hugo Black thirty-hour bill. Urban liberalism, a fixture in the state and local movements for twenty years, now became a hallmark of the national movement as well. In advancing its agenda of social reform, the New Deal could count on organized labor as a steady ally. As for New Deal efforts at industrial recovery, these rendered irrelevant any lingering principled argument against public intervention on the organizing front. If the National Industrial Recovery Act (1933) granted to industry the right to self-regulation through codes of fair competition, how could labor be denied the right of self-organization under Section 7a? This logic was leveled primarily against objecting open-shop employers, but it served also to silence the voluntarists within the trade-union movement.

The two-year struggle to make Section 7a effective, led by the revived AFL, ended with the adoption of the National Labor Relations Act (Wagner-Connery Act) in 1935. The Wagner Act protected the organizing activities of workers from employer interference, set up rules and procedures for determining representation, and required employers to bargain with unions so chosen under the law. Broad, effective powers were lodged in a quasi-judicial National Labor Relations Board for administering and enforcing these rights. The labor movement had called into existence this public system of regulation so as to secure the private collective-bargaining functions that had always been at the heart of pure-and-simple unionism.

What kind of labor politics were appropriate to this New Deal settlement? Clearly not the independent variety that had sprung from the postwar crisis. The Great Depression spawned a profusion of opportunities for independent action—the Socialists, briefly resurgent in 1932; the Communists, a vigorous presence throughout the decade; a revived farmer-labor politics in Minnesota and elsewhere in the West; a succession of non-Marxist movements, from the League for Independent Political Action (1929) to Philip LaFollette's National Progressives of America (1938). As in the past, industrial conflict gave rise to labor parties in many cities, and the internal struggle over industrial unionism in 1934–35 likewise produced much sentiment in favor of independent politics (as evidenced by the flurry of resolutions at the AFL convention of 1935). Despite all this ferment, there was never any chance that the trade-union movement would pick up where it had left off in 1924. The real question was not about independent politics at all but about the degree of change in labor's relationship to the two-party system.

The historical bases of labor nonpartisanship had long been shifting. Waves of immigration, from the 1840s, had gradually recast the American labor force along ethnocultural lines that flowed ever more strongly into the Democratic camp. At the same time, the intensity of party loyalty, deep-rooted in the political culture of nineteenth-century America, eroded rapidly in the twentieth century, at least insofar as can be measured by declining voting rates and by erratic voting behavior at the polls. Overt partisanship became less risky to trade unionism. (The 1928 election, with the religious passions aroused by Al Smith's candidacy, probably was a break from this tendency: hence the special pleas by AFL President William Green for strict nonpartisanship "to avoid the danger of splitting [workers of diverse faiths] into groups over particular political issues.") Most important was the growing perception of the Democratic party, already evident in the Progressive years, as the party of the workers. The Great Depression dramatically accelerated this class differentiation between the parties. Hoover stood discredited; the New Deal, triumphant. In the hold that he exerted on working people, Franklin D. Roosevelt was unique among American presidents. This truth brought into being the American Labor party in New York; thereby socialist voters who could not abide the Tammany Democracy would be enabled to vote for FDR in 1936. Nor had labor unions ever before appealed to workers to sign up because "The President Wants You to Organize."

The rupture of the labor movement in the mid-1930s to some degree forestalled the evolving connection with the Democratic party. With the departure of the progressive wing in 1935 into the Committee for Industrial Organization (CIO; renamed the Congress of Industrial Organizations in 1938), the AFL fell into the hands of old-line conservatives. The more activist politics associated with the rival CIO became branded as illegitimate (hence cooperation by AFL state and city affiliates was formally prohibited in 1938). Once free of AFL constraints, on the other hand, the trade-union progressives rapidly stepped up the pace of their political activity. During the 1936 campaign, they formed Labor's Nonpartisan League (LNPL). Specifically committed to the reelection of Roosevelt, the LNPL tremendously increased labor's part in electoral politics, both in the volume of money contributed (roughly $750,000) and by the organizational resources brought to bear at the grass roots (the CIO organizing drives were virtually suspended in the last stages of the 1936 campaign).

The full meaning of this break from traditional nonpartisanship took some time to emerge. The CIO leader, John L. Lewis, the driving force behind the LNPL, overreached himself after Roosevelt's triumphant reelection. Roosevelt rejected Lewis's claims to favored treatment in the industrial wars that followed the CIO breakthroughs in auto and steel in early 1937. Lewis's apparent ambitions to be Roosevelt's running mate in 1940 were not taken seriously. Differences over foreign policy—Lewis was fiercely isolationist—brought the conflict to a head. When Lewis endorsed the Republican Wendell Willkie in 1940, he was in effect asking the industrial-union movement to chose between himself and Roosevelt. The CIO chose Roosevelt. Lewis left the CIO presidency (as he had pledged to do if Roosevelt won) and soon broke with the CIO. Instead of Lewis's vision of labor as a pivotal independent political force, the CIO committed itself to the Democratic party. The political arm that it formed in 1943, the Political Action Committee (PAC), improved on the LNPL model as both money raiser and campaign organization. The key CIO leaders, Sidney Hillman and Philip Murray, made no bones about the purposes for which these means had been raised: to advance the cause of the New Deal democracy.

The testing time for this party attachment came in the early cold war era. A new third-party movement sprang up, sparked initially by liberal disillusionment with Harry Truman's bungling of the reconversion program but carried forward by critics of the Truman administration's anti-Sovietism. The emergence of Henry Wallace's Progressive party reopened fundamental political debate within the CIO. The third-party issue turned partly on customary calculations of labor's interests. An antiunion reaction swept the country after the war. The Republicans carried both houses of Congress in 1946, pushed through the Taft-Hartley modifications of the Wagner Act over Truman's veto in 1947, and stood poised to seize the White House in 1948. It was the worst of times for a third party to be taking votes from the Democrats. Mixed in with these entirely practical considerations was a deepening crisis within the CIO over communism. Associated earlier with independent politics, left-wing unionists had given unswerving loyalty to the Roosevelt administration during the war and had, indeed, taken the lead in branding as unpatriotic and divisive the modest third-party activity within the wartime labor movement. With the onset of the cold war, the popular front abruptly ceased, and CIO communists committed themselves to the Progressive party. The third-party issue merged with anti-communism within the CIO. For the communist-led unions, this meant expulsion in 1950. For the CIO, it put the seal on the attachment to the Democratic party.

Although spared its rival's inner crisis, the AFL moved inexorably in the same political direction as the CIO. Very much the same kinds of forces were operating on the Federation—a new generation of leaders, a much larger and more diverse membership, organizational interests hardly less threatened by the Taft-Hartley Act. The AFL set up its own political arm, Labor's League for Political Education, and contributed nearly as much to the 1948 campaign as did the CIO. The symbol of traditional nonpartisanship fell finally in 1952, when the AFL formally endorsed the Democratic candidate, Adlai Stevenson. Converging political interests helped pave the way for merger in 1955. Seventeen million strong, the AFL-CIO was a political force to be reckoned with, but one committed irrevocably to the two-party system.

Labor in Modern American Politics

Seeking to characterize labor's place in modern American politics, the political scientist J. David Greenstone found it necessary in 1969 to coin a new phrase; he called labor "an organized constituency" of the Democratic party. Unlike an ordinary interest group, the AFL-CIO took it upon itself both to reshape the party and to speak for constituencies well beyond its own trade-union membership. Labor's large role within the Democratic party, thought Greenstone, was "a partial equivalence to the Social Democratic [formerly socialist] party-trade union alliance in much of Western Europe."

Democratic candidates relied heavily on labor's funds. In presidential campaigns, roughly 25 percent might come from unions. Hardly less important was the campaign work of the AFL-CIO political arm, the Committee on Political Education (COPE). Operating nationwide at every level of the country's political structure, in highly unionized areas COPE was organized down to the precincts. It was capable of mobilizing armies of volunteers—191,000 in the week before the election of 1968, for example. A high degree of professionalism, however, actually characterized its work: full-time directors not only for the states but also for major cities and key congressional districts; a heavy reliance on union staffers during campaign months; and a sophisticated technical capacity. Labor had become the most important electoral organization within the Democratic party.

A steady purpose guided this massive union contribution. "We felt that instead of trying to create a third party—a labor party," Walter Reuther of the United Automobile Workers (UAW) told a British journalist in 1960, "we ought to bring about a realignment and get the liberal forces in one party and the conservatives in another." The withholding of labor support from such steady friends as Wisconsin's Robert M. LaFollette, Jr., and Oregon's Wayne Morse helps to account for the demise of the progressive Republican tradition after the 1940s. Within the Democratic party, organized labor adapted old nonpartisan methods—rewarding friends, punishing enemies—to the end of encouraging the party to put up liberal candidates. Nor was the liberalizing party force of the unions limited to the nominating process. They also tried to foster potential Democratic constituencies by registration drives in ghetto areas and by encouraging minority leaders and organizations. Practiced most vigorously in black Detroit, such activities took place in urban areas across the country. It was far beyond the scope of an interest group, remarked Greenstone, to help "aggregate groups that are much more completely in the *party's* political constituency rather than in the ranks of union members themselves."

These efforts at party transformation in turn were linked to large social goals. Here, too, organized labor developed along lines that defied political science categories. Following the election of John F. Kennedy in 1960, and even more so after his assassination, labor came into its own as a legislative force. In Washington, the labor movement maintained a formidable lobbying operation, including rich support facilities in research, publicity, and communications. In two ways, the deployment of these resources went beyond ordinary pressure-group activities. First, the union effort generally occurred within a coalition of forces, with labor doing much of the initiating and organizing, and always shouldering the operational burden. In the drive for Medicare, for example, unions helped build up the grass-roots organizations of the elderly, a labor official ran the umbrella National Council of Senior Citizens, and the crucial technical and financial backing came from the AFL-CIO. Equally distinctive was the reliance on labor by the Democratic leadership. In congressional battles in which party leaders hesitated to exert direction, labor stepped in and took over some part of their role, for example, on the issues of job discrimination and poll tax in the civil rights bills of 1964 and 1965, and, to a fuller extent, in defense of the Supreme Court decision on the reapportionment of state legislatures from rural-conservative attack. Had it been willing to give way on the Dirksen reapportionment amendment in 1965, in fact, the AFL-CIO likely could have gained repeal of the hated right-to-work provision of the Taft-Hartley Act. It refused to do so, thereby sacrificing for the general welfare its own narrow interest on an issue to which labor attached immense importance.

American trade unions, as the British political scientist Vivian Vale remarked in 1971, constituted "by far the largest and most stable body supporting liberal causes in the United States today." By pitching their political efforts to the broader party constituency rather than strictly to their own membership, added Greenstone, they were acting in an "aggregating" way "often thought to be a distinguishing attribute of major political parties in two-party systems." Yet if it was something more than an interest group, organized labor was something less than the controlling force within the Democratic party. And it was less by conscious and deliberate choice.

No national trade-union leader of the modern era was more politically aggressive, more committed to "a realignment [that would] get the liberal forces in one party and the conservatives in another," than Walter Reuther. Yet Reuther explicitly opposed "the labor movement trying to capture the Democratic Party." In fact, the AFL-CIO occupied no official place within the Democratic party. It did not claim the kind of representation that the Trades Union Congress, for example, exercised within the British Labour party. Labor leaders were active in party affairs; upward of three hundred might serve as delegates at Democratic national conventions. But they came as party people selected by the same processes as any other delegates, not as representatives sent by the AFL-CIO. And there was this final fact: the labor movement—even the CIO during the 1940s—never abandoned its formal espousal of nonpartisanship. At its merger convention, the AFL-CIO "reaffirm[ed] labor's traditional policy of . . . supporting worthy candidates regardless of . . . party affiliation. . . . We seek neither to capture any organization *nor will we submit our identity to any group in any manner.*"

Those italicized words perhaps provide a touchstone for understanding how labor defined its place within the modern political system. If the preempting political culture fixed the limits in the nineteenth century, in the twentieth century those limits derive more from within the labor movement itself. Under the pure-and-simple logic of Samuel Gompers, organized labor came to see itself as a secondary institution, committed above all else to preserving its separateness and independence. In politics, long after the other sources had faded, nonpartisanship remained as an expression of labor's modest self-conception, as a reminder of ties that went back to Samuel Gompers. "Our goals as trade unions are modest," AFL President George Meany had said in 1955, the year of the merger, "for we do not seek to recast American society. . . . [W]e seek a rising standard of living." And in 1966: "The labor movement program is 'practical.' . . . We avoid preconceived notions and we do not try to fit our program into some theoretical, all-embracing structure." For a movement thus closely defined, its own integrity came first.

Nor was there, in the end, anything final about the large place that organized labor occupied in the political system in the 1960s. The conditions of its political participation, enduring for two decades after World War II, now began to shift. This was evident first in the terms of political debate—initially in the rupture of the cold war consensus inaugurated with the Vietnam War; then with the host of new domestic issues, from the environment to the right to life, that cut across liberal-conservative lines; and finally in accelerating economic problems not susceptible to New Deal-Keynesian solutions. The result was a breakdown in the postwar liberal coalition and, to some degree, in labor's own unity on public issues. The aggregating role that Greenstone had ascribed in 1969 to organized labor could no longer be well performed in the decades that followed.

Within the party system, too, disturbing changes were under way. By the early 1970s, the Democratic party was no longer capable of meeting labor's expectations for a predictable return on its political efforts. Party reform after 1968 undercut the ability of the established party leadership to control the national conventions. Beyond the "opening up" of formal procedures, there were the equally important advances in the techniques of campaign organization and media manipulation. It became increasingly easy for an outsider to capture a nomination and run successfully for office with little regard for the preferences of the regular party leadership and little support among the party cadre. The full significance of these changes became obvious to labor after the Democrats returned to power in 1976. Despite an all-out effort on behalf of Jimmy Carter and despite comfortable Democratic majorities in the

Congress, the AFL-CIO could not put across its ambitious program, not even the labor-reform bill (aimed at making the National Labor Relations Act more effective) on which it had heavily banked. What the country needed, complained the progressive bloc that coalesced around the UAW, was "political parties that are accountable, issue-oriented, and disciplined to abide by their platform commitments."

Labor's programmatic defeats signified, finally, an even more serious problem—its own erosion as an organized movement. During the 1970s, many unions fell on hard times, partly because of the resurgence of antiunion activity, even more because of structural changes cutting into the unionized sectors of the economy. Unable to keep up proportionately with the growth of the labor force since the mid-1950s, union membership began to suffer an absolute decline from 1975 onward. One effect was to weaken labor's commitment to general-welfare advocacy. In adversity, its own needs as an interest group became more pressing, its political capital more limited. The reversion to interest-group politics was accelerated by the changing composition of the labor movement. For public-employee unions, a major component by the 1970s, politics was inherently a self-interested activity, since it was the arena in which their terms of work were fixed. The decline in union strength, moreover, cut pervasively into labor's political authority, evident even in its influence over its own members (only 56 percent voted the national Democratic ticket in 1980).

The failure of the labor-reform bill of 1978 served to touch off a period of introspection and debate over labor's political future. The historic options were once more considered. UAW President Douglas Fraser's denunciation of the major parties after the labor-reform loss gave rise briefly to talk of a new third-party effort. A return to nonpartisan tactics was also broached, by no less a progressive unionist than Jerry Wurf of the American Federation of State, County, and Municipal Employees. This was predicated on the emergence of sympathetic Republican candidates—a hope scarcely fulfilled by the nomination of Ronald Reagan in 1980. Perforce, labor's place remained with the Democratic party.

In 1981, bent on restoring the earlier terms of political exchange, the AFL-CIO helped to engineer a major rollback of the party reforms of the McGovern era. This was preparatory to a sharp break with the past that the AFL-CIO was now prepared to make: this time, in 1984, it would pick the reliable candidate it sorely wanted—Walter F. Mondale—and campaign openly for his nomination. By entering what was a party process, the labor movement was making itself captive to the compromises a party has to make in hopes of building an electoral majority. In the mid-1980s, with the powerful currents that were running against New Deal liberalism, it was no minor thing to abandon the programmatic independence that even the ritual form of nonpartisanship it practiced gave to the labor movement. Moreover, by crossing this defining boundary, the AFL-CIO was putting the labor movement to a test it had been loath to face even at the height of its power. That the executive council had acted with little rank-and-file preparation only compounded the risks.

The AFL-CIO did manage to summon up the resources to get Mondale the presidential nomination, but only after demonstrating how slight a hold it had on its ranks: in the primaries, 30 percent of the union vote had gone to Gary Hart, 20 percent to Jesse Jackson. And, in Jackson's Rainbow Coalition, there arose a claimant for the role the labor unions had traditionally played; they found themselves displaced from the left wing of the party, uncomfortably doing battle with the new champions of the minorities and the poor. Having prevailed in that unhappy struggle, organized labor signed on to what the *Congressional Quarterly* called "economically the most conservative Democratic platform in fifty years." All to no avail. Walter Mondale was overwhelmed by President Reagan in November, gaining a mere 41 percent of the popular vote and the electoral votes only of Minnesota and the District of Columbia. The consensus, both within the Democratic party and inside the AFL-CIO, was that being labor's man had hurt Mondale by tagging him as the candidate of a "special interest." Most humiliating was the fact that the AFL-CIO had failed to deliver the votes for labor's own candidate: a lower percentage (53 percent) of union households voted for Mondale in 1984 than had voted for Jimmy Carter in 1980. And among blue-collar workers generally (the middle fifth of voters with average annual earnings of $19,000), a clear majority had gone to the Republicans. Afterward, a chastened movement reverted to its traditional stance, but with its political capital largely spent and contemplating a Democratic party anxious to distance itself from its New Deal past and bent on contesting the Reaganite grip on the suburban middle class.

In 1960 Walter Reuther had expressed what seemed to him the limits of labor's political aspirations—"to learn to work within a party without trying to capture it.'' Today's labor movement does not seek to extend those limits. They are, as things presently stand, more capacious than organized labor needs for the reduced means it can bring to bear on the political system.

BIBLIOGRAPHIC ESSAY

Irving Bernstein, *Turbulent Years: A History of the American Worker, 1933–1941* (Boston, 1970), the standard work on labor during the 1930s, is the starting point for understanding the expansion of labor's political role under the New Deal. David Brody, ''On the Failure of U.S. Radical Politics: A Farmer-Labor Analysis,'' in *Industrial Relations,* 22 (1983), is an exploratory essay that seeks to show, through a comparison of farmer and labor movements, why organized labor rejected independent politics in the twentieth century. John D. Buenker, *Urban Liberalism and Progressive Reform* (New York, 1973), is a comprehensive study of the relationship between Progressivism and urban liberalism that throws much light on how organized labor was drawn into the reform movements of the early twentieth century. John R. Commons *et al., History of Labor in the United States,* 4 vols. (New York, 1918–35), the pioneering work in the field, is still an invaluable source for the details of labor's role in American politics. Melvyn Dubofsky and Warren Van Tine, *John L. Lewis* (New York, 1977), is the definitive biography of the CIO leader; it is crucial for understanding the expansion of labor's political role during the New Deal era. Nathan Fine, *Labor and Farmer Parties in the United States, 1828–1928* (New York, 1928), is a useful survey, despite its age, of third-party politics and is informative especially about the movements of the post–World War I era. Gary M. Fink, ''The Rejection of Voluntarism,'' in *Industrial and Labor Relations Review,* 26 (1973), surveys the literature on political activity at the state and local levels of the labor movement during the first decades of the twentieth century and concludes that voluntarism had little appeal at those levels. Leon Fink, *Workingmen's Democracy: The Knights of Labor and American Politics* (Urbana, Ill., 1983), contains case studies of local political activity that both reveal the vitality of reform labor politics in the 1880s and suggest the restraints on any permanent development of that activity. Its important reevaluation of the Knights of Labor places the movement and its political manifestations in their local setting. Eric Foner, *Free Soil, Free Labor, Free Men: The Ideology of the Republican Party Before the Civil War* (New York, 1970), is an important study that shows how the Republican party adapted the workingmen's ideology to the cause of free soil, thereby powerfully attracting the labor vote to its camp.

Ronald P. Formisano, *The Transformation of Political Culture: Massachu-*

setts Parties, 1790s–1840s (New York, 1983), is an ambitious effort to explain the emergence of a mass political culture capable of absorbing the early impulses toward independent labor politics. James C. Foster, *The Union Politic: The CIO Political Action Committee* (Columbia, Mo., 1975), is the standard work on the political activity of the CIO in the years when it was an independent industrial-union movement. Joseph C. Goulden, *Meany* (New York, 1972), a biography of the longtime head of the AFL-CIO based on extensive interviews, contains much valuable information on labor's political role in the modern era. J. David Greenstone, *Labor in American Politics* (New York, 1969), is based on extensive fieldwork. This is the fullest study of the political role of the labor movement at the peak of its mature strength during the 1950s and 1960s. Gerald N. Grob, *Workers and Utopia: A Study of Ideological Conflict in the American Labor Movement, 1865–1900* (Evanston, Ill., 1961), is a useful history of the formative period of the American labor movement that draws too sharp a line between trade unionism and labor reform but is nevertheless informative on the role of politics in the struggle to define the future course of the labor movement. Michael F. Holt, *Forging a Majority: The Formation of the Republican Party in Pittsburgh, 1848–1860* (New Haven, 1969), is a revealing study of how an emerging mass party incorporated the labor vote, solidly buttressed with statistical evidence of voting patterns. Walter Hugins, *Jacksonian Democracy and the Working Class: A Study of the New York Workingmen's Movement, 1829–1837* (Stanford, Calif., 1960), is the best of the many case studies of the Jacksonian labor movement and its relation to American politics. Marc Karson, *American Labor Unions and Politics, 1900–1918* (Carbondale, Ill., 1958), is a standard work, notable especially for its stress on the Catholic church in holding the labor movement to a conservative political line. Stuart B. Kaufman, *Samuel Gompers and the Origins of the American Federation of Labor, 1848–1896* (Westport, Conn., 1973), an important study that traces pure-and-simple unionism back to its Marxist origins in the 1870s, shows how Gompers and his circle directed the emerging trade-union movement away from independent politics.

John H. M. Laslett, *Labor and the Left: A Study of Socialist and Radical Influences in the American Labor Movement, 1881–1924* (New York, 1970), is the standard work on the role of socialists within the American labor movement, valuable especially because it focuses on individual unions rather than on the AFL. Bruce Laurie, *Working People of Philadelphia, 1800–1850* (Philadelphia, 1980), is a detailed local study that places early labor politics in its social and economic context. Allan J. Lichtman, *Prejudice and the Old Politics: The Presidential Election of 1928* (Chapel Hill, N.C., 1979), is a highly sophisticated statistical analysis of voting patterns during the 1920s. It is especially important for revealing the continuities between the Progressive vote of 1924 and the New Deal vote a decade later. David Montgomery, *Beyond Equality:*

Labor and the Radical Republicans, 1862–1872 (New York, 1967), is the definitive study of the breakdown of the alliance between Republicanism and the labor movement and of the emergence of labor-reform politics in the post–Civil War era. This is a pioneering study of the social roots of the nineteenth-century labor movement. Selig Perlman, *A Theory of the Labor Movement* (New York, 1928), is a seminal effort at accounting for American labor "exceptionalism." Although its explanatory force has weakened in recent years, the book's characterization of American trade unionism remains highly influential. Edward Pessen, *Most Uncommon Jacksonians: Radical Leaders of the Early Labor Movement* (Albany, N.Y., 1967), is valuable both for its assessment of the literature on the Jacksonian workingmen's parties and for its treatment of the leaders and their ideas.

Michael Rogin, "Voluntarism: The Political Functions of an Antipolitical Doctrine," in *Industrial and Labor Relations Review,* 15 (1962), a provocative essay on the political ideology of voluntarism, argues that voluntarism was an important buttress of the status quo inside the labor movement and that it did not actually represent the political realities at the local level. Nick Salvatore, *Eugene V. Debs: Citizen and Socialist* (Urbana, Ill., 1982), is the most recent and best biography of Debs, valuable especially for throwing light on the strain of radical politics that resulted from disillusionment with conservative trade unionism. Bruce Stave, "The 'LaFollette Revolution' and the Pittsburgh Vote, 1932," in *Mid-America,* 49 (1967), is an important case study that reveals the impact of the Progressive campaign of 1924 on the labor vote and on the New Deal revolution that began in 1932. Philip Taft, *The A. F. of L. in the Time of Gompers* (New York, 1957), and *The A. F. of L. from the Death of Gompers to the Merger* (New York, 1959), are the standard histories, essential for understanding the political policy of the modern labor movement. Sean Wilentz, "Artisan Republican Festivals and the Rise of Class Conflict in New York City, 1788–1837," in *Working-Class America: Essays on Labor, Community, and American Society,* Michael H. Frisch and Daniel J. Walkowitz, eds. (Urbana, Ill., 1983), is a superb example of the application of social history methods to the study of labor history. By a close study of artisan festivals, Wilentz reveals the social origins of Jacksonian labor politics. Robert H. Zieger, *Republicans and Labor, 1919–1929* (Lexington, Ky., 1969), an important book, revises the standard view that the Republican party was hostile to organized labor during the 1920s. It reveals Herbert Hoover as a progressive anxious to conciliate labor and fit it into his vision of a modern corporate order.

Since this essay originally appeared in 1984, the scholarship on labor politics has been exceptionally rich. For the nineteenth century, the republicanist sources of working-class politics have been actively explored and debated. The opening salvo was Sean Wilentz, "Against Exceptionalism: Class Consciousness and the American Labor Movement,'' *International Labor and Working Class History*, no. 26 (1984), accompanied by his major study, *Chants Democratic: New York City and the Rise of the American Working Class, 1788–1850* (New York, 1984) and by a later foray into historical narrative, ''The Rise of the American Working Class, 1776–1877: A Survey,'' in J. Carroll Moody and Alice Kessler Harris, eds., *Perspectives on American Labor History: The Problems of Synthesis* (DeKalb, Ill., 1989). For a penetrating critique, see Daniel T. Rodgers, ''Republicanism: the Career of a Concept,'' *Journal of American History*, 79 (June 1992). Equally important have been studies of the relationship of the labor movement to the state, among which the most notable are Christopher Tomlins, *The State and the Unions: Labor Relations, Law, and the Organized Labor Movement in America, 1880–1960* (New York, 1985); Leon Fink, ''Labor, Liberty, and the Law: Trade Unionism and the Problem of the American Constitutional Order,'' *Journal of American History*, 74 (December 1987); and William E. Forbath, *Law and the Shaping of the American Labor Movement* (Cambridge, Mass., 1991). Two recent books usefully place American labor politics in a comparative context: Ira Katznelson and Aristide R. Zolberg, eds., *Working-Class Formation: Nineteenth-Century Patterns in Western Europe and the United States* (Princeton, N.J., 1986); and Gary Marks, *Unions in Politics: Britain, Germany, and the United States in the Nineteenth and Early Twentieth Centuries* (Princeton, N.J., 1989). David Montgomery, *The Fall of the House of Labor: The Workplace, the State and American Labor Activism, 1865–1925* (New York, 1987) treats in depth the linkage between work relations and labor politics through the critical war years. On farmer-labor politics, the most important recent book is Richard M. Vallelly, *Radicalism in the States: The Minnesota Farmer-Labor Party and the American Political Economy* (Chicago, 1989), which stresses the limitations of state-level politics as power shifted to the national arena. A valiant effort is made to reconcile class and ethnicity as political variables in Richard Oestreicher, ''Urban Working-Class Political Behavior and Theories of American Electoral Politics, 1870–1940,'' *Journal of American History*, 74 (March 1988). For the New Deal period, four exemplary contributions are Stanley Vittoz, *New Deal Labor Policy and the American Industrial Economy* (Chapel Hill, N.C., 1987), a sophisticated reconsideration of the corporatist interpretation of the Wagner Act; David Plotke, ''The Wagner Act, Again: Politics and Labor, 1935–1937,'' *Studies in American Political Development*, 4 (1989), a systematic treatment of the entry of organized labor as a key element in an emergent New Deal ''political order''; Lizabeth Cohen, *Making a New Deal: Industrial Workers in Chicago, 1919–1939* (New York, 1990), a probing study of the transformation of immigrant workers into industrial unionists and New Dealers; and Steven Fraser, *Labor Will Rule: Sidney Hillman and the Rise of American Labor* (New York, 1991), a life-and-times biography of labor's key architect of New Deal economic policy and the CIO-Democratic alliance. In two provocative articles Karren Orren makes the case for the centrality of the labor movement for the postwar liberal democratic state: "Union Politics and Postwar Liberalism in the United States," *Studies in American Political Development*, 1 (1986); and "Organized Labor and the Invention of Modern Liberalism in the United States," *Studies in American Political Development*, 2 (1987). For a robust radical critique from the perspective of the 1980s, see Mike Davis, *Prisoners of the American Dream* (London, 1986). A provocative collection of essays covering that same ground is Steven Fraser and Gary Gerstle, eds., *The Rise and Fall of the New Deal Order, 1930–1980* (Princeton, N.J., 1989).

3

Shaping a Labor Movement

Among the constants of industrialization, none seems more certain than the impulse toward collective action by workers. Essential uniformities underlying modern industrialism have given a common character to the labor movements of all the western nations. Even so, those movements have varied widely, and nowhere more markedly than in the United States. Nowhere else has the labor movement focused so militantly on narrow job interests, nowhere else has it so insisted on insulating labor's concerns from the political sector nor been so disinclined to question the standing order or to define its mission in class terms. No other movement has had quite so hard a struggle to establish its legitimacy and to organize its constituency. In the following essays, I seek to explore three of the historical strands that bound the American labor movement to its particular fate.

Ideology*

Consider the teachers' strikes that have become a familiar part of the opening of the school year around the United States every September. Negotiations stall. The union sets a strike date. The school superintendent places a notice in the local press for substitutes. There is never any lack of applicants. School remains at least formally open while the teachers picket outside. And then there is a settlement and they go back to work.

*From *Dissent*, 36 (Winter 1989), 71–77. Reprinted with permission.

To relate this scenario to an Australian audience, as I had occasion to do several times during a semester at Sydney University, is invariably to evoke titters of laughter or a shocked silence, followed by a flood of questions. How was it possible for a public official to try to break a strike? What kind of people were Americans that they would scab on one another? And, anyway, where was the labor movement? Why was there no sympathy strike to keep the schools properly shut down? This incredulous reaction exposed to me in an especially forceful way what any observant American visitor to Australia quickly discovers— the immensely different place accorded the labor movement in the two societies.

By "place" I mean not so much the role that trade unions play as the regard in which they are held by the larger society. This is admittedly a difficult distinction. By any international standard, trade unionism is powerful in Australia. In 1990 union membership stood at 56 percent of the labor force. A Labor government had been in power since 1983. The Australian Council of Trade Unions is not only the primary constituent of the Labor party but is independently a principal in making national economic policy by means of an accord with the government in 1983 aimed at improving the competitiveness of the lagging Australian economy. The amazement of Australian audiences at my tale of American teachers' strikes certainly arose in some measure from a healthy respect for the power and militancy of Australian unionism. But their response also reflected the regard they had for the labor movement. The difference with the United States is perhaps best captured by how trade unions are treated under the labor laws of the two countries. Under the Australian arbitration system, it is assumed that workers will be represented by unions; registration involves only the question of which union is appropriate for a given group of workers. The central thrust of American labor law, on the other hand, is to determine whether or not workers want union representation. If trade unionism is taken as a given, then strikebreaking—inherently a life-threatening attack on a union—is almost by definition a bad thing, and especially abhorrent at the hands of public officials such as superintendents of schools.

The Australian comparison is no more than a device for bringing my subject into focus. It perhaps sharpens our sense of the quite different— and lesser—regard in which the labor movement is held in America, but not with any precision. For that, we must turn to a more systematic presentation of evidence. Since 1936, public opinion about organized labor has been continuously and ever more elaborately surveyed. In a detailed survey of how unions have fared in public opinion polls, the sociologist Seymour Martin Lipset finds "a dismal picture for organized labor."

In ratings of the ethical and moral practices of twenty-five occupational groups in the early 1980s, labor leaders stood at the bottom. In a 1979 poll that asked whether it would be acceptable for a labor leader to become president, 53 percent said no, 30 percent said yes. For business executives, the findings were 25 percent no, 59 percent yes. (To refer back to the Australian comparison: the Labor prime minister until 1992, Bob Hawke, had earlier served as head of the ACTU.) In 1978, the Roper poll asked "whether you think the country would be better or worse off if certain groups had more influence and freedom to do what they think best." For organized labor, 64 percent thought the country would be worse off, only 10 percent thought better off. This was the worst showing of the seven groups listed.

Nor is the labor movement seen as at one with the working class. In fact, a sharp divergence obtains here. In a 1976 poll, for example, 82 percent expressed positive feelings toward workers, 32 percent toward unions. And while nearly two-thirds thought labor unions exerted too much influence in politics in 1976, only 4 percent thought the same of "workingmen," while 53 percent thought the latter had too little influence (compared to 5 percent for unions). Consistently, opinion polls register concern over the power of the labor unions. Over half rated them too powerful in 1976. In 1985, despite a decade of labor setbacks, 46 percent still thought so.[1] Thus, from a variety of angles, public opinion research draws us to this conclusion: in America trade unionism is regarded as a suspect institution to some degree at odds with the larger society.

It is suspect, Lipset suggests, because its collective character places organized labor at odds with the value system of the larger society. Lipset's point can be readily demonstrated in the historical record. The individualistic values embodied in American law, for example, kept labor in persistent legal trouble during the nineteenth century. In the early labor conspiracy cases, the main charge was unlawful coercion of individual workers who were unwilling to abide by union standards. Later in the century, the labor injunction was justified as a legitimate protection of property rights of employers threatened by union power; and the yellow-dog contract, by the equally fundamental right of contract between consenting individuals. Trade unionists opposed to the absolute freedom of contract, wrote Woodrow Wilson in 1907, had "neither the ideas nor the sentiments needed for the maintenance or enjoyment of liberty." Until political expediency caught up with him, the future president pronounced himself "a fierce partizan [*sic*] of the Open Shop and of everything that makes for industrial liberty."

Or listen to Edward Atkinson, a Rhode Island manufacturer, explaining to an audience of workers twenty years earlier why it was against their interest to form a trade union. "If you put first-class spinners and weavers in the same place with second-class spinners and weavers, without discrimination, it will be just like packing first quality and second quality goods in the same bale; they will all be sold for just what the seconds are worth." The workingman should not aspire to a collectivity uniting everyone at the level of the least, but to "an even chance in the use of the only thing we all have in common, whether we be rich or poor—the use of his own time. The man who comprehends the use of time, and who keeps control of his own time, his hands, and his brain, will come out on top every time." And then the peroration: "There is always plenty of room on the front seats in every profession, every trade, every art, every industry. There are men in this audience who will fill some of those seats, but they won't be boosted into them from behind; they will get there by using their own brains and their own hands." There were certainly women in attendance as well—at least half of Rhode Island's labor force was female, probably more in the textile mills—but in Atkinson's time to speak of economic opportunity meant addressing a masculine concern.

We do not know whether his audience of workers found Atkinson's message persuasive; or whether hard experience had taught them to doubt the reality of "front seats" for any of them, or even of the likelihood of a fair reward for a hard day's work in the mills; or, indeed, as much recent scholarship would suggest, whether the textile workers did not hold a rival ethic of solidarity and mutuality. But the force with which he made his case bespeaks Atkinson's own immense confidence in an ethic of competitive individualism.

The existence of that value system cannot, however, in itself explain the dubious regard in which trade unionism came to be held in American society. What is left out is the element of human agency. There is, in fact, a particular history of how the American labor movement tried to define its place in the larger society and of why this resulted in the hostility recorded in modern opinion polls.

In 1834, the General Trades' Union of Boston put forth a "Declaration of Rights" that began: "When a number of individuals associate together in a public manner for the purpose of promoting their common welfare, respect for public opinion, the proper basis of a republic[an] form of government, under which they associate, requires that they should state to their fellow citizens, the motives which actuate them, in adopting such a course." Sound familiar? It is of course an echo of the opening words of the Declaration of Independence. "With the Fathers of our Country," the Boston unionists continued, "we hold that all men are created free and equal; endowed by their Creator with certain inalienable rights, that among these are life, liberty, and the pursuit of happiness."

These rights were expressed not through Atkinson's competitive individualism but were linked instead to a producer ethic. "Labor, being the legitimate and only real source of wealth, and the laboring classes the majority and real strength of every country, their interest and happiness ought to be the principal care of Government." Just the reverse had happened in practice. "We already behold the wealthy fast verging into aristocracy, the laboring classes into a state of comparative dependence." And the effect, disastrous to a healthy republican society, was to deny to "the working class that standing in the community to which their usefulness entitles them." The purpose of the labor movement was to reverse this unnatural process, "until we behold our young men aspiring to the character and title of virtuous and intelligent mechanics, as the most certain means to obtain the respect and confidence of their fellow citizens."

The nineteenth-century labor movement thus attached its cause to the country's republican heritage—to equal rights, to citizenship, to the vision of a virtuous society of independent producers. For many years, the Fourth of July was a workers' holiday, celebrated by them with such toasts as: "The Working Men, the legitimate children of '76, their sires left them the legacy of freedom and equality. They are now of age and are laboring to guarantee the principles of the Revolution." If we lack nineteenth-century opinion polls, we have much else that suggests the resonance of labor's republicanism in the larger society.

So compelling was the free labor ideology that it was appropriated by the emerging Republican party during the sectional crisis of the 1850s. "Labor is prior to, and independent of capital," said Lincoln.

And his fellow Republican William Evarts: labor is "the source of all our wealth, of all our progress, of all our dignity and value." For a time, David Montgomery has argued, the labor movement assumed that the political struggle against slavery marked the opening stage of a larger battle for the achievement of its own republican vision. "What would it profit us, as a nation," asked the labor leader William Sylvis in 1865, "were we to preserve our institutions and destroy the morals of the people; save our Constitution and sink the masses into hopeless ignorance, poverty, and crime? . . . Remember . . . that all popular governments must depend for their stability and success upon the virtue and intelligence of the masses."

That translated into the demand for eight hours, which became the central goal of the National Labor Union that Sylvis founded in 1866. But the Republican party, if long on rhetoric, came up short when confronted by a demand that would have to be paid for out of the pockets of capital. The National Labor Union foundered on the discovery of this harsh truth. But it foundered even more on its own institutional weaknesses.

From the very beginning, the movement had searched without success for an institutional strategy for labor republicanism. Its natural venue was politics, but in a system dominated by two mass parties little scope could be found for independent labor politics. There is a long and fascinating history of experimentation with labor parties stretching back to the workingmen's parties of the 1830s, but it is a history of nearly unvarying failure, in which the NLU's National Labor Reform party was but the last. The programmatic problems were equally troubling. How was an exploitative industrial order to be transformed into the cooperative commonwealth? The nostrums that were forthcoming—agrarianism, eight hours, greenbackism, cooperation—never quite made the grade. They were productive of brilliant theorizing and flashes of popular enthusiasm, but not of practical results. And there was an intractable organizational problem. A movement founded on a producerist ethic had to be open not only to wage earners but to all "producers." What structure would accommodate and discipline a constituency that included nearly anyone who felt like joining up?

The last great assault on these problems was undertaken by the Knights of Labor, which enjoyed a spectacular success in the first half of the 1880s and suffered an equally spectacular collapse in the second half.

At this juncture, there occurred one of those rare moments in which the history of a social movement is made by conscious choice. The key actors were a small circle of trade-union radicals, among them Samuel Gompers. Mainly German Marxists, they were not locked into the tradition of republicanism. They thought in terms of class struggle and recognized, as J. P. McDonnell had remarked, that they faced a harder task than their European brothers because "in the United States our capitalist enemy resides in the breast of almost everyone." Out of debates within the First International, moreover, they had identified the trade union as the only effective means of fostering working-class development in America.

In founding the American Federation of Labor in 1886, they were bent on defining a labor movement that would survive in the American environment. "We do not wish to raise a structure whose foundations are rotten, being built up by repeating the errors of others who have preceded us." The pure-and-simple philosophy that guided them was captured most succinctly by Gompers's colleague in the Cigarmakers' Union, Adolph Strasser, in testimony before a Senate committee:

Q. You are seeking to improve home matters first?
A. Yes, sir; I look first to the trade I represent; I look first to cigars, to the interests of men who employ me to represent their interests.
Q. I was only asking you in regard to your ultimate ends.
A. We have no ultimate ends. We are going on from day to day. We are fighting only for immediate objects—objects that can be realized in a few years.
Q. I see that you are a little sensitive lest it should be thought that you are a mere theorizer. . . .
A. Well, we say in our constitution that we are opposed to theorists, and I have to represent the organization here. We are all practical men. . . .

Visionary thinking was to be avoided. "The ills of our social and economic system cannot be cured by patent medicine," Gompers wrote. He did not dismiss the possibility of larger change. In more radical moments, he could still speak of trade-union unity as "the germ of the future state." But such thinking had to be put aside. "I am perfectly satisfied to fight the battles of today, of those here, and those that come tomorrow, so their conditions may be improved, and they may be better prepared to fight the contests or solve the problems that may be presented to them. . . . Every step that the workers make or take, every vantage point gained, is a solution in itself.''

Such a movement would eschew independent politics, which caused internal dissension and distracted the movement from its main tasks. Unions should never seek ''at the hands of the government what they could accomplish by their own initiative and activities.'' Nor could there be a place for any but wage workers, organized by trades and led by fellow workers. All of this was grounded on this rock-bottom Marxist maxim: ''Economic organization and control over economic power were the fulcrum which made possible influence and power in all other fields.''

Thus on all the issues in which labor republicanism had gone in one direction—on politics, on program, on constituency—pure-and-simple unionism went in the other. By lodging its principles in the new AFL, Gompers meant to make them the exclusive basis for trade-union organization. In so doing, of course, he boldly exposed to public view his pure-and-simple brand of labor movement—in which economic power was everything, in which organization served above all as the basis of economic power, in which the cement of organization was the immediate interest of the members.

If Gompers's approach was well-calculated to build a viable trade-union movement, it did so by distancing that movement from traditional republican values. Trade-union leaders by no means denied republicanism its centrality in American society or, indeed, in the lives of workers as citizens. But not as the basis for the labor movement.

Here, then, was a central paradox of American labor history: to embrace the republican values of the larger society was to have a labor movement that would not work. And to have a movement that would work required some degree of disengagement from those American values. It was Gompers's genius to see what had to be done,[2] and he can scarcely be faulted for the choice he made.

The labor movement has lived with that choice ever since. I do not mean to suggest that history stopped with Gompers. Even in his lifetime, the AFL expanded, grew ethnically and ideologically diverse, established links to the state, and became a significant force in American politics. During the 1930s, in the heyday of the CIO, the labor movement seemed on the brink of social-democratic transformation, and, after that moment faded, long remained a central actor in liberal Democratic politics. Yet organized labor never abandoned what was essential in the pure-and-simple formulation, a truth perhaps more evident during hard going—as in the 1920s or the 1980s—than in flush times. And, by the same token, it never managed to reclaim the moral legitimacy given the nineteenth-century movement by labor republicanism.

How heavy has that liability been for the modern labor movement? Enormous, if one accepts the argument advanced by Lipset in a companion essay to his public-opinion analysis.[3] Until the 1930s, trade unionism had normally been confined to about 10 percent of the nonagricultural labor force. Then union density began to grow, reaching a high point of nearly 33 percent in 1953. This was, Lipset suggests, an exceptional event, reflecting a shift in the country to more collectivist values as a result of the Great Depression. Since the 1950s, affluent America has drifted back to the older value system of individualism, and the result has been an erosion of trade-union strength down toward pre-New Deal levels. Union representation fell below 18 percent of the nonagricultural labor force during the 1980s, and in the private sector down toward 10 percent. Lipset finds a significant correlation between a key indicator of public opinion—the Gallup survey of approval/disapproval of unions, which moved from a disapproval rating of 14 percent in 1957 to a record high of 35 percent in 1981—and the decline in union density over that period.

The burden of Lipset's argument, however, is not statistical but comparative. There has been no lack of explanation for labor's dramatic decline since the mid-1970s—the deregulation of major markets, the shift to a service economy, the faltering competitiveness of the manufacturing sector in an increasingly internationalized economy, a labor law inimical to labor's organizing efforts. Plausible as these reasons may be, in Lipset's view they lose much of their force when applied cross-nationally, for they do not seem to explain in any clear pattern how the labor movements of other industrial economies have fared. What remains, then, are differences in national values.

The anchor for this broad claim is a detailed Canadian-American comparative analysis. At the very time that the union sector in the United States was shrinking, in Canada it was growing. Roughly equal in the mid-1950s, both movements experienced a similar slow downward trend until the mid-1960s, then sharply diverged. Canadian union density currently stands at 40 percent, well over twice that of the United States. Yet no two national movements have been more alike. They have common historical roots. Canadian unions mostly began as the ''international'' segments of American national unions. While a process of disassociation has been under way—most recently in the case of the Auto Workers—institutional structures and rules remain pretty much the same.

Canadian labor law, moreover, is patterned on the National Labor Relations Act. In one respect, Canadian law has been seen by critics of the NLRA as much more favorable to union representation. Most provinces will certify unions on a show of dues-paying membership; the others mandate very quick elections. In the United States, there are normally long delays that enable employers to mount antiunion campaigns. Lipset, however, minimizes the significance of these problems. He cites research that shows little impact of delays or employer opposition on election outcomes and ascribes the low current rate of union success—45 percent—to the declining sympathy for unions in the population as a whole.[4]

The economic settings, finally, are also in many ways similar, with many common employers, a comparable level of industrial development, and many economic links. In fact, business conditions in Canada —unemployment, inflation, low productivity—were even less favorable to trade unions in the 1980s than in the United States, and Canada shifted even more decisively from a manufacturing to a service economy.

The vigor of the Canadian movement can only be explained, Lipset concludes, by a more sympathetic national value system. "As compared to her more populous neighbor, Canada is a more elitist, communitarian, statist, and particularistic (group oriented) society." Canada never had a liberal revolution. Its national existence, indeed, derives from its rejection of the American Revolution. The clerically led French Canadians were equally impervious to the French Revolution. The dominant Canadian tradition has been a kind of Tory paternalism that, as Henry Phelps Brown describes it, "stressed authority and hierarchy, but with these went solidarity and benevolence, which occupy some common ground with collectivism."

Although part of a North American movement, the Canadian unions historically showed a more collectivist bent, advocating state intervention when the AFL was preaching voluntarism, and, since the 1930s, providing the core support for the independent social democratic politics that has evolved with the New Democratic party. Differing value systems have different organizational outcomes, says Lipset. "The American social structure and values foster the free market and competitive individualism, an orientation which is not congruent with class consciousness, support of socialist or social democratic parties, or a strong trade union movement."[5]

Lipset's analysis is undeniably incomplete. Values for the most part do not have direct consequences but are mediated through the many institutional and social-economic forces acting on trade unionism. And even where Lipset asserts a direct connection, much remains to be clarified.

While there may be a statistical correlation, for example, it does not necessarily follow that any real relationship exists between national approval ratings of labor unions and the proclivity of workers to vote for union representation in certification elections. Public opinion polls show a significant discrepancy between negative attitudes to unions as institutions and valuations of the need for unions—for example, in the 56 percent affirmative responses to the statement: "If there were no unions, most employers would move quickly to exploit their employees."[6] The discrepancy suggests a conclusion different from that drawn by Lipset, namely, that workers do not have to like unions in principle in order to opt for them in practice.

Nor is it clear that worker preferences are the decisive factor. Union organizing expenditures, for one thing, have declined relative to the size of the nonunion sector. By most accounts (if not Lipset's), employer opposition has been highly effective, not only during representation campaigns but also in resisting good-faith collective bargaining after unions have won representation elections. Less than two-thirds of first-time negotiations result in signed contracts. None of this, moreover, takes account of the rate of attrition of the trade-union base as industrial plants close and the service sector expands. The AFL-CIO estimated in 1983 that it had to organize over a million new workers each year just to stay even.[7]

Much of the complexity of the organizing process clearly has not been captured in Lipset's analysis. But there is still no escaping the force of his thesis. At some fundamental level, the crisis of American trade unionism derives from the dubious regard in which it is held by the larger society.

There are no obvious ways to change this. Labor's tendency, doubtless more reflexive than calculated, to try to regain the moral high ground by taking on the Americanist coloration of its adversaries—for example, by its embrace of anti-immigration nativism in the 1890s, or by Gompers's strident patriotism during World War I, or, to some degree, by the militant anticommunism of the Cold War era—never paid off where it most counted, that is, in moderating the antiunion forces in the country.

The labor movement can perhaps do a better public-relations job explaining how its activities advance the cause of social justice. But if Lipset is right, collectivist values are no longer in the ascendant. And, in any event, organized labor can lay less claim to the social-justice mantle today than it could in the Roosevelt, or even the Johnson, era. As a pure-and-simple movement, labor has the least leeway when its power is eroding and its membership declining. This was true in 1929, when it seemed to many critics no more than "a life raft . . . for skilled labor," and is equally true today. Under duress, American unions husband their resources to defend what they have. In the early 1990s, job security for the membership becomes the top bargaining goal, and in politics nothing is more important than an adjustment of labor law to outlaw the permanent replacement of strikers.

There is always, of course, the possibility that the larger environment will shift once more. On October 19, 1987, the stock market crashed; 22 percent of its value vanished in a single day. At the AFL-CIO convention a week later, a reporter hears, amidst anxious talk about an economic contraction, some hope "that the collapse in stock prices would call into question the individualist ethos of the Reagan era and create an environment far more sympathetic to the labor movement's insistence on the importance of social solidarity." Time will tell. But, if the bounds of constraint do shift—as they did in an earlier great depression—they seem unlikely to break. The United States is not Canada; and it is not Australia.

Career Leadership*

In an essay in 1928, the labor writer J. B. S. Hardman imagined a conversation between a union president (XYZ) and His Younger Self (HYS).

---

*From Frederick C. Jaher, ed., *The Age of Industrialism in America* (New York: The Free Press, 1969), 288–303. Copyright © 1969 by The Free Press, a division of Macmillan, Inc. Reprinted with the permission of the publisher.

> HYS: . . . Look what you have become. Is that what I meant to grow into?
> XYZ: Why, a leader of labor, that was your dream.
> HYS: No, old man, you are not a leader of labor, you are a labor leader.
> XYZ: What is the difference?
> HYS: All the difference in the world. One is a fighter, the other a professional.[8]

The hypothetical Younger Self was drawing a distinction vital in the history of American organized labor. Its leaders became professionals: they were paid, they worked full time, their offices became careers. Peculiarly an attribute of pure-and-simple unionism, professionalism helped shape the conservative movement.

American trade unionism took permanent form in the last decades of the nineteenth century. As pure-and-simple doctrine prevailed over reformism, as the organizational structure crystallized and the trade unions stabilized, the career leaders emerged. The International Association of Machinists, for instance, began in the South in 1888 as a fraternal-benevolent order plus some reform notions derived from the Knights of Labor. Inside of half a dozen years the Machinists became, as their historian Mark Perlman put it, "a job-oriented trade union." The IAM simultaneously developed a career officialdom. When he took office in 1893, president James O'Connell assumed that people should be paid, and paid adequately, to do the union's work. The lack of an expense account bothered him. "This is certainly an injustice to your executive officer," he complained at the 1895 convention. "You should not ask him to expend the greater portion of his salary for hotel bills. . . . " O'Connell also urged the IAM to hire organizers. The first were appointed the next year to cover Chicago, New York, Cleveland, and Lynn, Massachusetts. The International Association of Machinists completed the professionalization of its leadership when full-time officers replaced the lay members of the executive board in 1925.[9]

The same process occurred at the local level. The early butchers' unions, for example, suffered from the rapid turnover of officers. They resigned to enter business or, as one unionist complained in 1902, refused "to keep their old offices, for they were tired of the hard work they had done for our local." The answer was to pay for leadership. "It is going to cost us a great deal at first," another member reasoned, "but in my opinion it is the only way that we can make a success of the union. . . . We will have a man in the field all the time, and he is a hustler. . . . " One by one, the surviving butchers' unions arrived at that conclusion. In the 1920s, the powerful Chicago local employed "high class fellows . . . who could go out and do business." The secretary received $150 a week, the business agents, $100. "The local's business representatives," an admiring visitor from the West Coast reported in 1926, "were recognized as men of affairs and . . . all of them make their rounds in modern cars."[10] Such career men had long since become familiar figures in the labor circles of American cities.

Professionalization normally proceeded unremarkably from cumulative administrative decisions and thus rarely became an explicit issue in the conflict between trade and reform unionism. The United Brotherhood of Carpenters and Joiners provided the important exception. Peter J. McGuire, who founded the national union in 1881 and organized many of the local bodies, was a labor reformer. He saw trade unions not as ends in themselves but as a means "to educate our class, to prepare it for the changes to come, to establish a system of co-operative industry in place of the wage system. . . . " Meanwhile, the carpenters' locals and district bodies in the 1880s began to employ business agents, a notoriously hard-headed crew whose vision ended with wages, hours, and working conditions. McGuire and the business agents clashed over fundamental differences, among them the creation of a national officialdom. The business agents pressed for salaried, full-time national officers and organizers. At the time, only the secretary-treasurer— McGuire—received an income from the national union. For more than a decade, Secretary McGuire used his powerful hold on the rank and file to fight off the local professionals. They finally brought him down, old and sick, on charges of malfeasance in office in 1902 and drove him out of the organization. Then at last the carpenters followed the leadership pattern already fixed among national unions in the American movement.[11]

In the formative years, the opponents of pure-and-simple unionism seemed typically indifferent to building careers from their labor activities. Their work was selfless and idealistic; or, curiously, combined with other ambitions. Terence V. Powderly never conceived of the top post of the Knights of Labor as a permanent career, nor even as a full-time one while he held it. In 1882–83, Powderly served simultaneously as mayor of Scranton, county health officer, the operator of a coffee and tea business, and Grand Master Workman. And he also jockeyed openly for political appointment, an ambition he finally fulfilled after supporting William McKinley in 1896.[12]

After 1900, contrasting attitudes toward career leadership became more sharply defined. The new radical unions abhorred professionalism. They feared what one member of the Western Federation of Miners called "the peculiar point of view which always comes to a man that occupies an executive position for any length of time." Militancy would shrivel under that influence. So the independent Butte Mine Workers' Union, adopting a constitution in 1914, permitted only one paid officer (the president), compensated him only for days worked, and limited him to a single term of six months.[13] The Industrial Workers of the World incessantly fought careerism. When the organization was one year old, President Charles O. Sherman was ousted and his office abolished. "The labor fakirs," Vincent St. John later explained, "strove to fasten themselves upon the organization that they might continue to exist if the new union was a success." The "decentralizing" faction carried the point to a logical conclusion in 1913: eliminate all national offices and the national convention as well. "We are . . . working to overthrow this [wages] system and we . . . claim . . . that the rank and file of the proletariat will have to do this themselves." The demand went too far even for the IWW. Still, if organized activity required leadership, the corrupting consequences had to be fought and the careerists constantly rooted out.[14]

So career leadership as a normal and accepted phenomenon was restricted to pure-and-simple unionism. Equally significant, the tendency was especially marked in the American movement. Consider the extent of professionalism in the trade unions of six countries in the post–World War II era: in the United States, the ratio of full-time officials to union members was 1 to 300; in Denmark, 1 to 775; in Australia, 1 to 900; in Sweden, 1 to 1,700; in Norway, 1 to 2,200; in Britain, 1 to close to 4,000.[15] By a wide margin, the American movement maximized the number of career places in its structure. What was there in the American situation that encouraged this distinctive characteristic of American trade-union leadership?

Part of the answer rested in attitudes that American labor shared with the larger society. The sociologist Seymour Lipset has pointed to "the achievement-equalitarian syndrome" of American society. "The emphasis on pecuniary success, combined with the absence of the kind of class consciousness characteristic of more aristocratic societies . . . served to motivate workers to use the labor movement itself as an avenue to financial and status gain." Lipset's thesis finds support in the comparison with English experience. In his illuminating book, *Weekend in Dinlock,* Clancy Sigal noted that Yorkshire miners viewed career union leaders with "unbounded, if tolerant and humorous, contempt, the measure being that a man loses worth according to the distance he puts between himself and the coal face." When asked what "social standing" other people ascribed to union officials, English labor leaders revealed a significant contradiction. Most thought a middle-class level or higher. But many also were disturbed by the question, and a few even doubted its propriety: union leaders ought not to be set above the rank and file. "If they 'aspired' to some other 'social standing' they would be betraying the trust put in them by their fellow members," one officer wrote.[16] Such disapproval had little force in a society that expected its citizens to rise as far as they could; that denied the importance of class distinctions; and that expected voluntary associations, trade unions included, to pay their functionaries. American social values thus encouraged unionists to seek and the labor movement to provide advancement through leadership careers.

The pure-and-simple thrust of American trade unionism, in addition, created a need for careerists. In his excellent study of the Carpenters' Union, Robert A. Christie arrived at this explanation for the early appearance of the business agents. The local unions initially undertook to combat the piecework system favored by building contractors, and then to organize and control the local labor market. The Carpenters quickly discovered that only full-time, paid functionaries could handle these demanding tasks.[17] That conclusion followed wherever trade unions allocated jobs, maintained apprenticeship programs, policed agreements, and protected employers against nonunion competition. Collective bargaining—the primary union function—made an especially heavy demand for officers skilled in formulating, negotiating, and interpreting contracts. Even at an early point, the issues could be complex—the sliding scale in the iron industry, for example—and bargaining itself always called for an experienced, knowledgeable hand. Hence the plea of the Syracuse butchers' union to the national office for "someone to help get our Next Contracts signed. There is no one here who is experienced in this line."[18] Company unions suffered on this score. Studying the experience of the Colorado Fuel and Iron Company, one investigator concluded that many steelworkers "felt that they themselves lacked the training and experience to be able to meet company officials and other specialists . . . on an equal footing. They needed the aid of union officials who have become expert in representing the interests of the wage-earners.''[19] The relationship worked in reverse as well. The radical unions, disliking careerists, had less need for professionalism: they also rejected collective bargaining.

So, in essential ways, career leadership grew from basic characteristics of American labor: its social attitudes and its narrow economic orientation. The influences, however, ran both ways. Professionalism affected the nature of the labor movement. The career factor did not operate alone; it was a contributing, secondary influence. But in that limited way, assuredly the career needs of labor leaders did serve as a determinant to the American movement.

Powerful motives were at work. In addition to its avowed function of representing American workers, trade unionism raised a fortunate number entirely out of the blue-collar class. In the mid-1940s C. Wright Mills made a pioneering study of top labor officials. They turned out to be predominately working class in origin. Only one in ten came from families in the middle class of professionals, executives, and entrepreneurs. At the time they embarked on trade-union careers, 75 percent themselves worked at trades.[20] The labor movement gave them a chance—perhaps the most accessible to American workers—for steep upward mobility. The sharp break occurred at the first move into either of the two paid jobs, organizer or business agent, available to beginning careerists. Job security increased, income rose, and, above all, the white-collar world of offices, suits, and flexible schedules opened up. Rewards rose commensurate with progress up the ladder. Not counting expense accounts, salaries reached $9,500 and above for one-third of all union presidents in 1944, and $7,500 and over for the same proportion of other national officers. Their style of life became, as C. Wright Mill observed, ''like that of any middle-class businessman in an urban area.''[21] Nor should the sweet satisfactions of power and influence be discounted. The stakes of office, running as high as they did, could not fail to influence the decisions of American labor leaders.

Radicals grew vociferous on this point. Eugene Debs (who once boasted sardonically of his ''modest distinction'' as the only national leader ever ''to resign his office after being unanimously re-elected and given the privilege of fixing his own salary'') explained the AFL reaction to the IWW: ''Who is it that is so violently opposed to the Industrial Workers? It is not the rank and file of the trade unions. It is their officers. And why . . . ? For the reason that when the working class are really united a great many labor leaders will be let out of jobs. . . . Let me say to you that their interests are primarily in keeping themselves there.''[22] Polemical as the attack was, it rested on a solid respect for the officeholding influence. That partly explained why many radicals preferred dual-union tactics over boring from within. Daniel De Leon warned "that the pure and simple leaders give jobs to Socialists for the purpose of corrupting them. . . . " The IWW agitator Joseph Ettor in 1914 answered the borers-from-within in the same way.

> The theory that what is needed to save the [American] Federation [of Labor] is the energetic and vigorous men who are now in the I.W.W. is on a par with the "socialist" advice of how to save the nation . . . roll up our sleeves and become active politically within capitalism. . . . We tried, but the more we fooled with the beast the more it *captured us*. . . . We learned at an awful cost particularly this: That the most unscrupulous labor fakers now betraying the workers were once our "industrialist," "anarchist," and "socialist" comrades, who . . . were not only lost, but . . . became the supporters of the old and [the] most serious enemies of the new.[23]

What could be more telling testimony to the power of careerism: that it kept radicals at a distance from the trade unions.

The career influence pervaded the American labor movement. The economic orientation itself reflected the inclination of the American worker and, at best, labor leaders could only encourage that powerful bent. It was more important that they directed the economic impulse into channels that best met career needs.

Many union objectives were obtainable through government action. Yet until the 1930s the American Federation of Labor staunchly opposed most labor legislation. Public measures were desired only for defensive reasons—for instance, to curb the courts and immigration—and for groups incapable of acting in their own behalf. Law, Gompers was arguing in 1914, should "free people from the shackles and give them a chance to work out their own salvation." Among its other sources, voluntarism sprang from the career requirements of trade-union leaders. Legislation had this drawback: it minimized the functions of the unions and their officials. Compulsory unemployment insurance, William Green warned, would "pull at our vitals and destroy our trade union structure."[24] When the New York retail butchers' unions finally won a state Sunday closing law in 1901, a prominent official privately warned that they were thereby cutting away their own ground. The butchers soon came to the same conclusion; the regulation of hours, at first pursued through political means, became the subject of collective bargaining.

Economic action, not legislation, satisfied two essentials for professional leadership. First, it built up the permanent, dues-paying membership on which careers depended. Workers had to receive "something tangible for their money" that would "induce [them] to join the Union or to keep themselves in good standing after joining."[25] No activity did this better than collective bargaining, although insurance benefits were also important for many unions. The objective was, in any case, clear enough. As Hardman's hypothetical union president said, "It pays our people to belong to the organization." Second, collective bargaining was the taxing, continuing activity that required a professional hand. By monopolizing the collective-bargaining functions, officials maximized the volume of career-creating work. American unions wanted nothing to do with the European (particularly German) works councils that took over representation at the plant level.[26] Nor, on the other hand, would trade-union leaders share their economic responsibilities either with government agencies or with the American Federation of Labor (hence its relative unimportance in the American movement).

Nonpartisan politics likewise best fitted the career needs of the leadership. Of course, strong practical and ideological reasons argued against an independent party, but so did the logic of professionalism. A labor party would rest on a broad constituency and create jobs of a different kind and in a different framework. The prospects for political careers would certainly expand for individual trade-union leaders. (Even under nonpartisanship, some unionists did enter public life, more often through appointment than election.) But a regular channel, secure and predictable for careerists, could not be erected between the union hierarchies and even a successful labor party. That had proved the case in Great Britain.[27] Nor did a trade-union career provide the kind of base, as did law and business, that would remain secure while a person pursued politics. As in England, a labor party would doubtless be exploited by the middle-class intellectuals and thus violate Gompers' injunction—itself an aspect of professionalism—"that leadership in the labor movement could be safely entrusted only to those . . . [with] the experience of earning their bread by daily labor."[28] On the other hand, union officials did go into local politics, through independent organizations and, more regularly, within the established parties.[29] At the local level, no conflict existed between a union career and political involvement; both could occur simultaneously and in fact be connected. Labor's political ends in the state and nation, however, were better pursued through the nonpartisan, lobbying activities that did not force a departure from the career base in the trade unions.

The career influence also played on the internal life of American labor unions. Characteristically, live politics gave way to one-party government as a union matured. The ruling group tended to become permanent and opposition, illegitimate. The formal democratic process remained, but not the substance. This instance of Michel's "iron law of oligarchy" sprang largely from the monopoly of political weapons by the administration and from the indifference and isolation of the rank and file. But it resulted also from the professionalization of leadership.[30]

For one thing, officials acquired the skills of the politician no less than those of negotiator and organizer. Consider, for example, the thoughts of Hardman's President XYZ on his way to an international labor conference in Europe:

> All in all it was not quite easy to put the trip matter straight. Brother A had to be promised the post of representative on the national Advisory Council, and B served notice that he meant to get a seat on the General Executive Board at the next convention. That would mean a good deal of trouble next spring. . . . The Pennsylvania boys would have to be "satisfied," and that would upset the balance of power. . . . It was not easy to sidetrack [B]. Yes, there was that bank possibility for which he was likely to fall and which, if things went right, would take him out of the field. . . . In the meantime one would do well to watch the game very closely. XYZ . . . knows of what material human beings are made . . . Ambition must be played on. . . . The larger the number of people involved, the more intricate the political game. . . . One must calculate, bargain, gamble, buy, sell. . . . No, XYZ would let no one snatch things from under his hands. And once an issue is raised he will fight it out. . . . In politics only the terms of a deal may be negotiated, not the issue of leadership.[31]

Here, honed by years of experience, was the fine political edge that ensured control of America's trade unions.

Beyond the skills, professionalism created the primary motives for oligarchical rule. The free play of the democratic process could only hinder their job, as labor leaders conceived it. "The administration of labor is an art," said Hardman's hypothetical XYZ, "and it requires knowledge. . . . Centralized action. . . . No open forum exercises.''[32] It was not only a leader's sense of competence pitted against aspiring rivals and the uninformed membership. To the professional leader, opposition spelled factionalism. His organization would lose economic force and, simultaneously, would face irresponsible demands and strikes. Collective bargaining could not be properly directed under those disturbing circumstances. To build a stable relationship with an employer, an astute official might assume the delicate role of mediating union and management interests. If he had broader concerns—for instance, a desire to gain employer support for organizing purposes—he might at times even lean toward the company position on a contested point. As a prerequisite for such a role, of course, he needed the free hand that came only from unquestioned one-party rule.[33]

Finally, for career leaders, high personal stakes were involved. What would defeat mean? To return to a manual job meant an intolerable decline in status and income. In a few unions, such as actors' or printers', the gap between leaders and members remained narrow, and little was lost in the return to the trade. These unions, significantly, retained the democratic process. The International Typographical Union, in fact, evolved a genuine two-party system. The other alternative for the defeated leader, the one usually taken after the early years of the labor movement, was to leave the union.[34] But the labor leader was a political man, not a bureaucrat. Unlike his management counterpart at the bargaining table, he could not circulate without fundamentally altering his future. For his career depended on the support he commanded inside his union—a nontransferable commodity. A post with another union would necessarily be appointive and dependent. A management job signified, in addition, that he was selling out. These hard choices compelled the labor leader to follow a course that would preclude defeat. And the democratic process paid the price.

The leadership view of union members as a dues-paying clientele exerted a broad influence. Jurisdiction, for one thing, naturally became a matter of large importance. Labor unions mapped out their boundaries precisely and exclusively, and even so fought endlessly among themselves over disputed territory. The clientele idea also encouraged the peculiar emphasis on security arrangements—the union shop and the checkoff—which would stabilize and guarantee membership. Finally, it helped shape the approach to organizing the unorganized. The Machinists wanted to send a man into the East because ''it would be a profitable investment for us to make earnest efforts to organize that section. . . . ''[35] The conception of organizing as a kind of business venture—so much invested, so many members gained—clearly reflected the idea of membership as a clientele. And that narrow calculation, among other things, explained why the attempts to organize the mass-production industries consistently fell short.

Did the influence of career leadership extend to the industrial unions that emerged during the 1930s? A special situation dominated those first years. To a large extent, the unionizing impulse came from the ranks, and with it a marked resistance to outside direction. Control, asserted one CIO man, should rest in "the whole body, in one, acting as one. All of these collectively comprise your leadership." The outlook resulted, among other things, in the spontaneous strikes of the mid-1930s and in the opposition to appointed officials within the Auto Workers, Rubber Workers, and other emerging industrial unions. The recruitment of officers was likewise abnormal. The rank and filers and left wingers who were catapulted into leadership were motivated—to use Lipset's distinction—more by a calling than by career ambitions. In 1941 a local UAW official who had lost his post wrote:

> I have given serious thought as to whether to accept an organizational job outside of auto at this time, and I don't think it advisable as there is a job to be done and if I leave it means I would be running away from it. It's no use running some place else and losing here. . . . I am now back in the shop at $48.00 per with my nose to the grindstone as an electrician and the first week has been a tough one although most of the boys made a large fuss and were glad to see me. My chief Steward resigned so that I could be elected in his place so that I could be in a position to function for the Union immediately. Boy, did that get the managements [*sic*] goat.[36]

Although the calling still dominated, clearly the career influence was working among such fresh recruits to labor leadership. There was, moreover, an unusual circulation of professionals into the new unions, mainly from the Mine Workers and Clothing Workers. Their counsel and, where they were able to sustain it, their rule followed closely the standard, professional line.

If the early CIO seemed to have the character of a social movement, from the start it was also in the main line of American trade unionism. The industrial unions always aimed for collective bargaining, and they were fighting for that alone in the bitterest strikes of the 1930s. The

CIO was more concerned with political and social issues than was the AFL, but by a matter of degree, not kind; and the distance narrowed with the passage of time. The industrial-union leaders similarly functioned as full-time, paid officials. Although some part of the original calling remained, in time they did not differ essentially from their counterparts in the AFL. Here, as earlier, the demands of bargaining unionism forced professionalism on the leadership. Indeed, the pressures intensified because modern problems, centralized negotiations, and the expanded role of government—the National Labor Relations Board and then the wartime regulation of labor relations—required more skills and time from union officers. But, again, becoming professional, they developed the career needs that would influence CIO organization in the same ways as these had the AFL unions.

The force of that influence is of course beyond exact measurement. Career leadership never worked alone, nor could it be counted as decisive, but assuredly it contributed in a pervasive way to making American trade unionism what it is today.

Ethnicity*

For the half century prior to World War I, the shaping years of the national labor movement, the foreign-born consistently made up roughly a seventh of the American population. Within the labor force, however, they were a much larger presence. In 1910 immigrants constituted 25 percent of the employees in transportation, 36 percent in manufacturing, and 45 percent in mining. If white-collar jobs are excluded, the concentration of foreign-born workers becomes still higher, running in many manual occupations from 50 to more than 75 percent. Immigrants made up nearly 58 percent of the wage earners in twenty principal mining and manufacturing industries in 1909. And when their American-born children are included, it becomes apparent that during the industrializing age the nation's working people were predominantly of recent origin in the United States.

The relative lack of an indigenous labor supply had distinguished the American industrial experience from the start. Unlike England, the

*From *Harvard Encyclopedia of American Ethnic Groups* (Cambridge: Harvard University Press, 1980), 609–18. Reprinted with permission.

United States could not draw on a numerous population of artisans and laborers to man its new factories. In the early days the giant cotton mills north of Boston recruited Yankee farm girls; textile producers in Rhode Island and elsewhere relied on family labor for mill work and on the putting-out system for weaving cloth. Some industries—such as the boot and shoe manufacture around Lynn, Massachusetts, and the machine-tool production in the Connecticut Valley—were able to rely on chiefly local labor. In general, however, as industrialism gathered force, the need for hands far outran native sources of supply. More than any other force, it was this persistent shortage of labor that drew thirty-five million immigrants to the United States in the century ending with World War I. The Great Migration must be seen as primarily economic, ebbing and flowing along with the business cycle, drawing disproportionately on males of working age, and in its details, largely shaped by the changing needs of American industry for particular kinds of European workers.

The dependence on outside sources of labor did not end when the mass immigration from Europe was checked, first by World War I and then by the restrictive laws of 1921 and 1924. An exodus from settled farming areas had been under way throughout the nineteenth century, and while much of it went westward, the movement was also persistently cityward. The decline of immigration after 1914, however, made internal migration more decisively industrial in its direction. The half-million southern blacks who moved north during World War I, for example, boosted the black portion of the labor force in the Chicago packinghouses from 3 percent in 1909 to over 20 percent in 1918. By 1930 over 25 percent of the nation's black males were engaged in industrial occupations, compared to 7 percent in 1890. Similarly, Appalachian whites became a major source of labor for defense industries during World War I and for such growing manufacturing centers as Detroit, Michigan, and Toledo and Akron, Ohio, during the 1920s.

These successive waves of newcomers did not enter the industrial system in a random way. Many of the western Europeans were seasoned artisans and industrial workers bringing applicable—and in the earlier years, essential—skills to American production. The more advanced British economy made an especially large contribution. Skills gave a distinctive ethnic stamp to the nineteenth-century occupational structure—the Welsh in anthracite mining and tin plate manufacture, the

Scots in bituminous mining, Cornishmen in copper and lead mining, the English in iron, steel, and textiles, Germans in traditional crafts, Scandinavians on the Great Lakes boats, Russian Jews in the needle trades. Those who came without skills also found specific niches in the economic system. Rural Ireland was the main source of common labor in the pre–Civil War period. In Boston in 1850, for example, over 80 percent of the laborers were Irish. Starting as cartmen, longshoremen, and ditch diggers, the Irish moved into the factories and gradually up the scale of the expanding industrial economy. In 1855 they formed a substantial part of the skilled artisan class of New York City (40 percent of the carpenters, 50 percent of the blacksmiths, 60 percent of the masons and bricklayers). Similarly in industry and mining: by 1885 half the Irish involved in accidents in three Pennsylvania anthracite districts were classified as skilled miners, a proportion equal to that of the English and Welsh. As mechanization and mass-production techniques advanced in the late nineteenth century, dependence on European craft skills lessened, while the need for ordinary workers accelerated, which was one of the reasons for the remarkable shift of immigration from northern to southern and eastern Europe. In 1907 Slavs and Italians made up over 80 percent of the common labor in the Carnegie Steel Company. The low-paid, heavy work in northern industry and transportation became the virtual preserve of the ''new'' immigrants in the early twentieth century.

Ethnicity cut deeply into American occupational patterns not only because of the varied skills of the immigrants. Within trades and industries, ethnic groups tended to cluster together in certain industrial locales and even within individual factories and mines. Settlement patterns worked to the same effect. French Canadians crossing the border did not normally venture beyond upper New England; Mexicans confined themselves mainly to the fields and mines of the Southwest, the Chinese to the Pacific Coast. In a city such as Milwaukee, Wisconsin, settled mainly by Germans, the trades were heavily German in composition (in 1860, 58 percent of the tradesmen were German, ranging from 42 percent of the machinists to 54 percent of the carpenters and 74 percent of the butchers). To some degree, ethnocultural characteristics, especially among preindustrial groups, determined the choices of occupation. The *padrone* system naturally led Italian peasants into construction and roadwork. Eastern European Jews flocked into the needle trades, not only because of prior experience but also because the subcontracting and homework fitted (or could be made to fit) family, religious, and group needs in the tenement districts of the great cities.

There were, finally, persistent constraints imposed by the larger society on the job opportunities of particular groups. The blacks suffered most severely. Of all the minority groups in late-nineteenth-century Boston, for example, blacks alone experienced no significant degree of upward mobility and remained confined, generation after generation, in menial and unskilled work (laborer, servant, porter, janitor). When blacks began to move into northern industry in much larger numbers after 1914, the experience was repeated: they were relegated to the most onerous and undesirable jobs. Although no other group (except the Asians in the West) was so completely handicapped, prejudice always played a part in pressing despised groups—from the Irish in the 1830s to the Latinos in our own time—into the bleaker corners of the economic system.

Work in the United States was inscribed indelibly by ethnicity, and in consequence, so would be any American labor movement. How could such a movement capitalize on the strengths inherent in the ethnic groups and skirt the dangers of diversity and mutual antagonism? The answers to those central questions do not exhaust the subject, for the immigrant workers were not passive agents. They impressed the experiences from their own pasts on the American movement. This was most obvious among those who derived from a European working-class background and brought knowledge of European trade unionism and those who arrived dedicated to European radical ideologies, such as many of the Germans, Finns, and Russian Jews. But even those with no industrial past played an active part in shaping the labor movement. Why these immigrants joined and how they acted collectively were related to what they had known back home.

The origins of the American labor movement went back to the 1790s and possibly earlier. As the line became sharper between journeyman and employing craftsman, the cordwainers, printers, carpenters, and other artisans formed the first American trade unions. The basic unit of the labor movement—the local union of workers of the same trade—emerged. So did the basic economic thrust: protection of wage rates and labor standards, control of access to the trade, and exertion of economic power through the strike. During the 1830s the movement broadened into citywide organizations that united the local unions for purposes of mutual defense and political action. In the third stage of development twenty years later, national unions began to take root as local unions became aware that the transportation revolution was nationalizing the labor and product markets in their trades. After the Civil War the movement took the first tentative steps toward federation in order to define its larger purposes and cope with issues beyond the scope of city central bodies and national trade unions. This formative labor activity was inspired by economic forces within American society, and the basic tendencies of the movement sprang from the native environment. The participants themselves, however, were mostly European in origin.

In Illinois immigrants participated in the labor movement out of proportion to their numbers. Although foreign-born workers constituted 40 percent of the state's industrial labor force, they constituted over two-thirds of the union membership in 1886. Pondering this discovery, the Illinois Bureau of Labor Statistics stressed the immigrants' class consciousness and craft identity: "The foreign workman . . . has no possibilities beyond a given sphere, and is trained and developed within it. Thus environed, his career and ambitions lie in the paths his fathers have trod, and his associations with his fellow craftsmen make the trade-union his natural and necessary place." Many of the industrial immigrants had been union men at home. It was, in fact, a regular practice of English unions to encourage unemployed members to emigrate by providing information and free passage. A few English unions, such as the Amalgamated Society of Engineers, even set up American branches to serve their overseas members. "Everybody belonged to unions, it was taken for granted as a normal part of life," recalled John Brophy, an Anglo-American miner who later became an important twentieth-century labor leader. His early success at organizing a miners' union in South Fork, Pennsylvania, he ascribed "to the fact that the miners were almost all of British origin . . . The British immigrants brought with them not only experience in British mines but also, like my father, the experience of British unions." There were regional variations, and probably greater native participation earlier in the nineteenth century, but in general American trade unionism was very much a movement of immigrant workers during the formative years.

Their presence helped surmount the organizational fragility of the movement. In every depression, unions that had been built up in prosperity foundered. As late as the 1870s economic crisis nearly put the

labor movement out of business. Of some thirty national unions operating in 1873, fewer than ten survived the depression, and even the
strongest of these suffered severely from lost membership and defunct
locals. Samuel Gompers doubted that total membership exceeded
50,000 in 1878. It was not only their industrial past that made immigrant
workers a stabilizing influence; ethnic bonds also served to cement labor
organization. Wherever foreign-language immigrants clustered in a single trade, they tended to organize along ethnic lines. In New York City
German artisans in the 1840s organized social clubs and mutual-aid
societies, some of which evolved into trade unions. The New York
German unions maintained their own central labor body, the Arbeiter
Verein. The same kind of separate activity occurred in other cities with
large German populations. The tendency to organize along ethnic lines
eventually expressed itself formally in such bodies as the United Hebrew
Trades, the United German Trades, and the Italian Chamber of Labor.
From ethnic loyalties, too, roots were thrust down into the larger community. Through its large Irish membership, the Molders' Union of
Troy, New York, had ties to the Irish fraternal orders, the Catholic
church, and local politics. In its struggles with the stove manufacturers
in the 1860s and 1870s, the Molders' Union could count on sympathy
from the police (largely Irish) and public officials and on support from
the Irish-American population. In an age when the vitality of trade
unionism was still bound up in local community life, such ethnic link-
ages were an abiding source of strength to the labor movement.

The immigrant presence also exerted some force—subtle and im-
measurable, to be sure—on the ultimate direction of the labor movement. From the 1830s through the 1880s the movement alternated
between economic unionism and labor reform. It would be inaccurate
to suggest any neat correspondence separating native and immigrant
workers on this issue. For one thing, many of the utopian proposals—
from land reform in the 1830s to cooperation later in the century—
either derived from or closely paralleled European ideas, and the reform
impulse that periodically took command always attracted a foreign-born
following. Half the leading figures in the National Labor Union between
1862 and 1872 were British, as were eleven of twenty-five major leaders
of the Knights of Labor at the peak of its power in 1886. And labor's
ambivalence about its direction was genuinely internalized, existing
within the minds of individuals as well as dividing organizations. Yet
if one thinks of tendencies, the immigrants seemed less susceptible to

the lure of broad reform than American workers. The goal of a cooperative commonwealth was grounded in notions of antimonopolism and of a producer society expressive of an American animus against industrialism. Such an appeal might reasonably be expected to exert its main force on native-born people who were experiencing a sense of loss and deprivation in the face of the economic changes then transforming American life.

That this was actually the case is suggested by the 1886 survey of the Illinois Bureau of Labor Statistics. Native-born participation was much stronger in the reformist Knights of Labor (43 percent) than in the trade unions (20 percent). Of nearly 35,000 Illinois residents who belonged to Knights assemblies, over 15,200 were native born; of some 54,200 in trade unions, only 10,700 were native born. This difference cannot be explained by the fact that the Knights of Labor was open to middle-class as well as manual occupations. Only 1,260 Illinois members (3.5 percent) fell into the former category, not enough to make any appreciable difference, even if all had been native born. On the other hand, the inclusive recruiting policy of the Knights, especially during the wave of enthusiasm of 1885–86, brought in large numbers of unskilled workers—over a quarter of the total in 1886—who were disproportionately of recent immigrant origin. The only two ethnic groups more heavily represented in the Knights than in the trade unions were Poles and Bohemians, almost entirely Chicago workers in the stockyards and heavy industry. The remaining membership of the Knights, representing the same occupations covered by the unions, thus was even more thoroughly American in composition.

Class-conscious by background and often trade-union by experience, industrial immigrants found comparatively uncongenial a reform philosophy that denied the significance of class and minimized those elements of militancy (including the strike) and craft identity that were at the heart of trade unionism. By the same token, the immigrants gave to American trade unionism much of the weight it needed to prevail over labor reform.

The industrial immigrants also helped set the ultimate direction of the labor movement by providing leadership. Of 77 American labor figures who were prominent between 1860 and 1875, 45, or 58 percent, had been born in Europe—13 in England, 11 in Ireland, 9 in Germany, 5 each in Scotland and Wales, 2 in France. A more comprehensive survey of 150 leaders prominent between 1870 and 1895 reveals that

48 percent of those whose birthplaces were known had been born abroad. Many of the immigrant leaders came as seasoned industrial workers and unionists. The Irish activists, for instance, generally arrived via English industry rather than, as most of their compatriots did, directly from the countryside. Of the foreign-born leaders of the 1870–95 period, nearly two-thirds arrived in the United States after the age of fourteen, and as many as half of these had engaged in labor activities at home. Among this group were such pioneering figures as Thomas Phillips of the Knights of St. Crispin and the Knights of Labor, John Siney and Chris Evans of the Miners, John Jarrett of the Iron and Steel Workers, and Adolph Strasser of the Cigar Makers. Equally notable was the preponderance of Britons among the nineteenth-century foreign-born leaders—two-thirds of them (not counting Canadians) for the 1870–95 period, and an even higher proportion for the earlier group. Experience and predilection alike led them to put a particular stamp on American trade unionism.

"England has been the model," remarked French economist Pierre Émile Levasseur after surveying the American labor movement of the 1890s. "The ideas . . . cross the ocean with the tide of immigration." Britons figured prominently in the origins of at least twenty-four of the major national unions in the United States. When the Miners' National Association was formed in 1873, the Scotsman John James followed the constitution of Alexander Macdonald's Miners' National Association in Great Britain. English unions served as the models for, among others, the Boilermakers, Granite Cutters, and Carpenters and Joiners. Especially influential was the example of English "new model" unionism, with its stress on benefit systems, high dues, centralized control over local unions, and collective bargaining (a term the Americans borrowed from the British). The demonstration union for these policies in the American movement was the Cigar Makers, whose leaders boasted that they had "borrowed . . . most particularly from the English trade unions." Efforts at federation were similarly inspired. The Federation of Organized Trades and Labor Unions (1881) was explicitly modeled on the British Trades Union Congress, and so was its permanent successor, the American Federation of Labor (1886). It was fitting that the temporary president of the FOTLU was a Welshman and that two Englishmen nominated a third, Samuel Gompers, for the presidency. Gompers himself honored Britain "as the cradle of our now universal movement."

But if structure and policy derived from British models, American trade-union philosophy traced its roots to quite different foreign sources. Ever since the 1840s, the Germans had been the principal bearers of European radicalism to the United States. The implanting of modern socialism after the Civil War was distinctly the handiwork of German immigrants, especially in New York City, where, for the four years until it expired in 1876, Karl Marx's International Workingmen's Association was based. Marx favored trade unionism as the means for building the class consciousness and economic power of the workers, while the followers of his rival, Ferdinand Lassalle, stressed political action. Although the issue was essentially tactical—should unions be the first step, or should all energy go into creation of a political party?—the debate was carried on furiously both in Europe and within the narrow confines of the German socialist community in the United States (but with some participation by others). The formation of the Socialist Labor party in 1877 signaled the triumph of the Lassalleans and set the future course of American socialism toward politics.

As it happened, several key future unionists—Adolph Strasser, J. P. McDonnell, P. J. McGuire, and Gompers—participated in the socialist controversy over politics and trade unionism. During that time they hammered out the philosophical position defining American pure-and-simple unionism (the term *pure-and-simplism* was used during the debate): first, a determined focus on concrete, short-term objectives; second, a reliance on economic power rather than politics; third, a membership limited to workers and organized on strictly occupational lines; finally, as Strasser said in 1883, a rejection of "ultimate ends . . . we are opposed to theorists." These ideas Gompers and his colleagues brought with them into the trade-union struggle and into the launching of the American Federation of Labor. Although it had been couched originally in Marxian terms of class struggle, pure-and-simple unionism cast off its radical moorings and, under Gompers's skillful hand, became the guiding philosophy of a profoundly conservative movement.

From a sectarian debate conducted mainly in German had come a set of ideas that would permanently distinguish American trade unionism from its European counterparts. Originating intellectually in a narrow corner of immigrant America, pure-and-simple unionism derived much of its compelling logic from labor's need to function within the wider world of immigrant workers. Central to Gompers's purpose was securing the common ground, narrow though it might be, on which workers of the most diverse persuasions and nationalities might unite.

The difficulty of building worker solidarity within an ethnically divided labor force had long been apparent. A half-century earlier, in the 1830s, Philadelphia workers had experienced a remarkable surge of militant organization. Not only the skilled trades but mill hands, laborers, and hand-loom weavers formed unions, which joined together to form the General Trades' Union of Philadelphia. After a general strike in 1835 secured the ten-hour day, the Trades' Union swelled to over fifty locals representing ten thousand members, and with its aid, Philadelphia workers won a series of stirring victories. The Panic of 1837, however, initiated a rapid decline in labor's strength and, within a year, the General Trades' Union collapsed. As the depression deepened, a religious revival swept through the distressed ranks of the Protestant artisans, who eagerly embraced the cause of temperance. Irish Catholic weavers and laborers, the target of this enthusiasm, angrily protested the intrusion on their personal liberty. Meanwhile desperate strikes, punctuated by violence and rioting, deepened ethnic tensions. A dispute over Bible reading in the schools brought matters to a head in May 1844. Triggered by Irish attempts to disrupt nativist meetings in their neighborhoods, an anti-Catholic riot swept through Kensington, leaving in its wake heavy casualties and burned houses. In politics the lines became sharply drawn, with the artisans in the nativist American Republican party, the Irish workers in the Democratic party. Catholic and Protestant gangs and fire companies fought pitched battles on the streets for years afterward. Class unity had fallen apart in an ugly shambles of nativism and bigotry.

The Kensington riots were a microcosm of the ethnic forces besetting working-class life in the nineteenth century. Fear of cheap competition almost invariably inspired settled workers to resent the next wave of immigrants, and when the newcomers entered as strikebreakers—a common event—job rivalries took on a murderous intensity. Mixed in with economic fears were ethnic tensions, which unions persistently complained were exploited by open-shop employers. An endless catalogue could be drawn up of conflict between Cornish and Irish hard-rock miners, Yankee and French Canadian textile workers, Irish and English anthracite miners, white and black locomotive firemen, Italian and native laborers, and so on.

Ethnicity also exerted a potent influence on political behavior. Studies of late-nineteenth-century politics are consistent on this point: whether a man voted Democratic or Republican depended much less on whether he was a worker (even taking into account occupation and industry) than on whether he was a Catholic or an evangelical Protestant, an Irishman or a Yankee, a black or a southern white. Even the socialist parties, participating as they presumably were in an international class struggle against capitalism, actually were rooted in specific ethnic communities. In the 1880s, an uneventful political era by modern standards, electoral participation and party loyalty (as measured by voting behavior) stood at record levels because of the potent ethnocultural content of political life. Artfully aided by the major parties, this political mode proved highly resilient in the face of class interests activated by the depression of the 1890s.

Pure-and-simple unionism was strongly mindful of the ethnocultural realities of American working-class life. The AFL ruled "that party politics, whether they be democratic, republican, populistic, prohibition, or any other, should have no place" in its conventions. By rejecting any form of independent or partisan politics, the Federation was abandoning a claim on its members' loyalties that it could not successfully have asserted in any case. At the same time, nonpartisanship would insulate the labor movement from the ethnocultural issues that divided American politics. Even if such an issue might unite workers politically, the result was hardly likely to be consonant with the purposes of the labor movement. Thus anti-Chinese sentiment in California spawned an independent labor politics in the 1870s, but it was so corrupt and opportunistic as to blight the California labor movement for years thereafter. This did not mean that organized labor stayed out of public life— that choice it never had—but that it pursued its necessary political objectives through lobbying and nonpartisan tactics that kept it free of the ethnocultural web of American politics.

Pure-and-simple unionism focused aggressively on the narrow job concerns of workers. The ruling principle, as Gompers always said, was that trade unions "should open their portals to all wage workers irrespective of creed, color, nationality, sex or politics." However these differences might divide them in the larger world, workers on the job were united by a common purpose: to maximize the return on their labor. And they were equally united by a common need: to act collectively to force fair treatment from employers. All questions of union structure and strategy were put to this economic test: will it enhance the bargaining position of workers? The ethnic basis of organization, frequently the essential first stage of unionization, normally gave way to more strictly economic units once collective bargaining began, either by a process of amalgamation or, as in the garment trades, by subordinating ethnic locals to the control of a joint board. Even such auxiliary bodies as the United Hebrew Trades were accepted only grudgingly by the AFL. To do so, Gompers remarked, was "theoretically bad but practically necessary." Relentlessly economic in its means and ends, pure-and-simple unionism negotiated a path through the tangle of conflicting loyalties inherent in American working-class life, asserting an absolute claim to what related to the job and excluding the rest. It goes without saying that Gompers was responding to other demands of nineteenth-century America, but clearly the genius of his formulation lay in its attack on the ethnic dilemmas facing the labor movement.

As it turned out, Gompers's success was more fully realized in theory than in practice. In 1888 the International Association of Machinists (IAM), a key union, sought affiliation with the AFL. Southern in origin, the IAM had a whites-only clause in its constitution. Gompers rejected the application.

> Wage workers ought to bear in mind that unless they help to organize the colored men, they will of necessity compete with the white workmen and be antagonistic to them and their interests. The employers will certainly take advantage of this condition and . . . even stimulate race prejudice. View it in a common sense manner . . . not with the old prejudices . . . but study it in the light of the historical struggles of the peoples of all nations, and you will find that I am right.

This reasoning did not move the Machinists, however, and within a few years the AFL caved in. The IAM struck the offending clause from the constitution but not from the ritual, and blacks continued to be barred from the union. By 1900 even this sham collapsed. Anxious to bring in the railroad unions, which were notoriously antiblack, the AFL admitted the Order of Railroad Telegraphers and the Brotherhood of Railway Trackmen despite their constitutional racial bars. Then in 1902 the affiliated Stationary Engineers added an amendment excluding blacks. The Federation had already amended its constitution in 1900 to permit the chartering of federal unions for blacks who were not admitted into white unions. Whatever hopes Gompers might have harbored for future benefits from these accommodations, the harsh reality was that he was presiding over a virtually lily-white movement. In 1902 blacks constituted hardly 3 percent of the total union membership and were largely segregated in the ineffectual federal unions. Black organization in the coal mines and on the New Orleans docks stands out as the lonely exception. Nearly two-thirds of all white unionists belonged to unions that had either no black members or negligible numbers.

The Federation's dismal record exposed underlying weaknesses in the pure-and-simple formulation. Issues, such as race, that stirred deep emotions could not be left outside the union hall. Nor were trade-union leaders, oriented as they were to economic interests, capable of meeting racism on a compelling moral plane. The vicious repression of blacks in the South in these years did not evoke official concern within the AFL. Gompers assured white workers who, "like many others may not care to socially meet colored people," that "there is no necessity to run counter to social distinctions." Organizing blacks, Gompers insisted, was "a proposition of the most eminent practicality . . . a bald business proposition." At the turn of the century, as it happened, the threat of black competition did not loom large. Ever since Reconstruction, relentless pressures had forced blacks out of their traditional southern jobs as artisans and down into menial and segregated work in both North and South. The New Orleans city directory of 1870 listed 3,460 blacks in a variety of skilled trades; not 10 percent remained in those occupations in 1904. By the time the AFL faced the issue, blacks were so confined economically as to pose no present danger to the trade unions, notwithstanding their use as strikebreakers. Ironically, racism and pure-and-simple tactics now tended to coincide rather than conflict. Craft unions had always tried to restrict access and control labor markets. What more efficacious way than along the color line?

Gompers may have perceived the longer-term dangers in this course, but he lacked the authority to counteract them. Because the national unions performed the key economic functions of the labor movement, they were conceded the rights of "trade autonomy." "To the union of the trade belongs absolute jurisdiction on all matters connected with that trade," Gompers admitted in his quarrel with the Machinists. "The recognition of this cardinal principle, however, did not deny us the right of expressing the sentiments of trade unionism against any matter involving the general interest of the labor movement." But if trade autonomy did not prevent Gompers from talking, it assuredly did deny him the capacity to act. In the end, Gompers justified his handling of the race issue (beyond an increasing tendency to blame the blacks themselves) precisely on the grounds of trade autonomy: the AFL had no authority to instruct the national unions on the management of their affairs. The treatment of black workers would one day return to haunt the labor movement, but in the meantime, its failure could be taken as symptomatic of a larger incapacity to live up to the precepts of pure-and-simple unionism. Where ethnocultural divisions cut deeply, labor's economic focus and institutional structure proved unequal to, if not downright destructive of, the task of uniting workers.

At the turn of the century, labor faced no crisis from the excluded blacks. The same could not be said of the eastern and southern Europeans flocking into American industry. Contemporaries drew a sharp quali-tative distinction between the old and the new immigration. Contempt for the Irish, virulent seventy-five years before, had long since died out, and the Irish now occupied a respectable place in the ranks of American workers. The other older immigrants had generally been treated with a good deal of respect all along—the Germans and Scan-dinavians for their skills and industrious habits, the Britons for those qualities and because they were regarded as compatriots. The new im-migrants, on the other hand, seemed distinctly alien, ignorant of English, exotic in their habits, largely devoid of industrial skills, herding apart in crowded, noisome neighborhoods. It was a telling commentary that a Welsh miner, himself by no means certain that he would remain in America, referred derisively to Slavs and Italians entering the mines as "foreigners."

The perceived differences, moreover, were given an ominous per-manence in the racist thought of the early twentieth century. The pre-vailing belief, rooted in the "science" of eugenics and dignified in the writings of respected scholars, was that ethnic characteristics were in-herited rather than culturally determined. The Dillingham Commission, established by Congress in 1907, undertook a vast survey of the new immigrants that was intended to document the various inferiorities mak-ing them undesirable additions to the American population. (That the data showed otherwise did not stop the commission from drawing the expected conclusions.) So the racist antipathies traditionally directed against blacks were now to some degree leveled at the new immigrants as well.

For the labor movement, the immigrants were different from the blacks in key ways. For one thing, immigration could be closed off at the source. The AFL already claimed much of the credit for the Chinese Exclusion Act of 1882, and during the 1890s the Federation became a fervent advocate of a literacy test for entering immigrants. This, Gompers argued in 1902, "would exclude hardly any natives of Great Britain, Ireland, Germany, France, or Scandinavia. It will shut out a considerable number of South Italians and of Slavs and other[s] equally or more undesirable and injurious." When the Immigration Act of 1917, which imposed a simple literacy test, failed to have that effect, attention turned to the device of a quota system, and the AFL eagerly endorsed it.

There can be no question but that the labor movement was instrumental in bringing about the reversal of America's historic open-door immigration policy. Why labor favored restriction is less clear. The leading historian of the AFL, Philip Taft, has argued forcefully that the Federation was acting strictly—and properly—from economic motives. An overcrowded labor market, constantly replenished by outsiders eager to work at any price, was bound to undermine labor standards and the effectiveness of trade unionism. This was the incessant claim of AFL spokesmen. But there is no doubt about the racist coloration of their thinking. Unionists made no bones about their race animus toward the Chinese, and they were clearly intent not only on reducing the numbers of eastern and southern Europeans but on eliminating "undesirable immigration." They applauded the distorted findings of the Dillingham Commission. (It should be pointed out, however, that the commission went out of its way to underscore the economic fears of the labor movement.) The AFL had no qualms about a quota system calculated on the blood mix of the population as it was in 1920. The racist assumptions behind this national policy were not objectionable to Gompers. As he wrote in his autobiography (completed in the same year as the Johnson Immigration Restriction Act), it was about time that people understood "the principle that the maintenance of the nation depended upon the maintenance of racial purity and strength."

The flow of new immigrants ended, but millions had already entered the country. They were present in force in American industry. They confronted the labor movement with a challenge of far greater magnitude than did the blacks prior to World War I.

American trade unionism at the turn of the century was a movement of skilled workers. While efforts to organize the unskilled had not been lacking—the Knights of Labor and the American Railway Union were only the last in a string of failed experiments—those workers still remained beyond the bounds of trade unionism. The dominance of the craft unions, together with rules and structure designed to their specifications, rendered the AFL incapable for practical purposes of acting on its early promise to reach all workers. No place was likely to be made for the unskilled so long as the central premise of craft unionism remained intact: namely, the indispensability of the skilled, all-round worker. Industrial progress was relentlessly undercutting this worker's position, however. In field after field his importance was being eroded by the use of machinery, the subdivision of labor, and the techniques of scientific management. Some unions did devise effective defenses— the Typographers, for example, by asserting bargaining rights over the linotype machine, and the Carpenters by tight control over local labor markets and over machine-made wood products. But for the many unions incapable of such holding actions, craft exclusivity was called into question. They could not deny, as the Butchers' Union conceded after entering the Chicago stockyards in 1900, that technological change "places the skilled workman at the mercy of common labor and makes it necessary to organize all working in the large plants under one head."

By the time the crisis arrived, the mass of new immigrants had joined the unskilled ranks of American industry. In 1904 the AFL sent a team of organizers into the iron and steel industry, where only fifteen years before, the once-proud Amalgamated Association of Iron and Steel Workers had been accounted the model craft union. "We find on investigation that the number of skilled steel workers ha[s] been greatly reduced on account of improved machinery. . . . On the other hand, a large number of the unskilled workers are foreigners, hardly able to speak or understand the English language, thereby complicating and retarding our efforts. All told, the field is not a promising one." This pessimism was not entirely misplaced. Nothing in their agricultural past had prepared the immigrants for trade unionism. Mostly intent on saving money and returning to the native village, green arrivals did not find the arguments of organizers persuasive. But with time and industrial experience, the immigrants disproved the stereotyped view that they were hopelessly docile. Their peasant origins, which stressed group decisions and communal approval, actually made them notably militant strikers and loyal unionists in coal mining. Similarly, the success of the garment unions after 1909 was rooted in the fact that it was a largely Jewish work force. The obtuseness of the trade unions on this point to some degree testified to the more deep-rooted problem: the ethnocultural chasm separating English-speaking workers—both leaders and rank and file—from the southern and eastern Europeans.

What this meant for trade-union policy cannot be separated out and given precise weight. For one thing, craft identity exerted a stubborn hold in its own right. Convention halls witnessed agonizing debates over the wisdom of broadening the membership. To admit specialists and helpers, IAM delegates protested, would "ruin" the machinists' trade and undermine "our dignity." Some unions—the Window Glass Workers, for example—were so immobilized by craft sentiment as to fail utterly to respond to basic technological advances. Trade-union conservatism was fostered also by the institutional rigidities of trade autonomy and exclusive jurisdiction and by the vested interests of existing memberships and entrenched leaders. The results were often such cosmetic responses as the creation of second-class membership for the less skilled or formal broadening of jurisdiction unaccompanied by actual organizing programs. But these inherent tendencies within the labor movement were certainly nourished by the knowledge that the less skilled were mainly the eastern European immigrants.

There are enough instances to suggest that if trade-union logic clearly called for broader organization, prejudice might be thrust aside. In the coal mines, where immigrants entered easily and rose swiftly in the miners' ranks, the UMWA organized them (and blacks) and prospered thereby. The Mine Workers operated as a genuinely multilanguage, multiracial organization in the early twentieth century. When the Butchers' Union concluded that the Chicago packinghouses could not be organized without the unskilled, it did not long hesitate to take them in, even though they were overwhelmingly of recent Slavic origin. And during World War I, a uniquely opportune time, the labor movement managed to mobilize very considerable resources and enthusiasm for organizing the unskilled in steel, meat packing, and other mass-production fields. Even if a union was fainthearted or obstructive, this did not necessarily preclude the organization of immigrant workers. The men's clothing workers unionized themselves almost in spite of the old-guard United Garment Workers and, finding themselves barred from influence there, split off in 1914 to form the Amalgamated Clothing Workers under the leadership of Sidney Hillman.

In the end, the governing factor was the trade-union calculation of profit and loss. The mass-production sector, in which the immigrant workers were heavily concentrated, proved nearly invulnerable to trade unionism. The employers not only had the technological advantage, they wielded enormous economic power by virtue of corporate business organization and strong trade associations, and they could normally rely on the support of the state and the courts. Most important was their ruthless determination to protect the open shop at any cost. The power balance shifted decisively to the side of management in the early twentieth century and, in so doing, placed a deadly pall on the trade-union movement. Although labor shortages and government protection evoked a union resurgence during World War I, the crushing failures of the postwar period produced an abiding defeatism. Thereafter the labor movement effectively abandoned the immigrant industrial workers.

The wartime influx of southern blacks cut still another gap between workers that the trade unions could not bridge. New to the industrial scene and justifiably suspicious of organized labor, blacks largely resisted appeals to unionize. Terrible race riots in East St. Louis, Illinois, in 1917 and in Chicago in 1919, plus a host of violent incidents elsewhere, etched in blood animosities that would not fade for a generation. Black workers generally stayed on the job during strikes and thereby contributed to labor's defeats in the postwar years.

The mark of pure-and-simple unionism had been its intention to bring together in job-conscious unity workers of the utmost ethnic diversity, but this unifying function was lost along with the capacity to organize the mass-production sector. Confined essentially to the skilled trades, American unionism took on a more fixed ethnocultural character. Fully a third of the union leadership after 1900 was Irish born or of Irish descent, including the presidents of over fifty national unions and at least half the AFL vice presidents at any one time. The Catholic church, acting especially through the Militia of Christ, began to exert a marked influence on the AFL in these years. As the ethnically mixed United Mine Workers and clothing unions weakened during the 1920s, organized labor moved closer to cultural homogeneity. In the ethnically and racially diverse working-class world the labor movement lost its capacity to serve as a common ground and became instead an island for a minority of American-born northern European workers.

The American left exerted little counterforce on the trade unions. Since the 1890s, the main radical thrust had been into politics. The Socialist party did have a considerable trade-union following, mounting up to as high as a third of the delegate strength at the AFL convention of 1911 and including key national unions and central labor bodies. The Socialist trade-union program called for industrial unionism and militant organizing work. A strong resolution in 1912 urged the unions to begin "organizing the unorganized, especially the immigrants who stand in greatest need of organization." But this was more a symbolic than a real stance. The moderate Socialist leadership accepted the AFL as the legitimate labor movement and minimized differences in the vain hope of winning over the Federation. Despite its own ethnic constituencies, moreover, the Socialist party did not take much interest in the immigrant industrial workers, and toward blacks and Asians its views were hardly more advanced than those of the AFL. Class-conscious rhetoric notwithstanding, Socialist trade unionists in practice acted like any other unionists. The persistent deterioration of their standing within the labor movement after 1912 ended any lingering prospects that the Socialists might revitalize American trade unionism.

For the left-wing minority that despaired of bringing about change from inside the Federation, the answer was a rival movement. In 1905 the Western Federation of Miners, Daniel DeLeon's Socialist Labor party, and left-wingers from the Socialist party formed the Industrial Workers of the World (IWW), which proclaimed itself "an organization broad enough to take in all the working class." In a rampantly intolerant age, the IWW was singularly free of prejudice. Its doors were wide open to Asians as well as to eastern Europeans, and it held the AFL in contempt for "calling them 'undesirable' class[es] of immigrants, and . . . agitating for laws to bar them from America." Sensitive to their needs, the IWW employed foreign-language organizers, published materials in many languages, and aggressively asserted the worth of every worker, "no matter what his religion, fatherland, or trade." With its syndicalist philosophy, the IWW was more successful as a shock force to lead the immigrants when they rose in spontaneous strikes—for example, at McKees Rocks, Pennsylvania, in 1909, Lawrence, Massachusetts, in 1912, Paterson, New Jersey, in 1913, and on the Mesabi Range, Minnesota, in 1916—than as a builder of permanent organization among immigrant workers. Beginning in 1913 the IWW shifted its attention to the harvest workers, miners, lumbermen, and itinerant construction workers of the West, far from the main centers of immigrant employment. Crushed by federal repression during World War I, the IWW left as its legacy not so much substantial success among minority workers as an ideal of working-class unity that still commands respect.

The Socialists and the IWW pursued alternative strategies for opening up the labor movement: the former by working within the AFL, the latter by starting up a separate movement. The Communist party, the principal vehicle of American radicalism from 1919 onward, tried both strategies, but with even less success. Partly because of the impact of the Bolshevik Revolution, the Communist following initially consisted very largely of recent immigrants—of the total membership in 1919, over 75 percent was eastern European, including 25 percent Russian. Although most of the Russians soon dropped out or left for home, the immigrant character of the membership persisted through the 1920s, when Finns, Jews, and eastern Europeans made up roughly 80 percent of the total. Ties to ethnic fraternal and cultural associations were a crucial source of support.

The Communists had been too disorganized and self-absorbed to play any part in the labor struggles of 1919–20, but in 1921 they recruited William Z. Foster, who had been the key man in the AFL meat-packing and steel campaigns, and embarked on a program of boring-from-within the AFL. In 1925 the autonomous language federations that the Communists had inherited from the Socialist party were abolished, and the basic party unit became the ''shop nucleus'' so as to focus organizational activity more directly on the economic struggle. Far from having a liberalizing effect on the labor movement, the Communists sparked bitter internal battles that decimated such unions as the International Ladies' Garment Workers and the United Mine Workers. The AFL, scarred by postwar losses and the Red Scare of the 1920s, reinforced its identification with ''Americanism'' (including ties with the American Legion and the anti-Bolshevik National Civic Federation). Linked in the public mind with the foreign born ever since World War I, the Communist threat fortified the AFL in its growing inclination to steer clear of the immigrant workers. In 1928 the Communists abandoned their boring-from-within strategy and launched the rival Trade Union Unity League, which sought to hammer-from-without. Its efforts in mass-production fields were not notably successful but did not go wholly to waste; it provided a cadre of experienced organizers for the industrial-union drives of the later 1930s. But in the short run Communist rivalry only tended to confirm the private belief of conservative unionists that the labor movement ought to be reserved for the English-speaking workers in the skilled trades.

Great events intervened to confound that restricted view. The depression injected a desperate militancy into the ranks of workers and reduced the resistant power even of corporate business. With the coming of the New Deal under President Franklin Roosevelt, labor found sympathetic allies and ultimately legal protection of the right to organize and to engage in collective bargaining. Life stirred in the old ideal of a labor movement for all workers. The AFL was actually hard pressed to break out of the encrustations of its own past—so much so as to force an impatient minority to launch the rival Committee for Industrial Organization (CIO). Embedded in the complex causes of the split were contrasting racial and ethnic attitudes. Throughout this period the AFL stubbornly rejected the pleas of black organizations for a liberal racial policy, even defeating their efforts to have antidiscrimination language written into the New Deal collective-bargaining legislation. The old-line leaders' reluctance to mount a strong organizing drive reflected their disdain for the mass-production workers—"rubbish," one craft official called them. On the other hand, the industrial-union minority consisted precisely of those unions—the Mine Workers and the garment unions—that traditionally had been multiracial and multinational. The cause they espoused called for structural reforms that would foster an open labor movement. As the Urban League rightly observed, there was "little hope for the black worker so long as the AFL remains structurally a craft organization." The industrial form of organization, said the CIO, had as its "basic principle . . . organization of all workers regardless of skill, race, nationality, religion or politics."

The CIO adroitly applied that precept in its organizing campaigns. The first CIO organizer sent into Detroit (a UMWA veteran) laid out a comprehensive plan to reach the immigrant auto workers: "Obtain information on the approximate location of the numerous nationalities. . . . Approximate population, names and addresses of the fraternal and social organizations maintained by these groups. Endeavor to contact such groups. . . . By the use of organizers who speak foreign languages we will be able to reach the large foreign-speaking elements in our community." The CIO drive in steel was equally attentive to these considerations. At a CIO conference on October 25, 1936, delegates from seventeen fraternal orders and several hundred lodges in the steel towns around Pittsburgh, Pennsylvania, pledged their support, including public endorsement, sponsorship of mass meetings, and enlistment of the foreign-language press in the CIO cause. For a rally of Jones and Laughlin steel workers in January 1937, the CIO was able to provide speakers in Polish, Lithuanian, Russian, and Serbo-Croatian, and to list the endorsement of fraternal orders covering virtually every immigrant group in the industry.

The passage of time was meanwhile creating other changes. In the steel industry, European-born workers declined from 50 percent of the labor force in 1910 to 30 percent in 1930, and these workers were steadily rising from the bottom ranks; by 1930 less than half were in unskilled work, compared to two-thirds in 1910. In fact, European-born and native whites were equally numerous in the unskilled labor force in 1930. As the immigrants grew "to middle age in the industry" (in the words of one CIO publicist) and were joined by their sons, the distinction between "hunky" and "English-speaking" began to lose its corrosive force, and longstanding ethnic barriers to organization began to crumble.

Ethnic identity still exerted a powerful influence on unionization in mass-production industry. A detailed study of one Detroit auto-parts plant between 1936 and 1939 reveals this progression: the first to join were the young second-generation workers, who became militant union-ists; then the older Polish and Ukrainian workers, initially hesitant, but ultimately intensely loyal; next, the scattered Appalachian workers, who tended to be strongly pro- or anti-union on moral grounds; and finally, the skilled workers of northern European descent, who had to be coerced into the union. The progression was not immutable; at the Detroit plant of Midland Steel, the skilled men of northern European extraction took the union lead between 1936 and 1939, only to be displaced in a factional battle by the second-generation semiskilled workers in 1940. However, there were certain underlying consistencies. For one thing, ethnic char-acteristics did exert continuing influence on labor organization. Thus the Appalachian leadership of President Homer Martin, who had once been an evangelical preacher, put a strong stamp on the early United Auto Workers. At the plant level ethnicity largely determined social groupings in which workers moved toward organization, and ethnic ties sometimes led to forms of ethnic unionism reminiscent of much earlier times. This happened, for example, among the copper miners of the Southwest, where Mexican-American fraternal orders, with links to unions across the border, persisted during the period of disorganization and served as the nucleus for the union revival in the early 1940s.

The black migrants to northern industry, like the eastern Europeans, had become seasoned workers by the 1930s, but racial barriers did not lessen so readily. Black workers continued to be distrustful of white fellow workers and to feel a special reliance on the good will of employers. As with its approach to the immigrant workers, the CIO responded by hiring black organizers and seeking support from the larger black community. For the first time the National Association for the Advancement of Colored People (NAACP) and the National Urban League unequivocally endorsed trade unionism. Early in the steel drive, the CIO held a national conference in Pittsburgh that drew two hundred representatives from black organizations and local unions to hear Philip Murray promise that the CIO would tolerate "no discrimination under any circumstances within its organization." Despite the range of support elicited by the CIO, its strategy was less successful among blacks than among immigrant workers. The organizational network reaching down to African-American workers was relatively weak, and the black churches, which had the strongest working-class following, remained on the whole unsympathetic to the union cause. But the balance between racial divisiveness and labor unity slowly shifted as the CIO scored collective-bargaining victories and demonstrated its genuine commitment to racial equality.

The evolution of trade unionism into a bastion of privileged labor was reversed by the industrial-union thrust. In 1938 the CIO proclaimed itself an independent movement—the Congress of Industrial Organizations—and proceeded to challenge the AFL on all fronts. The formidable competition provoked a remarkable revival throughout the labor movement. Such craft unions as the Machinists, Electrical Workers, Teamsters, and Meat Cutters began to organize vigorously on broad industrial lines and to reach a multiplicity of workers not easily accessible to the CIO unions. The AFL resurgence restored the basis for a single labor movement that was the defender of all workers. When the AFL-CIO was formed in 1955, it included millions of workers who twenty years earlier had found no place in organized labor. By the mid-1950s, the nativist force that had fostered exclusivity had largely exhausted itself, partly by the cycle of time and the passing of the immigrant generation, partly by the disrepute into which racist thought had fallen, especially since World War II. If the AFL-CIO applauded the excision of national-origins principles from American immigration policy in 1965, so did many other groups that had once decried the flood of "undesirable" immigrants.

Although ethnicity no longer constituted a real test of the egalitarianism of the labor movement, however, race still did. In its constitution the AFL-CIO pledged itself "to encourage all workers without regard to race, creed, color, national origin, or ancestry to share equally in the full benefits of union organization." Two black officials sat on the first executive council, and the administrative structure included a civil-rights section responsible for eliminating discriminatory practices "at the earliest possible date." But unlike corruption and Communism, discrimination was not designated as grounds for expulsion. And shortly the AFL-CIO proceeded to admit two railroad brotherhoods—Loco-motive Firemen and Railroad Trainmen—despite racial bars in their constitutions.

This faltering start reflected the persisting constraints acting on the modern labor movement. Not even the CIO in its most militant period had been immune to conventional trade-union calculations. Confronted by racism at the local level, industrial unions had generally moved cautiously, weighing the enforcement of principle against the cost in larger organizational interests, and not always coming down on the side of principle. The significant upgrading of black workers during the 1940s—the percentage employed as craftsmen and operators rose from 16.6 in 1940 to 28.8 in 1950—sprang much more from wartime labor shortages than from union activity. As employment conditions tight-ened, the CIO moderated its battle for full job equality, and it accepted the accommodations required to achieve a united labor movement. To one industrial-union president in 1958, the persistence of segregated southern locals constituted "practical problems" that had to be handled "in a realistic manner."

By the end of the 1950s the NAACP was attacking the AFL-CIO for failing "to eliminate the broad patterns of racial discrimination and segregation in many affiliated unions." After A. Philip Randolph openly split with President George Meany at the AFL-CIO convention in 1959, black unionists formed the Negro American Labor Council to exert continuing internal pressure on the labor movement. Black criticism of trade unionism was now directed at a laggard ally, not, as had been true prior to 1935, at an enemy of economic opportunity for black people. By contrast to those earlier years, organized labor now acted basically as a progressive force for racial equality. This tendency was much strengthened by the civil-rights revolution of the 1960s. But in-sofar as labor's thrust toward racial equality was rooted in internal changes, the main credit must go to the industrial unionists whose efforts opened the labor movement to all working people, irrespective of race, nationality, or creed.

That development, in turn, altered the political orientation of American trade unionism. Its nonpartisanship had been dictated by, among other things, the diversity of party loyalties among American working people. From the early 1920s onward, however, a major political realignment set in, especially among those ethnic groups that the CIO later reached. First by its identification with personal liberty during the intolerant 1920s and then by the enormous appeal of the New Deal, the Democratic party made heavy inroads among Catholics, recent immigrants, and, finally, even among the traditionally Republican blacks. So powerful was President Franklin Roosevelt's hold on these groups that the CIO exploited its ties to him in its organizing drive among steel, auto, and other industrial workers. The mass entry of such workers into the labor movement greatly weakened the logic of political nonpartisanship. Although the movement had been tilting toward the Democratic party ever since the Progressive Era, the events of the 1930s brought about the alliance that has lasted to the present day. And labor's eroding spirit of militant voluntarism was fatally undermined by the infusion of millions of workers favorable to New Deal social-welfare programs.

In this evolution, ethnicity acted as a remote influence, affecting the party preferences of union members and through them labor's political orientation. This probably characterizes the modern relation between ethnicity and the labor movement, although there are instances of direct interaction. The unionization of Chicano farm workers under Cesar Chavez offers a classic example of the power of ethnic identity as the basis for labor organization. In the South racial differences still can be made a barrier to unionization, and across the country in low-wage industries there are exploited ethnic groups—Mexicans, Puerto Ricans, Chinese, blacks—who replicate the organizing problems faced by the labor movement in the basic industries half a century ago. Nevertheless, as the great European migration to the United States grows more distant, so does the impact of ethnicity on the labor movement. So long as ethnic identity continues to be felt in American life—as social scientists believe it still does on succeeding generations—it will also act on the inner dynamics of the labor movement. But ethnicity derives its meaning today mainly in the form of a legacy: the enduring character of the American labor movement is rooted in the historical fact of a working class drawn from beyond the American industrial order. In the American ethnic experience, the significance of the labor movement likewise takes the form of a legacy: for the diverse, alien peoples flocking to this country, the trade unions in their imperfect way served as a primary vehicle for working-class unity and for entry into the American environment.

Since the concluding sentences of this essay were written in 1978, the sense of completion they conveyed has been overtaken by events. Even at that time, the pace of immigration into the country was quickening. By the 1980s, the numbers entering approached the high mark of immigration during the first decade of the twentieth century. In 1990 there were more foreign-born residents (19.7 million) than at any time in the nation's history. Moreover, the recent shift in the sources of immigration is even more striking than the shift from northern to southern and eastern Europe of a century earlier. As late the 1950s, two-thirds of all immigrants were still coming from Europe. By the 1980s, Europeans made up scarcely 10 per cent of the total. Over a third were Asians, and most of the rest Hispanics from Mexico and Central and South America. In California, which received as many immigrants in the 1980s as had New York State between 1901 and 1910, non-Hispanic whites will be a minority group by the end of the century.

For the labor movement, ethnicity can no longer be thought of as a "legacy," for it is again a live question, in some respects more challenging than ever before in labor's history. For today the elements of diversity that have to be encompassed are markedly greater. To ethnicity and race, there must be added the question of gender, no longer of marginal concern to a labor movement 35 percent of whose members are now women. And, at a time of slackening growth and drastic economic restructuring, the economic context is likewise more complex and problematic. The economic changes of the past decades have, in turn, powerfully set back the progress of African Americans and created new divisions between white and black workers. Even so, the basic question facing organized labor labor is not so different from that faced by a craft movement a hundred years ago when the industrial work force was being filled by Slavs, Italians and east European Jews: can a movement that took shape to organize an ethnically divided working class of an earlier age summon up the means to reach a new working class arriving from Asia and Latin America?

Notes

1. Seymour M. Lipset, "Labor Unions in the Public Mind," in Lipset, ed., *Unions in Transition: Entering the Second Century* (San Francisco, Calif., 1986), 287–322.

2. For instructive reading on this point, see the edition of Gompers's papers now being published. Stuart B. Kaufman, ed., *The Samuel Gompers Papers* (Urbana, Ill. 1986–).

3. "North American Labor Movements: A Comparative Perspective," in Lipset, ed., *Unions in Transition,* 421–52.

4. Lipset, "North American Labor Movements," 432–33.

5. Quotations in Lipset, 442, 443, 452. For other illuminating essays on Canada and the United States, see Christopher Huxley et al., "Is Canada's Experience 'Especially Instructive'?" in Lipset, *Unions in Transition,* 113–32; and Noah M. Meltz, "Labor Movements in Canada and the United States," in Thomas Kochan, ed., *Challenges and Choices Facing American Labor* (Cambridge, Mass., 1985), 315–34.

6. Lipset, "Labor Unions in the Public Mind," 300.

7. See, e.g., Richard B. Freeman, "Why Are Unions Faring Badly in NLRB Elections?" in Kochan, ed., *Challenges and Choices,* 45–65, and "Discussion," 67–71; John J. Lawler and Robin West, "Impact of Union Avoidance Strategy in Representation Elections," *Industrial Relations,* 24 (Fall 1985), 406–20; William T. Dickens, "The Effect of Company Campaigns on Certification Elections," *Industrial and Labor Relations Review,* 36 (July 1983), 560–75.

8. J. B. S. Hardman, "Stakes of Leadership," in Hardman, ed., *American Labor Dynamics* (New York, 1928), 163.

9. Mark Perlman, *The Machinists* (Cambridge, Mass., 1961), 21, 187, 294, 297, App. I.

10. Amalgamated Meat Cutters and Butcher Workmen of North America, *Official Journal* (June 1902), 15–16; Amalgamated Meat Cutters, *Proceedings* (1926), 79–80. *Butcher Workman* (November 1926), 7.

11. Robert A. Christie, *Empire in Wood* (Ithaca, N.Y., 1956), 62–64.

12. Jonathan Grossman, *William Sylvis, Pioneer of American Labor* (New York: Columbia University Press, 1945), 189, 262, and passim; N. J. Ware, *The Labor Movement in the United States, 1860–1895* (New York, 1929), 80–84.

13. Vernon H. Jensen, *Heritage of Conflict* (Ithaca, N.Y., 1950), 182, 343.

14. Paul F. Brissenden, *The I.W.W.: A Study of American Syndicalism* (New York, 1928), 137, 308–9.

15. Seymour M. Lipset, *The First New Nation* (New York, 1963), 192. In checking Lipset's source for Great Britain, H. A. Clegg, A. J. Killick, and Rex Adams, *Trade Union Officers* (Oxford, 1961), 38, I found errors in transcription that led Lipset to put the ratio at 1:2,000.

16. Lipset, *Nation,* 189; Clancy Sigal, *Weekend in Dinlock* (Boston, 1960), 73; Clegg, Killick, and Adams, *Officers,* 72–73.

17. Christie, *Empire,* 61–65.

18. W. R. Satterlee, Local 1, to Patrick Gorman, January 5, 1938, files, Amalgamated Meat Cutters and Butcher Workmen of North America.

19. Ben M. Selekman, *Employes' Representation in Steel Works* (New York, 1924), 172.

20. C. Wright Mills, *The New Men of Power* (New York, 1948), 88–95. Mills's survey does show, however, that while labor leaders were drawn from the blue-collar class, they also tended to have relatively more education and to come from skilled jobs.

21. Philip Taft, "Understanding Union Administration," *Harvard Business Review*, 24 (Winter 1946), 253–57; Mills, *New Men*, 103. On the high status of trade-union leaders in the popular estimate—equal to that of executives and proprietors—see C. C. North and P. K. Hatt, "Jobs and Occupations: A Popular Evaluation," in L. Wilson and W. A. Kolb, eds., *Sociological Analysis* (New York, 1949), 46–73.

22. *Speeches and Writings of Eugene V. Debs,* introd. by A. M. Schlesinger, Jr. (New York, 1948), 181, 444.

23. Quoted in Brissenden, *I.W.W.,* 88, 308–9.

24. Marc Karson, *American Labor Unions and Politics, 1900–1918* (Carbondale, Ill., 1958), 130; James O. Morris, *Conflict Within the AFL* (Ithaca, N.Y., 1958), 139.

25. Amalgamated Meat Cutters, *Proceedings* (1899), 26, (1902), 31–32, (1904), 16–16a.

26. Adolph Sturmthal, ed., *Contemporary Collective Bargaining in Seven Countries* (Ithaca, N.Y., 1957), 174, 181, 183, 312–13. On the English shop-steward movement, see Walter Galenson, *Trade Union Democracy in Western Europe* (Berkeley, Calif., 1961), 45–47.

27. Walter Galenson, *Comparative Labor Movements* (New York, 1952), 93, also, e.g., on French unions' experience with the Socialists, see Galenson, 327.

28. Samuel Gompers, *Seventy Years of Life and Labor,* ed. P. Taft and J. A. Sessions (New York, 1957), 88.

29. See, e.g., Henry David, "One Hundred Years of Labor in Politics," in J. B. S. Hardman and M. F. Neufeld, eds., *The House of Labor* (New York, 1951), 90–112; Michael Rogin, "Voluntarism: The Political Functions of an Antipolitical Doctrine," *Industrial and Labor Relations Review,* 15 (June, 1962), 534–35.

30. See Philip Taft, *The Structure and Government of Labor Unions* (Cambridge, Mass., 1956), ch. 2.

31. Hardman, *American Labor Dynamics,* 160.

32. Ibid., 164–65.

33. See, e.g., David Brody, *The Butcher Workmen: A Study of Unionization* (Cambridge, Mass., 1964), ch. 6.

34. Seymour M. Lipset, "The Political Process in Trade Unions: A Theoretical Statement," in M. Berger et al., *Freedom and Control in Modern Society* (New York, 1954), 92ff; Ware, *Labor Movement,* 81; A. J. Muste, "Factions in Trade Unions," in Hardman, *American Labor Dynamics,* 340–41; Seymour M. Lipset, *Union Democracy: The Internal Politics of the International Typographical Union* (Glencoe, Ill., 1956), 239ff.

35. Perlman, *Machinists,* 297.

36. Frank D. Manfred to Michael F. Widman, October 9, 1941, CIO Papers, Catholic University of America.

4

Market Unionism in America: The Case of Coal

Among the forces driving America's remarkable industrial growth of the late nineteenth century, none was more powerful than the surging production of coal. By 1910 the 501 million short tons mined represented nearly 40 percent of the world's production and far exceeded the output of America's nearest European competitors. The coal industry provided 90 percent of the nation's energy, operated at a per-worker productivity rate three times that of either Germany's or Britain's,[1] and by every measure—cheapness, quality, availability—amply met the needs of the burgeoning industrial economy.

Contempories saw coal mining differently. They considered it, as Herbert Hoover once remarked, "the worse functioning of any industry in the country."[2] Hoover had, of course, a standard in mind. He was measuring coal-mining practice against the managerial revolution transforming American enterprise. Of all the sectors within the central industrial order, coal mining remained least touched by the great technological and organizational advances of the early twentieth century; and so, it followed, would be its labor relations. "It may be paradoxical ... since without coal there would have been no industrialism," remarked the economist Carter Goodrich in 1925, "yet it is true that, so far as the manner of work is concerned, mining is still in a way a

From Gerald D. Feldman and Klaus Tenfelde, eds., *Miners, Owners and Politics in Coal Mining: An International Comparison of Industrial Relations* (London: Berg Publishers, 1990), 47–117. Reprinted with permission.

'cottage' industry. The *indiscipline* of the mines is far out of line with the *new discipline* of the modern factories.''[3]

The market characteristics of coal set it apart from other sectors of heavy industry. The demand for coal was inelastic—that is to say, demand was determined much more by the level of business activity (or, in the case of the household market, by weather conditions) than by the price of coal. In theory, this meant that prices would be bid rapidly upward in time of short supply and rapidly downward in times of oversupply. In practice, the former condition rarely obtained; in fact, it occurred only in wartime or during national strikes. This was because of a peculiarity on the supply side of the coal trade. It was elastic on the upswing—ease of entry readily expanded production—but inelastic on the downswing—new operators preferred low or even unprofitable prices to shutting down their mines.[4] So that, despite the secular growth of coal demand, the normal condition of the industry was one of overcapacity and hence, in the absence of market controls, of extreme competition at low price levels.

In the anthracite sector, market controls did in fact come into play. Once the nation's premier industrial fuel, hard coal served mostly for home heating by the turn of the century. Produced in a geographically confined region of northeastern Pennsylvania and entering a fairly uniform and well-defined domestic market, anthracite was ripe for market control. The key actors were the anthracite railroads. They bought up most of the coal properties, perfected a cartel between 1898 and 1902, and thereafter set a price, f.o.b. the New York harbor, that remained virtually unchanged until World War I.[5]

The bituminous industry could not follow that course, however. Soft-coal reserves were far richer and more extensive, and impossible to engross. The enormous Appalachian field, containing the bulk of the nation's high-grade reserves, ran from northwestern Pennsylvania and Ohio all the way down to Tennessee, and there were important secondary fields in Indiana-Illinois, in Alabama, in the Southwest, in the Rocky Mountains, and in the Northwest. The industry was made up of a large number of operators—two for every three mines—totalling nearly thirty-five hundred in 1905.[6] They constituted, as the Chief Mine Inspector of Pennsylvania observed, ''a great army of antagonistic elements and unorganized forces . . . [who] continue to indulge in a cut-throat warfare.''[7] Nor did the railroads play the stabilizing role that they had in anthracite. On the contrary, in bituminous they tended to stimulate interregional competition. Anxious to build more traffic, and often with financial interests of their own in the developing southern Appalachian fields, the bituminous-carrying railroads set freight rates low enough to enable southern producers to compete in distant northern markets.

Bituminous was not wholly insulated from the consolidating processes affecting American industry generally in this period. Some properties were absorbed by vertically integrating steel firms and by other heavy consumers of coal. There was also a considerable amount of merger activity by such firms as Pittsburg Coal, Monongahela River Consolidated Coal and Coke, and the Consolidation Coal Company of West Virginia. But these were large only in a relative sense, each controlling only a few percent of the total output and even together incapable of much affecting the level of competition. The pattern of competition was not so much between individual operators—there had, in fact, always been considerable associational activity within specific fields—as between rival fields competing in a common market. It was for this reason that the issue of equitable railroad rates was so explosive for coal operators.[8] At the end of the greatest period of business consolidation in American history, the bituminous industry retained very much the competitive structure with which it had begun. And it was this industry, not anthracite, that really mattered. Bituminous output was four times larger than anthracite by 1910 and was central to the transportation and energy needs of the nation's industrial economy.

Competition in the marketplace translates into a labor policy transfixed by labor costs. That fact bore down with special force on coal mining for two reasons. First, mining was labor intensive, with wages accounting for between 60 and 75 percent of total production costs. Second, and no less important, market pressures acted in a wholly unmediated way on mine labor costs.

In this period, shop relations in American industry were being transformed by the managerial advances that, for convenience sake, we call Taylorism. In recent labor scholarship, Taylorism has been perceived primarily as a struggle for control of the workplace. By that definition, the coal miner remained singularly untouched. His control over the labor process went virtually unchallenged at the turn of the century and, indeed, for at least another three decades. But workers' control is only one dimension of modernizing work relations. The forces undercutting autonomous labor—mechanization, the redesign of jobs, the close supervision of work—also have the effect of insulating the wage bargain from market pressures. That is, insofar as capital can be substituted for labor, or work made more efficient by Taylorist methods, to that degree the cost pressures on the price of labor are diffused. But the obverse is equally true. Insofar as employers lack other means of reducing labor costs, they must perforce focus on the price of labor. This was the situation that obtained in coal, much magnified in bituminous by the intensity of competition, and that peculiarly defined its labor relations.

In coal mining, as the engineering expert Hugh Archbold remarked in 1922, the production process "still remain[s] practically the work of one man who makes a finished product." What the miner took off the coal face was, in effect, the product that the mine operators sold. Nor did the scale of operations compare with mass-production industry. In 1920 some 9,000 bituminous mines were in operation, on average producing sixty-thousand tons a year and employing seventy workers. The 702 largest mines—those whose output exceeded two-hundred-thousand tons a year—employed an average of three hundred miners. What pressures there were on mine management, moreover, did not derive primarily from production itself but from the maintenance side of mine operations—ventilation, safety, electrically driven haulage, and so on. In the mines of Allegheny County, Pennsylvania, the proportion of day (or company) employees grew from 10 to 25 percent of the underground work force between 1890 and 1930, and it was these employees who were subject to the supervisory control characteristic of American industry generally. Even here, the U.S. Coal Commission (1925) found management practice sadly lacking. "More definite planning and control of transportation and of all other underground operations are needed," remonstrated the Commission. "Progress must be toward functional methods of planning and control of the work of the men and machines such as have been introduced in industries other than coal mining."[9]

As for the miner, he was virtually on his own. In the late nineteenth century, a single supervisor, the mine foreman or pit boss, directed all underground operations. He did well if in his rounds he saw each miner once during the shift (a standard that, in fact, came to be mandated by some state regulations). Mine practice in America relied mostly on the room-and-pillar system. The mine was laid out from a main shaft (or, in hilly areas, from a horizontal "drift") from which entries (or corridors) radiated out along the coal seam. The attack on the seam was at right angles by cuts wide enough for one or two miners. The walls separating the lengthening "rooms" as the coal was taken off the face were cut through at regular intervals for ventilating purposes—hence the "pillars." Along a side entry twelve to fifteen hundred feet long, there might be twenty rooms.[10] Thus miners were widely dispersed at individual work sites, and not susceptible to close supervision.

Even substantially increasing mechanization did not significantly reduce the autonomy of mine work. By 1910 over 40 percent of all bituminous coal was mined by undercutting machine, removing from the pick miner the most skilled and physically demanding phase of his job. But machine undercutting was absorbed into, rather than transforming, existing work practice. Most telling was the fact that the machine runner and his helper were normally paid a tonnage rate, not on a day basis as were the company men.

Payment by tonnage was the lynchpin of the entire labor-relations system in American coal mining. It is important here to distinguish clearly between two different meanings of piecework—as payment for output in nineteenth-century artisan production and as an incentive mechanism on the redesigned, timed jobs of the modern workplace. Under the older meaning, the piece rate translated directly into the unit cost of labor, and that was precisely what payment by tonnage meant to coal operators: it was the direct labor cost on every ton of coal they sold. In its inquiries, the U.S. Coal Commission encountered a curious discrepancy. In the midst of mine practice that it found scandalously slack, the Commission noticed that "cost accounting and pay-roll records in coal mining are more systematic and uniform than in any other industry in the country. We question whether the plants, large and small, in any other business than mining would have had on file the unit-cost and pay-roll data which enabled coal operators without difficulty to fill out certain of the commission's questionnaires."[11] The reason, of course, was that in mining everything turned on that information. The tonnage rate was the cardinal datum of mine operation, and from its centrality we can extrapolate the leading characteristics of labor relations in coal-mining.

Consider, for example, these persistent points of tension between miner and operator: first, over the weighing of the coal; second, over dockage (i.e., deductions for dirty coal); third, over screening, which separated out the undersized coal for which the miner was not credited; fourth, where payment was by carload rather than weight, over the size of cars. Certain externalities also bore on labor costs. Because of the location of mines in remote or unsettled areas, operators frequently provided company housing and operated company stores. The monopoly profits incident thereto were folded into calculations of mine costs and were taken to be a part of the more general effort at shaving the price of labor. In open acknowledgment of this fact, an 1895 labor agreement actually cut the tonnage rate by five cents for those Pittsburg operators who abolished stores and paid in cash.[12]

Payment by tonnage meant also that the miner was, in the phrase of Carter Goodrich, "a sort of independent petty contractor" and therefrom flowed certain other points of tension in mining labor relations. One was over "deadwork." It was accepted that the preparation and maintenance of his room was the miner's responsibility. But where was the precise line between deadwork and compensable extra work caused, for example, by water in his room or by rubble in the haulways? Deadwork was always a sore point for the miner who got paid only for the coal he loaded. Payment by tonnage likewise lay behind the endemic problem of an adequate and timely supply of coal cars. If, as the U.S. Coal Commission estimated, the miner had to wait an average of an hour and fifty minutes each shift for empty cars, the time lost was his, not the operator's.

This brings into focus the functional differentiation at the heart of coal-mining labor relations. The term *operator* had a quite precise meaning. Miner owners "operated" the mine; they did not produce the coal; and, because they paid for it on tonnage basis, the labor process itself was not of primary concern. To be sure, low and irregular output did mean a slower recovery rate on their investment, higher overhead costs per ton, and delivery problems with customers. And miners were discharged for absenteeism, for dangerous or incompetent work, and for disruptive behavior.[13] But, within broad limits, the miner was his own man. "It seems to be very frequently the attitude of the industry," remarked Carter Goodrich, "that 'production is in the main the lookout of the miner' . . . and that how much he works and when are more his own affair than the company's."[14] Thus, although they came to work at a fixed time, miners habitually knocked off at their own discretion, and this notwithstanding an official eight-hour day from the late 1890s onward. At the mines observed by the U.S. Coal Commission, half the miners left early, as did a much higher proportion of the cutters.[15] Nor did the operator supply the miner with tools nor pay for powder and fuses. And because the miner invested his time in opening and developing his "room," it remained his by a kind of proprietary right. Even after an extended absence, no one ordinarily replaced him at his designated place at the coal face.

For his own safety, finally, the miner bore a heavy responsibility. The greatest hazard he faced—the cause of half of all mine fatalities—was roof falls. The primary preventative measure for this hazard was the proper timbering of his room. But timbering was deadwork, and every day the miner had to balance the risks against the unpaid labor expended on timbering. In their realm as mine operators owners had to strike a similar balance, only with rather different stakes in mind—the costs of repair, lost production, and higher insurance rates as against the costs of safer haulage and electrical systems and precautions against gas and mine explosions.

The statistics speak eloquently as how those calculations came out. The annual fatality rate ran at roughly four per thousand full-time miners in the early twentieth century, compared to three in Germany, one and a half in Belgium, and slightly more than one per thousand in France and Britain. Coal mining was everywhere a hazardous occupation, and always subject to great variations in mine conditions and practices, as, for example, the highly dangerous work of "pulling" the coal pillars in the American room-and-pillar system. Even so, a large residual can only be ascribed to the economics of the American industry. No evidence is perhaps more compelling on that score than a comparison of the adjacent states of West Virginia and Pennsylvania—the first a free-market environment, the second more highly regulated and constrained. For the years 1912–21, the fatality rate per thousand bituminous miners per year was 6.50 in West Virginia, 3.22 in Pennsylvania.[16] In some large measure, the 18,243 miners killed in those years bear witness to a labor system peculiarly defined by competitive market forces and unmediated wage/labor cost relationships.

In nineteenth-century coal mining, the unionizing current ran very strongly. Unvarnished industrial injustice was a lesson driven home on the unorganized miner, day in and day out, with every short-weighted ton of coal, extra bit of unpaid deadwork, or unfairly distributed coal car. In hard times, slashed tonnage rates brought the sense of grievance to white heat. Then, too, a special kind of mutuality came (in the words of the miners' union constitution) to "those whose lot it is to toil within the earth's recesses, surrounded by peculiar dangers and deprived of sunlight and pure air. . . . ''[17] The solidarity inside the mine was cemented aboveground by the close-knit community life of the isolated mining camps. And, given the early reliance on British miners, there were always seasoned trade unionists to serve as the nucleus for organizing activity.

Miners' unions go back at least to the 1840s, initially as local organizations, but quickly broadening in scope. The first national organization—the American Miners' Association—lasted only from 1861 to 1867, and its successors were equally short-lived, until finally, as a result of a merger of the National Federation of Miners and Laborers and National District Assembly No. 135 of the Knights of Labor, the United Mine Workers of America was formed in 1890. Although it barely survived the depression of the 1890s, the modern history of coal unionism begins with the UMWA.

The miner's work was, in Carter Goodrich's phrase, "a rough sort of craft." His tasks—undercutting the coal face by pickwork, drilling the holes for setting the explosive powder, loading the coal after "shooting" it from the face, timbering the roof and laying the track—involved skill and experience, but of a kind acquired on the job and picked up rather quickly by green hands.[18] With the introduction of the undercutting machine, the skill component of the job markedly fell, and fell still further as other tasks—shot-firing, for example—began to be transferred to specialists. Given payment by tonnage, moreover, the learning costs were mainly absorbed by the worker himself.

By the end of the nineteenth century, the labor supply was no longer much restricted by the scarcity of skills. On the contrary, the industry was drawing its labor force primarily from large pools of preindustrial workers. In the North, these were mainly peasant immigrants from eastern and southern Europe, who made up 46 percent of the work force in Pennsylvania's anthracite fields in 1920, and 49.6 percent in the bituminous. As the West Virginia and Kentucky mines developed, they built a labor force principally of mountain whites and poor blacks. The latter made up 20 percent of work force there in 1920, and over 50 percent farther south in Alabama. There was, finally, a built-in oversupply of experienced miners. Because of seasonal demand and an inability to shrink capacity, the industry matched supply to demand by irregular mine operation. The nation's bituminous mines averaged 207 days of work during the 1890s, with low of 171 days in 1894 and a high of 234 in 1899. The more prosperous decade that followed brought the average up only to 218 days.[19] Underemployment was thus a normal condition, creating a peculiar kind of labor reserve always available to the coal operator. Insofar as trade unionism depends on controlling the labor market, in coal mining the balance of forces ran persistently against labor's cause.

In the product market, on the other hand, the balance of forces cut rather differently. In 1868 the Workingmen's Benevolent Association, which had formed in the Pennsylvania anthracite fields, called a five-week suspension of work specifically to reduce the coal supply and force up coal prices. This remarkable action prefigured the market orientation that would become the hallmark of American coal unionism. The underlying assumption—that prices and tonnage rates were linked—the WBA acknowledged in the most explicit of ways: in the brief era of good feeling that followed the strike, it negotiated a sliding scale with the Anthracite Board of Trade, in which the tonnage rate moved along with coal prices.[20] There were as late as 1894 instances of direct action against an oversupplied market, but well before then union leaders had begun seeking a more orderly way of reducing the competitive pressures on the industry's labor relations. The key idea came in 1885 from Daniel McLaughlin, head of the newly formed National Federation of Miners and Laborers. At his instigation, the union issued an invitation to the nation's bituminous operators to "a joint meeting with the board for the purpose of adjusting *market and mining prices* and give each party an increased profit from the sale of coal."[21]

Only one operator responded to the first call, a handful to a second, but the third, at Columbus, Ohio, on February 23, 1886, produced sufficiently representative delegations from the major states (Pennsylvania, Ohio, Indiana, and Illinois) as to take up the question of an interstate agreement. A wage scale for these states was agreed upon, but other issues had to be left to a board of arbitration made up of an equal number of miners and operators. Although it collapsed in 1889, this first interstate agreement prefigured to a remarkable degree the collective-bargaining system that would take hold in the bituminous industry. In 1897, in a last-ditch gamble, the foundering UMWA called a national strike, and, to its astonishment, the bituminous miners came out en masse. The "spontaneous uprising of an enslaved people," President Michael D. Ratchford called it.[22] Out of that three-month strike came a temporary scale and a joint conference in Chicago the following February. For the next thirty years, the interstate joint conference would remain the basis for collective relations in the industry.

As an institution, the joint conference was emblematic of the hybrid union-management connection—at once adversarial and mutualistic—that sprang up in bituminous coal. The main business of the joint conference was of course the hard, often prolonged, bargaining over a new wage scale. The conference took the form, however, not of a bilateral negotiation, but of a kind of industry convention, with a credentials committee, committee on rules and order, and so on. By custom, the temporary chair was the UMWA president, the permanent chair a leading operator, the secretary, again, a unionist. The ritual celebration of mutual interest always accompanied the election of these officers by the entire conference—"not an arena where foe meets foe," as one speaker asserted at the 1899 conference, but "a friendly meeting-place of those who are interested for the benefit of all."[23] The adoption of the interstate scale likewise departed from the form of a bilateral negotiation. The agreement, once arrived at by the scale committee (i.e., the bargaining teams of both sides), was put to the vote of the conference, with approval requiring a unanimous vote on both sides. An agreement serves to bind the contracting parties. In this case, there were multiple contracting parties, not only union and industry but potentially competing segments within the industry. The objective of a unanimous vote by all four states was to bind these multiple interests, within the operators' ranks no less than between operators and union, to the interstate agreement. It was as much an industry as a labor agreement.

The underlying principle, implicit from the very outset but formally enunciated and accepted at the 1902 conference, was that of *competitive equality,* a term used thereafter by coal men. The objective was not to standardize tonnage rates—to take wages out of competition, in the current phrase—but on the contrary to treat them as the variable factor balancing other inequalities under which competitors labored, "so that," as one Illinois employer put it, "the operators in every district might exist, notwithstanding the different conditions that prevail; and so long as we work on these lines some miners will have to accept less wages than others."[24]

The crucial function of the interstate conference was to establish the framework through which competitive equality could be implemented within the four participating states—the so-called Central Competitive

Field. Four roughly comparable districts within these states—Pittsburg (thin vein), Indiana Bituminous No. 1, Grape Creek, Illinois, and the Hocking Valley, Ohio—served as the "basing points." The interstate conference negotiated the standard for the basing points. This then became the basis from which the districts and subdistricts within the four states negotiated their actual tonnage rates, taking into account inequalities in transportation costs and thin vein–thick vein differentials.[25]

The interstate agreement, always a very skimpy document compared to the district contracts, had to contend with powerful centrifugal forces. In fact, it was always difficult to bring all four states into agreement on a scale. Ohio had initially resisted a uniform basing-point rate, since it had historically enjoyed somewhat lower wages than the other states. In 1906, western Pennsylvania made concessions that disrupted the interstate framework, and Illinois, the best organized district, was always troublesome. That the interstate system prevailed in the face of these immense competitive pressures testified to its genuine achievement.[26] If imperfect, it worked well enough to persuade the operators that collective bargaining could indeed serve as the mechanism for leveling the playing field in their cut-throat industry.

And what did the miners receive in return? First, of course, recognition of their union despite an inherently unfavorable labor market. Then, the benefits of collectively determined terms and conditions of employment. If pick-mine earnings were unequal from district to district, at least they were so by consent rather than through the arbitrary action of the operators. With the basing-point system in place, moreover, the interstate conference served as the arena within which the pay standard would be regularly advanced (or, as in 1904, reduced) and other basic terms of work improved, beginning, in particular, with the adoption of the eight-hour day in the 1898 agreement. Most important perhaps was the swift eradication of the systemic forms of exploitation peculiar to coal mining. The interstate conference itself dealt directly only with the problem of coal screening, partly by mandating the standard dimensions of the screen, but then moving by 1916 to a run-of-mine basis (i.e., payment for a miner's total tonnage, but at a lower rate than for screened coal).

All other issues were left to the state and district joint conferences. The Illinois agreement regulated virtually every matter touching work in the mines—dockage for loading dirty coal, compensable deadwork and yardage, the price for powder and blacksmithing, the distribution of coal cars (every miner to get a fair share). Contractual infractions by either side were punished by a precise system of fines, a logical extension of the monetary nexus of work relations in the mines. In the case of unfair discharge, reinstatement invariably included back pay for the number of days of lost work. An elaborate process of adjudication enforced the contract, beginning at the mine site and rising by steps to the executive boards of the district union and state operators' association, with arbitration as the final resort. Arbitration was not compulsory, however, and if either side rejected it, the right to strike or lockout remained.[27] Nowhere in the pre–World War era was the logic of workplace contractualism pressed so far or the jealously held prerogatives of American management so constrained by contractually defined job rights as in the unionized mines.

But from the outset there had been, in the striking words of Selig Perlman and Philip Taft, "a gun pointed at the heart of the industrial government in the bituminous coal industry."[28] This was West Virginia. The state's rich coal reserves, left mostly undeveloped until the 1880s, thereafter came rapidly into production. Under the theory of competitive equality, the union's job was entirely clear. The Chicago agreement of 1898, indeed, specifically obligated the UMWA "to afford all possible protection to the trade . . . against any unfair competition resulting from failure to maintain scale rates." Because of its uncanny resemblance to an illegal conspiracy in restraint of trade, the clause was cut from subsequent agreements, but no one doubted that it remained an essential condition of the interstate system of collective bargaining. The joint conferences, as the operators remarked, "were the schools at which the miners for years received their education in the principle that the existence in the markets of competitive non-union coal was disastrous to their movement and well-fare, and that if they were to be able to continue their union relations with the operators . . . they must at all costs both force independent operators to accept union *conditions,* and prevent any union operators from breaking away."[29]

In nonunion West Virginia, the UMWA ran into a stone wall. The mountaineer-miners, little interested in collective action at first, participated in neither the 1894 nor the 1897 national strikes.[30] Thereafter, the legendary antiunionism of the West Virginia operators came powerfully into play. Many were rugged individualists of a frontier-capitalist stamp, of course. But what animated their fierce antiunionism was a market logic specific to the coal trade, in fact, the underside of the theory of competitive equality. If some competitors accept constraints, those who do not are gratuitously advantaged.[31] The very existence of competitive equality, one might say, gave West Virginia operators an incentive to be militantly nonunion. To that must be added the real locational disadvantage under which they labored: the unionized states were significantly closer to the key markets of the industrialized Middle West.[32] If we can credit what they said, the West Virginia operators suffered from a kind of economic paranoia, convinced that the joint interstate conference was conspiring not to force them accept to competitive equality but to drive West Virginia out of the coal business.[33]

They had, in any case, ample means for keeping that threat at bay—absolute control over the coal villages (including the power to evict miners), a private army of Felts-Baldwin guards, reliable allies in the courts and state government, and, not least, the stomach to see blood shed in their cause. The union may have missed its best chance by opting at the turn of the century to organize the anthracite region first.[34] Thereafter, the UMWA cannot be faulted for lack of trying, either in resources spent, or in the intrepidness of its organizers. Its hold on the Kanawha Valley, gained in 1902, could not be expanded and, after the bitterly fought Paint Creek–Cabin Creek strike of 1912–13, that too became problematic.

Year by year, the nonunion threat intensified. In 1913, West Virginia coal production surpassed seventy million tons, and, together with neighboring Kentucky's nineteen million tons, accounted for 20 percent of the nation's bituminous output. The significance of these data can be best understood by studying the impact on specific markets. The most important, the Great Lakes trade, supplied the nation's industrial heartland. In 1898, 86 percent of the coal shipped up the lakes originated in the union districts of Pittsburgh and Ohio. By 1913 this proportion had slipped to 67 percent, while West Virginia coal, negligible in 1898, accounted for 23 percent in that year. Eastern Kentucky, which first entered the lakes trade only in 1909, was shipping 2.6 million tons by 1921.[35]

At the outbreak of World War I, the collective-bargaining system of the Central Competitive Field stood in real and increasing peril. On their own, people on both sides of the table recognized, labor and capital lacked the capacity to bring order to the coal trade. Perforce, they turned to politics.

In the United States, as in Europe, coal mining has stood in special relation to the state. Even at the height of the rampant capitalism of the post–Civil War era, American courts consistently held that the safety of those who worked underground was a public concern. Beginning with Pennsylvania in 1869, every producing state passed and periodically revised and expanded its mine safety and inspection laws. But, if these laws demonstrated a special public interest, their history also revealed the even greater power of the industry's market forces.

State-by-state mining legislation suffered, of course, from a crucial structural flaw: it cut across the competitive pattern of coal markets. Insofar as the mine safety laws actually became effective, they did so in step with unionization: where collective bargaining expanded, so did vigorous state regulation.[36] During the Progressive era, in the wake of the Cherry Mine disaster of 1909, the popular outcry for reform became intense. Led by the American Mining Congress, the industry sought agreement on a uniform code for all the mining states—in effect, to take the cost of safety out of competition. The federal government, while encouraging that development, was itself denied by the Constitution (as then understood) the power to legislate over labor conditions in the industry. The U.S. Bureau of Mines (1910), the main result of progressive agitation, carried on useful research, provided technical assistance, and maintained rescue stations, but it lacked any regulatory authority over the mines. As for the industry's movement for uniform state laws, not surprisingly, it collapsed within a few years. While the mine safety record improved somewhat, primarily because of new workmen's compensation laws, the acknowledged state responsibility for the well-being of miners was far overbalanced by the competitive pressures within the industry.[37]

Perceived in strategic economic and geopolitical terms, as it was in some European capitals, coal could also be invested with a quasi-public character for reasons of state. Not in industrializing America, however. Coal's development, unlike the railroads', did not challenge the prevailing laissez-faire dogma.

After the turn of the century, labor troubles in anthracite did bring the government's power into play. With winter approaching and fuel dwindling for the eastern cities, the great anthracite strike of 1902 caused a national crisis. At that point, President Theodore Roosevelt intervened decisively and forced the operators to submit to a presidential commission, whose 1903 award, among other things, set up a permanent board of conciliation to adjudicate disputes between the miners and their employers. Under public auspices, an orderly labor-management relationship, exceptional by American standards, took hold in the anthracite sector. In bituminous, the federal government lacked a comparable incentive. The industry's very fragmentation militated otherwise. Major strikes, although frequent even after the interstate system began,[38] never closed off enough production to threaten the country's economy.

Nor, alternatively, could the industry's market problems be made to inspire public intervention or, to be more precise, not the right kind of intervention. The early twentieth century saw a marked expansion of federal regulation of the business economy. This development had nothing to do with the kind of unrestrained competition that was afflicting soft coal, however. The Roosevelt administration was responding to precisely the opposite problem—the sudden arresting of competition in those industries caught up by the merger movement of 1898–1903. The resulting antitrust campaign by Roosevelt and his successors served, ironically, to discourage the coal industry's own sporadic efforts at reducing competition by means of price-fixing pools, for example, or by joint sales agencies, or, after 1910, by open-price associations. Whether or not these schemes were challenged as conspiracies in restraint of trades (as some were) did in truth not greatly matter, for, as one leading operator remarked, they were "always made inoperative by the exigencies of business."[39] Operators and union leaders came increasingly to recognize that the soft-coal industry needed structural reform that dealt with the underlying problems of excessive capacity and unrestrained market pricing.

Joining with big-business interests, coal men in 1908 lobbied for the Hepburn amendments that would have relaxed the Sherman Anti-Trust Law and permited "reasonable" cooperative or joint activity under the supervision of the U.S. Bureau of Corporations. But some operators, doubting their industry's capacity to take advantage of such enabling legislation, advocated that a National Mining Commission be given "universal and complete jurisdiction over the mining business," with power to restrict entry, limit production, and fix prices.[40]

So sweeping a departure from American laissez faire was never in the cards. When a committee of operators appealed to President William Howard Taft in 1909, he told them (so they reported) that he "could see no escape from a continuance of the present system of vigorous competition.'' Nor did the industry's efforts in the Senate three years later fare any better. Not even Woodrow Wilson's far-reaching antitrust revisions of 1914 made any difference. The new Federal Trade Commission proved wholly unsympathetic: its concern was with the uncompetitive practices of big business, not the supercompetitive practices of small business.[41] In the national debate over antitrust policy, the problems of soft coal turned out to have been beside the point.

Then the war came, and all bets were off. Overnight, soft coal became an essential industry par excellence. Modern war, as one cabinet member said, had become "an industrial game, the foundation of which is coal." Without coal, "the war cannot be carried on."[42] In fashioning a strategy of industrial mobilization, the Wilson administration wanted to avoid overcentralization. It reserved for itself broad policy-making powers, while leaving the implemention of its guidelines on prices, priorities, and the like to the industries themselves. The war emergency thus opened a remarkable chance for industrial self-regulation, but that opportunity, as it turned out, was denied to soft coal.

The very competitiveness it was seeking to master confounded the industry's hopes. After 1915, prices pushed rapidly upward, tripling in the spot market by 1917 and, in the single month after the American entry into the war in April, jumping from $3.00 to $3.72 a ton. The inelasticity of coal demand was operating wholly to the industry's advantage, perhaps for the first time. The mechanism for dealing with such problems, under the Council of National Defense, was the tripartite industry group, and one was duly created for coal, the Committee on Coal Production. But by the time that body moved against the spiraling coal prices, political sentiment had turned on the industry. It seemed that the nation was being gouged by a predatory "coal trust" in its time of peril. "Government officials were condemning an essentially fragmented and leaderless industry as if it were a monopoly," remarks James P. Johnson.[43]

What followed was a monumental fiasco. Eager to capitalize on the antitrust enthusiasms set off by rising coal prices, the Justice Department had brought suit against members of the Smokeless Coal Operators Association of West Virginia for price fixing. The charge was that they had conspired to set a price of three dollars a ton for their coal. When the CND's Committee on Coal Production finally made its price-control announcement on June 28, 1917, the benchmark price was, lo and behold, three dollars a ton. Outraged by this apparent conspiracy, President Wilson immediately repudiated the three-dollar proposal, arranged to have coal included in the pending Lever food-control bill, and then personally fixed the maximum price for coal at two dollars a ton.[44]

Coal mining was taken over by the Fuel Administration. While other industries gained self-regulation under the War Industries Board, bituminous coal went through the war as effectively a nationalized industry. Coal executives did go to work for the Fuel Administration, and they helped to fashion a program of rationalized coal marketing and transportation that resolved a nearly castastrophic distribution problem. But at the war's end the industry, notwithstanding a newly created National Coal Association, was organizationally scarcely better off than it had been in 1914. On February 1, 1919, Fuel Administrator Harry A. Garfield (a college president, not a coal operator) lifted price and zone controls, wished the industry well, and expressed the hope that it would mend its ways and apply the war-induced marketing structure to peacetime operation.

The industry was not, as it turned out, so readily extricated from the government. Back in October 1917, under the aegis of the Fuel Administration, the joint interstate conference had granted a 15 percent wage increase under what became known as the Washington Agreement. Any further relief was denied the bituminous miners by the government despite persistently rising consumer prices and concessions to other workers (including those in anthracite coal). With the Armistice, a peculiar and intolerable anomaly appeared. Controls over the operators went off and coal prices jumped to record heights, but the wage freeze remained in effect, despite zooming living costs. It so happened that, under its terms, the Washington Agreement ran until either the end of the war or April 1, 1920, whichever came first. But the stalemate over the Versailles Treaty put off the formal return to peace, and the coal operators, while themselves enjoying unprecedented profits, insisted on holding the UMWA to the letter of the Washington Agreement. By the summer of 1919, the miners were up in arms, and wildcat strikes swept the coal fields.

Faced by a national coal strike on November 1, 1919, the Wilson administration intervened, resurrecting the wartime controls under the Lever Act (including the reimposition of maximum coal prices) in a futile attempt to put the genie back into the bottle. What it only managed to do, however, was to pit itself against the UMWA. On November 8, the union leadership bowed to draconian injunctions and ordered the miners back to work. It was a bitter moment for the UMWA, one that was never forgotten. Out in the fields, the miners resisted and only grudgingly trooped back into the mines. To settle the dispute, President Wilson appointed a special arbitration commission, which in early 1920 awarded the tonnage workers an increase of 31 percent and the day workers 20 percent. The discrepancy touched off a further wave of strikes that ultimately extracted for the day workers an increase to $7.50 a day, the union benchmark wage for the rest of the decade.

In the course of this struggle, the state's relationship to the industry fundamentally shifted. If the Republican administrations of the New Era had no stomach for the state socialism of wartime control, neither could they return to the hands-off attitude of the Progressive era. Coal had become a national problem. For one thing, the 1919 crisis had demonstrated that coal strikes could no longer be treated as private affairs. In subsequent strikes in 1922 and 1925, dwindling coal supplies and skyrocketing prices again forced public intervention, and reinforced the conclusion that the government had a stake in more harmonious labor relations in coal mining. Equally important, the health of the industry itself became a matter of public concern. The demoralized bituminous industry was too much at odds with the vision of modern industrialism celebrated by the New Era. The failure to stabilize that vital sector, remarked a trade journalist in 1927, was "the economic crime, as well as the prime folly, of an otherwise progressive age."[45] During the decade, there were no fewer than eight major investigations and a plethora of proposals for rescuing the industry. Unlike in the prewar years, unrestrained competition was now acknowledged to be the industry's core difficulty, and one that demanded some form of government intercession. The key Republican advocate of coal stabilization, schooled by the wartime experience, was Herbert C. Hoover, secretary of commerce under Harding and Coolidge, and then president in his own right.

The joint interstate system never recovered from the wartime upheaval. Competitive equality had worked under the conditions of relative economic stability that had prevailed in the prewar industry. Between 1903 and 1915, tonnage rates had advanced at an average rate of only 1 percent a year, the cost of living had moved up at about the same rate, and coal prices had fluctuated within a very narrow range. Given evenly distributed wartime pressures, the industry's bargaining system would have been strained, but, with wages frozen by the Washington Agreement, it broke down entirely in the 1919 crisis.

Although rescued by the arbitration awards of 1920, the damage to the interstate system was not so easily repaired. Rank-and-file militancy, slow to subside under any circumstances, was fed by the internal politics of the UMWA. Weakly led since the retirement of President John Mitchell more than ten years before, the UMWA was now coming under the rule of a genuine strongman, John L. Lewis. But Lewis's position was still uncertain, he had no popular mandate, and he was challenged by a host of formidable district leaders, all to the left of him and all appealing to a restive rank and file.[46] Out of this political cauldron had come the UMWA demands of September 1919: a 60 percent wage increase, a thirty-hour week, time and a half for overtime, double pay for Sundays and holidays, and, to top things off, the nationalization and democratic management of the mines. To the heightened expectations that these demands bespoke must be added the lost confidence in a mutualistic relationship with the operators. The operators, through their indecent behavior when they had held the whip hand under the Washington Agreement, had spent the good will built up by years of joint-conference negotiation.

Then the postwar boom collapsed, and the underlying weakness of the interstate system reemerged. Mine capacity had grown tremendously—by three hundred million tons between 1915 and 1920—and mostly in the southern Appalachian fields. Despite substantial union headway during the war, West Virginia and Kentucky were still imperfectly organized on Armistice Day. In the postwar reaction, the operators regained the initiative and, as in the violent Mingo County strike of 1920–21, relentlessly drove the UMWA back. So the nonunion competition persisted and, with every new mine, grew more threatening. What the market collapse of 1921 revealed was an added, tactical nonunion advantage: the capacity to move quickly in moments of economic crisis.[47] Unable to match southern wage cuts because of the contracts still in force, many union mines were literally swept out of the market in the terrible year of 1921.

By the time that ordeal was over, northern operators had turned massively against the interstate agreement. If they could not rid themselves of the union, at least they insisted on the freedom to bargain independently or by districts. In 1922, they refused to enter another joint conference. Ohio and Pennsylvania operators, said one of them, "felt that they must without restriction or limitation of any character make their own agreement with their own men in their own district."[48] It took a bitter twenty-week strike by the UMWA to enforce the interstate structure. But might alone had done it. The joint interstate concept no longer held the allegiance of northern operators. Any semblance of industry unity, briefly manifested in the National Coal Association, now broke down. Northern operators wanted to pursue their individual interests, they stopped thinking in industrywide terms, and they turned against government intervention or cooperation. By the mid 1920s, the competitive instinct had returned with a vengeance and the Central Competitive Field was reverting to nineteenth-century conditions.

At this moment, the burden of market reform passed to the United Mine Workers of America. But no longer on the basis of competitive equality. In certain ways, the concept had always been troublesome for the union, for while accepting in principle that all competitors ought be enabled to live, the UMWA also adhered as best it could to the goal of equal earnings and conditions for all its members. To strike a balance between these conflicting objectives had always been at the nub of district-level bargaining over tonnage rates.[49] Now the economic justification for variable labor costs itself began to erode. Competitive equality rested on the assumption of an ever-expanding market that would always make room for all producers. That crucial assumption broke down in the 1920s. The economy shifted away from heavy industry, the technology of coal utilization dramatically improved, and rival fuels commanded an increasing share of the energy market, roughly 30 percent by 1925, and growing. After sustained growth for half a century, the demand for coal leveled off.

"Too many miners and too much coal." With that phrase, John L. Lewis signaled the union's new economic program. "The butiminous industry is suffering . . . the pains incidental to a long-delayed adjustment," Lewis said in 1925. "When it is complete, there will be fewer mines and miners and it will be a prosperous industry."[50] Lewis intended to use the union's bargaining power to speed that outcome. The key, he felt, was a uniform, high-wage structure that would drive out "uneconomic mines, obsolete equipment and incompetent management." He wanted to encourage the mechanization of the more productive mines, assure an "American" standard of living to the remaining miners, and enable the industry to compete on even terms with gas and oil. "Any concession of wage reductions will serve to delay this process of reorganization, by enabling the unfit to hold out a little longer."[51] Thus Lewis's seemingly ruinous policy of "no backward step" in the face of nonunion price competition: to abandon the $7.50 standard meant abandoning his conception of an industry driven by high-wage labor.

Wage uniformity was necessarily a more remote goal, given the regional differentials and multitudinous tonnage rates built up under the practice of competitive equality. But Lewis now rejected its underlying principle—that the ability to pay should be a primary criterion of wage determination—and he would as best he could press toward the goal of an industrywide uniform wage structure. This partly explains (if it does not justify) his ruthless suppression of the UMWA's proud tradition of district autonomy during the 1920s: the centralized bargaining he envisioned required a centralized union. The 1924 agreement, the final effort at holding the interstate structure together, notably invaded the bargaining rights of the districts: by its terms, they were prohibited from seeking in any way to alter their district agreements.[52]

Lewis put forward his ideas in avowedly conservative, even Darwinian, terms. In 1923, he engineered the repudiation of the union's nationalization program. In the course of the decade, he systematically purged his left-wing critics from the secondary leadership. And in his book *The Miners' Fight for American Standards* (1925), he trumpeted his credo to the world.

> The policy of the United Mine Workers of America ought to have the support of every thinking business man in the United States, because it proposes to allow natural economic laws free play in the production and distribution of coal. . . . [The aim] is not to steal mines from their owners, but to make it possible for owners of economic and properly equipped mines, operated by free labor under an American system of government, to make reasonable and continuous profits.[53]

Nevertheless, John L. Lewis's program required the assistance of the state. Indeed, as the power of the union waned, that need mounted. Up to a point, the Republican administrations of the 1920s were amenable. Secretary of Commerce Hoover took very much the same view of the industry's problems as did Lewis. Hoover estimated in 1922 that there were twenty-five hundred more mines and two hundred thousand more miners than the nation needed. After weighing and rejecting a variety of public interventions, Hoover concluded by late 1923 that "the gradual elimination of high-cost, fly-by-night mines" could be best achieved through the industry's own efforts under conditions of industrial peace. So, at Lewis's urgent request, the secretary of commerce pressured the resisting operators, led by the key Pittsburgh Coal Company controlled by the brother of his cabinet colleague Andrew Mellon, into participating in another round of interstate negotiations. The resulting Jacksonville Agreement of 1924, which continued the $7.50 day for another three years, was almost as much Hoover's handiwork as Lewis's.[54]

But the Jacksonville Agreement did not hold. Under enormous pressure from the nonunion fields, it began at once to crumble. John L. Lewis had of course anticipated defections, but from the marginal operators, not from strongest firms (such as Pittsburgh Coal and Consolidation Coal) who in fact led the exodus. Their large holdings in nonunion fields gave them powerful leverage over the union. In a showdown, they could shift their production to the southern Appalachian mines and starve out the union miners.[55] What Lewis had thought would be a controlled attrition turned instead into a deluge that threatened to sweep his union out of the Central Competitive Field. His second miscalculation was in supposing that the Coolidge administration, as a virtual party to the Jacksonville Agreement, would help to maintain it. But when Lewis appealed to Hoover, the secretary of commerce coolly suggested that the union take any firms violating their contracts to court—useless advice twice over, since litigation was too slow a process, and, given the highly dubious enforceability of labor contracts, likely to fail in any case.[56]

When the Jacksonville Agreement expired in 1927, there were few operators prepared to negotiate a new contract. The UMWA called a last, futile strike and then instructed the districts to make whatever terms they could. The joint interstate system was dead and so, very nearly, was the union. Half a million strong in 1922, it had shrunk to under one hundred thousand by 1928 and, outside of Illinois and Indiana, had almost disappeared from the Central Competitive Field.

Liberated from union restraints, northern operators slashed wages and joined the desperate scramble for business. Coal prices, which had briefly stabilized in 1926, began to fall again, and, after the onset of the Great Depression in 1929, plummeted. At the depths, in 1932, prices at the pit stood at a bit more than a dollar a ton, compared to two dollars in 1926 and three dollars in 1922. From 1927 onward, the industry operated at a deficit; in 1932 over 80 percent of the surviving firms reported net losses to the Bureau of Internal Revenue.[57] As in the late nineteenth century, market pressures once more bore down directly on the wage bargain, slashing rates and restoring all those petty forms of cheating over weights, deductions, and charges by which operators could squeeze another penny from labor costs. But the mitigating effect of secular growth in demand of that earlier age was now over, and from 1929 onward, the trend was absolutely downward. Between 1929 and 1932, three hundred thousand miners lost their jobs. For those still employed, average hourly earnings fell from sixty-five to fifty-two cents, the work week from thirty-eight to twenty-eight hours. Hunger and privation spread across the coal fields.

John L. Lewis excoriated the owners of the industry:

> They have practically no form of organization. They have no code of ethics. They are simply engaged in a struggle to continue their existence and remain in business. Why, the larger interests of the country are preying upon the coal industry, buying its products at less than the cost of production, and compelling the operator to sell the blood and sinew and the bone of the hundreds of thousands of men who are engaged in industry, and to sell the future of their children. . . . [58]

When he spoke those bitter words in 1932, Lewis was no less impotent. His union was shattered, and he himself personally discredited. But bankrupt of ideas or will he was not. The core of his thinking had not changed since the mid-1920s—that a uniform, high-wage structure achieved through free collective bargaining would solve his industry's ills.

To get there, Lewis now recognized, required the massive intervention of the state, first, to guarantee the right of miners to collective bargaining so as to crack the hard nut of antiunionism that had defeated the UMWA's utmost efforts, and, second, to enforce strict controls on coal competition until the full power of collective bargaining could be brought to bear. Twice, in 1928–29 and again in 1932, legislation was introduced into Congress incorporating those ideas. Strenuously resisted by both Hoover and the industry, the Watson and Kelly-Davis coal stabilization bills stood no chance of passage. But they signified what distinguished John L. Lewis from the others. He at least had a conception of what had to be done. All he needed was a law.

With the launching of the New Deal, Lewis's chance came. His initial presentation of his coal stabilization plan to the new president on March

27, 1933, fared badly. Under the pressure of the banking crisis and the nation's emergency relief needs, Franklin D. Roosevelt at first thought that a program for industrial recovery could be put off until a later time. But as the Hundred Days proceeded, industrial recovery moved on to center stage, and Lewis and his economic advisor W. Jett Lauck made a critical decision: they would submerge their own plans in the more general effort to stem the deflationary spiral and stabilize American industry. It was largely due to Lewis, through Lauck's participation in the drafting process of April and early May 1933, that the National Industrial Recovery Act contained section 7a, which guaranteed to workers the right to organize and to engage in collective bargaining. Lewis had less luck with the bill's approach to market regulation. He would have preferred strict controls, via industrial boards empowered to allocate production and fix prices. Instead, the administration opted for a more mixed system of industrial self-governance modeled after the War Industries Board and favored by the progressive business interests represented by the U.S. Chamber of Commerce.

In the resulting National Industrial Recovery Act, the key mechanisms were the codes of fair competition, each to include the mandated labor provisions of sections 7(a) and (b), covering minimum wages, maximum hours, and child labor, but otherwise tailored to the regulatory needs of the individual industries. A government agency, the National Recovery Administration (NRA), was granted broad powers of oversight and enforcement. The codes, however, were to be written and administered primarily by the industries themselves, or, more precisely, by their trade associations.

Unlike the oligopolistic sector, the fragmented bituminous industry fought this chance for market regulation tooth and nail. The National Coal Association adopted, pro forma, an essentially empty model code, while the various districts drew up regulations that had in common only a rejection of the labor provisions of the National Industrial Recovery Act. By early August the NRA had before it a bewildering array of coal codes. To forge from these discordant elements an acceptable coal code—that is to say, industry-wide, capable of restraining the industry's competitive impulses, and in conformance with the law's labor provisions—seemed almost beyond the powers of the embattled NRA authorities, and, indeed, of President Roosevelt himself.[59]

At this juncture, a revived UMWA suddenly seized the initiative. Popular uprisings are among the most intractable, the most difficult of events for historians to fathom. But in the case of America's miners in mid-1933, the ingredients at least seem reasonably clear: first, long-festering grievances brought to a boil by the Great Depression; second, an authoritarian management briefly weakened and disoriented; equally exceptional, a political environment, symbolized by section 7(a), suddenly sympathetic to labor's cause; and, finally, a dramatic organizing drive into which John L. Lewis threw his union's last remaining resources. The upshot was the swift reorganization of the mining fields, not only the traditional areas of union strength but now also southern Appalachian and deep South territory and even the mining properties of the steel industry. Overnight, John L. Lewis became again, to use his own phrase, "captain of a mighty host."

So armed, Lewis moved aggressively on two fronts in Washington. He pressed the coal industry to accept an effective code and simultaneously demanded that it enter collective bargaining with his union. In these endeavors, Lewis found an indispensible weapon in the spontaneous strikes that swept the Pennsylvania coal fields during that August. Although beyond Lewis's control, the pressure from below gave him the leverage he needed at key points in the protracted NRA negotiations. "In the last analysis," remarks the principal historian of these events, "it would be a truly nationwide union that would compel the operators to agree on a single code." On September 21, 1933, three days after President Roosevelt signed that code, John L. Lewis and James D. A. Morrow, an industry leader of long antiunion standing, signed the Appalachian Agreement that both men called "unquestionably . . . the greatest in magnitude in the history of collective bargaining in the United States."[60]

In one decisive stroke, Lewis had set in motion the uniform, high-wage program whose pursuit had very nearly destroyed him and the UMWA in the 1920s. The Appalachian Agreement preserved the industry's traditional bargaining structure, with a pattern-setting central field and outlying fields that followed its lead. But now Illinois and Indiana, main components of the old Central Competitive Field, were cut out and relegated to the category of outlying fields, reflective of the long-term shift in competitive markets (and a contributing factor in the breakup of the joint conference system after 1924). The remaining parts of the old Central Competitive Field, western Pennsylvania and Ohio, were now joined to West Virginia, Virginia, western Maryland, northern Tennessee, and eastern Kentucky—that is, the entire Appalachian region—in a new central bargaining unit that represented 70 percent of total bituminous production and constituted the real heart of the industry.

The nonunion threat that had for so long defeated the UMWA was thus finally eradicated and, while the first Appalachian Agreement did concede a North-South wage differential, it was of a scale much reduced from the past. In 1934, northern West Virginia came up to the northern standard, and in 1941, after a bitter and protracted struggle, so did the rest of the southern Appalachian field. This uniformity applied, of course, only to the day workers. Tonnage rates remained fixed in the industry's history of district and local differentials. But the significance of this rate variation rapidly declined.

As Lewis had anticipated, his wage-bargaining strategy speeded mechanization of the mines. Coal-loading machines, the major innovation of the 1930s, deprived miners of their principal remaining manual task and ended their reign as contract-tonnage workers. The relationship was entirely precise: as mechanical loading expanded, tonnage work contracted. By 1945, it was down to 25 percent of mine labor and shrinking, and so, by definition, was the portion of variably compensated labor. And for the tonnage work that remained, the UMWA did all it could to reduce the historical differentials. Its most effective tactic, initiated in 1946, was to negotiate flat wage increases for all workers, tonnage as well as day workers, so that while base tonnage rates might vary, the repeated flat increments eventually narrowed the earnings differentials to practical insignificance.[61] Thus John L. Lewis came closer to the wage policy for which he had long battled—equal labor rates for all and no quarter to the marginal operators.

If competitive equality had fostered decentralization, the campaign for wage equality brought precisely the opposite result. District bargaining did not disappear, but it was increasingly emptied of significant content. Much that had earlier been left to the districts was now absorbed into the Appalachian Agreement: the grievance procedure, key terms of employment, and even the specification of tonnage rates by district.[62] District autonomy had been so undermined, in any case, that the distribution of bargaining functions scarcely mattered. Two-thirds of the districts were under virtually permanent trusteeship—Lewis's technique for seizing control over them—and hence run by his appointees, not by elected officials. As a result the union's formal representative bodies (for collective bargaining, most importantly, the National Wage Policy Committee) were relegated to the status of rubber stamps. Although pro forma demands for greater autonomy were regularly heard at UMWA conventions, so commanding, even mythic, had Lewis's standing become among rank-and-file miners that they acceded to a concentration of power in one man's hands that is probably unique in American trade-union annals. The only limitation on Lewis's rule, an outgrowth of the bitter internecine struggles within the UMWA before 1933, was the survival in Illinois of a minor dual union, the Progressive Mine Workers of America.

The coal producers, for their part, experienced a parallel, if much more imperfect, organizational development. The National Industrial Recovery Act, to begin with, demanded a degree of associational discipline beyond what the industry's rugged individualists had hitherto been willing to accept. The conception of an Appalachian Field was originally not the union's handiwork, in fact, but that of four key operators seeking to come to terms with the New Deal's industrial-recovery program. During the early code-writing period, these industry leaders formed two large regional organizations—the Northern Coal Control Association and the [southern] Smokeless and Appalachian Coal Association, which then combined to present a single, albeit antiunion, code covering the entire Appalachian region. Collective bargaining, implanted on this structure, cemented the unity of the Appalachian operators.

It was a fragile unity, however, with an ironic tendency to break apart at the very points when greater economic uniformity was being imposed on the industry. Thus the two signal breakthroughs on North-South wage differentials—with northern West Virginia in 1934, the southern Appalachians in 1941—split the associations representing those regions from the industry's bargaining structure. For the remainder of the 1940s, the Southern Coal Producers Association negotiated independently and indeed frequently took bargaining stances at odds with that of the northern Appalachian group. The outcome was, nevertheless, always substantial uniformity. The industry's organizational development had likewise come a long way, with an acknowledged industrial leadership in the North and South and a grudging acceptance of the reality of centralized bargaining.

One fight being waged by the miners in this period carried the UMWA out onto a much larger battleground. The captive mines, so called because they were owned by and their output entirely consumed by steel companies, had never been a factor in the industry's competitive markets, and, hence, never of primary concern to the union. But the organizing explosion of 1933 engulfed these mines, and the captive miners flocked into the UMWA. On economic issues, there was no problem. Although not participants in the Appalachian negotiations, the steel companies were always prepared to apply the standards of the Appalachian agreements to the captive mines. On the question of union rights, however, they parted company with the commercial mines. After 1933, most operators accepted collective bargaining unreservedly, and only a few scattered areas—notably, Harlan County, Kentucky—put up stiff and continuing resistance. But the steel industry, bulwark of the open shop, stubbornly withheld the formal acceptance that the UMWA demanded. It took years of strife to gain full recognition and, in 1941, an embittering year-long battle to extract the union shop from the captive-mine owners. Their hard opposition attuned John L. Lewis to the larger struggle of the nation's industrial workers for collective bargaining. Equally important, the captive mines forged a link in his mind between the fate of the steel workers and the fate of his own union: without the captive mines, the commercial miners would not be safe, and without the steel industry, the captive miners would not be safe. From 1935 onward, Lewis committed his union's resources and his own energies very largely to the titanic battle for industrial unionism. And it was at the head of the Congress of Industrial Organizations (CIO) in its triumphant hour that Lewis earned his enduring place in American history and contributed most signally to the American labor movement.

But the rock on which he stood was always the miners' union. And so long as the Great Depression persisted, its power depended on the fragile structure of price restraints put into place by the NRA. For all the swagger that John L. Lewis cultivated in this period, he was deeply fearful of any resurgence of cutthroat competition in the coal business. In late 1934, for example, as the expiration of the NRA approached, operators began to accept new contracts at below-code prices. An alarmed Lewis castigated the operators for following a "policy of monumental stupidity." Since they seemed "incapable of preventing their own commercial destruction," Lewis demanded NRA action to "meet this menacing situation." Although his demands were satisfied, Lewis had already resumed his campaign for a more centralized price-fixing program specifically for soft coal, and, given the power he wielded in New Deal politics, this time he succeeded. His first bill, the Guffey-Snyder Act (1935), was found, like the NRA itself in May 1935, to be unconstitutional, and the second, the Guffey-Vinson Act (1937), proved to be an administrative nightmare.[63] Nevertheless, these troubled laws worked well enough to sustain the level of coal stabilization achieved under the NRA.

There is no doubt about the effect of the New Deal intervention on coal prices, which, notwithstanding weak demand, rose from $1.29 per ton at the mine in mid-1933 to $1.75 in 1934, and to $1.95 by 1938. It was this upward push that enabled the industry to grant a seven-hour day in 1934 and wage increases raising average hourly earnings from 52 cents in 1932 to 80 cents by 1939.[64] Unquestionably, the New Deal underwrote the Appalachian collective-bargaining system, and, unquestionably, it did so in large measure at the earnest and unceasing behest of John L. Lewis.

On September 1, 1939, war broke out in Europe, and, once again, all bets were off. In a defense-driven economy, the mine workers did not need the state: New Deal market regulation became superfluous. Lewis's statist enthusiasms had, of course, always been strictly limited and, more to the point, strictly instrumental. By 1941, with the economy booming, Lewis was bent on exploiting the new balance of forces— hence the maximum drive for North-South wage uniformity and, in the captive mines, for the union shop. In that second, monumental struggle, Lewis had to overcome not only the powerful steel interests but also a disapproving President Roosevelt and his National Defense Mediation Board as well. This prolonged battle with the defense-period apparatus reminded Lewis of what he already knew: that in wartime the state was likely to become the mine worker's enemy. The bitter memory of World War I, etched in Lewis's mind, partly explains the isolationist stance he took after the Nazi threat began to engulf Europe. Disagreement on this issue, among other reasons personal and political, led to Lewis's famous break with President Roosevelt. But at bottom it was a matter of business or, more precisely, of the marketplace economics that always dominated Lewis's thinking. He vowed that his miners would not for a second time become "innocent victims of an ill-advised wartime economy."[65]

After Pearl Harbor, Lewis's worst fears were swiftly realized. The government moved, more decisively than in 1917–18, to impose anti-inflationary controls over the wartime economy. The National War Labor Board, which had been established to arbitrate industrial disputes affecting war production, soon took jurisdiction over wages as well. In July 1942, the NWLB enunciated its governing stabilization policy: the Little Steel Formula, which, based on an estimated price rise of 15 percent from January 1, 1941, to May 1, 1942, set 15 percent as the limit on wage increases counting back to the beginning of 1941. Since the miners had received an 18 percent increase on April 1, 1941, their wage rates would effectively be frozen for the duration of the war. Nor was there the *quid pro quo* that reconciled other industrial unions to wartime regulation: the UMWA had no need of the maintenance-of-membership protections held out by the NWLB as the reward for union cooperation.

Lewis was as patriotic as the next man, and as willing to support the war effort, but not at an intolerable cost to his coal miners. The Roosevelt administration had adopted "a paradoxical policy that runs to the premise of rewarding and fattening industry and starving labor," he protested. It was World War I all over again: rising living costs (inevitable, in Lewis's view, despite price controls and rationing), cost-plus contracts for business, frozen wages for workers. So far as he was concerned, Lewis told assembled Appalachian operators in March 1943, "the Little Steel formula has outlived its usefulness. . . . It can't last because it is so viciously unfair. It seeks to deny to labor what the government gives to industry, namely, the cost of living plus a profit." As for the War Labor Board, it had "fouled its own nest" and was best advised "to voluntarily resign and not cast its black shadow in the face of Americans who are merely hoping for a right to live and a right to serve in this emergency of our own country."[66] Thus, with the Appalachian Agreement due to expire on April 1, 1943, Lewis threw down a challenge of the most fundamental kind to the power and majesty of the American government.

On its face, such a contest might have seemed wholly one-sided. In wartime, the president can bring sweeping emergency powers to bear. He can also, with sufficient skill, mobilize enormous political and popular pressure against a dissident like John L. Lewis. And, if he is a Roosevelt, he can even isolate such a leader and make him a pariah in his own movement. All these things Roosevelt did, but Lewis was not disarmed. Above all, Lewis was backed—and in a certain sense, even instructed—by the rank-and-file miners, who, through the wildcat strikes that swept the coal fields from January 1943 onward, revealed to him their determination to resist on the ground the Little Steel Formula.

Lewis did defy the War Labor Board. When it took jurisdiction over the stalemated negotiations in late April 1943, the UMWA refused to attend its hearings, and when it handed down a final directive specifying a new agreement on June 18, Lewis rejected the order as an "infamous yellow dog contract" that "no member and no officer of the United Mine Workers would be so devoid of honor as to sign or execute."[67] On May 1, 1943, with 75,000 miners on strike, the government seized the mines, rendering the miners public employees, and strikes illegal. The War Labor Disputes Act, passed over President Roosevelt's veto by an infuriated Congress, then made such strikes criminal acts. Nevertheless, walkouts continued. Lewis proved adept at orchestrating the striking miners, and, as the government quickly discovered, there was no effective way of forcing them to work against their will. So, despite a good deal of trumpeting of its sovereign powers, the Roosevelt administration backed down. Secretary of the Interior Harold Ickes, the federal administrator of the seized mines, engaged in bargaining with Lewis and finally settled with him on November 3, 1943. By a complicated calculation involving additional work time and portal-to-portal pay (i.e., covering travel time within the mines for which miners had not hitherto been compensated) Lewis got the $1.50 a day increase he had been demanding.[68] Although he had not broken the Little Steel Formula, he had in fact triumphed over the wartime state.

Ironically, Lewis faltered not when its powers were at their peak but when they were being dismantled. In the first postwar round of negotiations, Lewis successfully repeated the tactics that had worked for him in 1943. After a six-week strike that created a desperate coal shortage, Lewis forced the Truman administration to seize the mines again on May 21, 1946, and, as in 1943, he then proceeded to extract from government negotiators an historic new "fringe"—a welfare-and-retirement fund financed by a five-cent royalty on coal tonnage—that evaded the wage stabilization guidelines established by the 1946 steel settlement. But five months later, Lewis declared the agreement he had made with the government terminated effective November 20, 1946, and demanded new negotiations.

This time President Truman, pushed too far and aware of the high political stakes, held firm. "The Administration must find out sometime whether the power of Mr. Lewis is superior to that of the Federal Government,'' declared one of the president's advisors.[69] The injunction Truman obtained—in a historic break from the national policy, going back to the Norris–LaGuardia Act of 1932, against using that legal weapon in labor disputes—required Lewis to rescind the termination declaration as a disguised strike order that violated the War Labor Disputes Act. Once pushed into the judicial system, Lewis lost all room for maneuvering. In contempt proceedings, the UMWA was fined a crushing three and a half million dollars, and Lewis branded (and fined ten thousand dollars) by the outraged federal judge as instigator of a strike that was "an evil demoniac, monstrous thing . . . a threat to democratic government itself."[70] Lewis had overreached himself and, beaten and humbled, he called off the strike. If he needed any further justification for the libertarian conclusions he was drawing,[71] it was the passage of the Taft-Hartley Act the following year, for which, it must be said, Lewis had to bear some considerable responsibility.

This protracted struggle inevitably took a heavy toll on the collective-bargaining system that had been constructed in the New Deal period. While the formalities remained—the Appalachian Agreement still served as the basic framework and negotiations did take place (and once, in the spring of 1945, came to successful conclusion)—the heart of the bargaining process had been cut out. At every critical stage, the coal operators had been shunted aside, their properties taken over and held by the government for lengthy periods. In practice, seizure proved less than draconian: only the hardy few who refused to cooperate were actually displaced by public officials in day-to-day operations.[72] But this did little to assuage the resentment of operators as they watched government negotiators trade away in "interim" agreements precedent-setting concessions on portal-to-portal pay, safety practices, and welfare benefits. Almost necessarily, the return of their properties at the expiration of the War Labor Disputes Act on June 30, 1947, ushered in a period of industrial conflict during which they tested out the uses of Taft-Hartley and the permanence of the union's wartime gains, in particular, the burdensome welfare-and-retirement fund financed by a royalty on their coal output. Yet, as it turned out, the stage was being set in that turbulent time for the completion of the system that had begun with the Appalachian Agreement back in 1933.

After a decade of war-driven demand, the coal market was by 1949 reverting to normal. The rivalry of other fuels, arrested during the war, resumed with a vengeance. The railroads, converting rapidly to the diesel-powered locomotive, were about to disappear as coal's best remaining market. And operators had to contemplate not the flat demand of the 1920s but the dread prospect of an absolute decline. As the problem of overcapacity reasserted itself, so did the persistent question of an industrial policy for soft coal.

The New Deal solution was foreclosed. There would be no returning to federally imposed market stabilization. The second Guffey law had expired unlamented in 1943, and, with the Keynesians in the ascendancy, the economic thinking it embodied was discredited and gone from the political agenda. For their part, neither the industry nor the union had any stomach for more government intervention. It was, in fact, the prospect of congressional legislation authorizing re-seizure of the mines that precipitated a sudden resolution of the last protracted round of struggle of 1949–50.

Intervention came from a different quarter. In basic steel, as elsewhere in the industrial economy, corporate leaders were in process of constructing their post–New Deal version of economic stabilization. For that reason, the troubles in coal had to be taken in hand. In a curious way, U.S. Steel's Ben Fairless was returning the compliment to John L. Lewis. To protect his miners in the 1930s, Lewis had moved to force collective bargaining on U.S. Steel. Now, seeking to perfect industrywide bargaining in basic steel, Ben Fairless found he needed stability in soft coal. To that end, Fairless and his associates began in 1947 to participate in the bituminous negotiations, and the captive mines for the first time came under the national agreement. To this was added a sudden spurt of consolidation within soft coal. In 1945, George Love merged three of the largest firms into the giant Pittsburgh Consolidation Coal Company, and he too had an interest in stabilizing coal's collective bargaining. Between George Love, who became the dominant force among the commercial operators, and U.S. Steel's Harry Moses, who exerted comparable influence over the captive-mine group, it became possible to bring virtually the entire industry, North and South, into the National Bituminous Wage Agreement of 1950.[73] Shortly thereafter, Love and Moses established the Bituminous Coal Operators' Association (BCOA), which, in alliance with the Southern Coal Producers' Association, effectively united the bituminous industry for purposes of collective bargaining.

Thus, almost improbably, what John L. Lewis had hoped for since the 1920s became a reality. The confrontational bargaining of the 1940s suddenly gave way to private, informal discussions between John L. Lewis and Harry Moses (who had resigned from U.S. Steel to become head of the BCOA). Expiration dates no longer applied: after one year, either side was free at any time to reopen the contract and the outcome took the form of "amendments" to the basic National Bituminous Wage Agreement. When Lewis and Moses came to a decision, the terms were announced with a flourish and automatically approved by their respective organizations.[74] National strikes, almost endemic in the previous decade, became virtually extinct. The only significant walkout occurred in 1952 during the Korean War and was directed not at the industry but at Truman's Wage Stabilization Board for scaling back a wage increase to which the BCOA had agreed.

Lewis's doctrine of high-wage uniformity had carried the day. Average earnings rose from $14.75 a day in 1950 to $24.25 a day in 1958, and royalty payments for the welfare-and-retirement fund added another 40 cents of labor cost to every ton of coal. Most telling was the conclusion drawn by economists studying the wage impact of trade unions: in soft coal, over 30 percent of earnings in the mid-1950s could be credited to the UMWA, "the largest effect . . . estimated for any industrial union."[75] That the industry shared Lewis's market reasoning was evident in the contractual provisions aimed at enforcing uniformity on the entire industry. Of these schemes, the most notorious was the "protective wage clause" of 1958, which committed all signatories not to buy or process coal from, nor lease coal lands to, firms not abiding by the national agreement.[76] Not surprisingly, the UMWA soon faced an antitrust suit charging "a conspiracy with the large operators to impose the agreed-upon wage and royalty scales upon the smaller, non-union operators, irrespective of their ability to pay. . . ."[77]

In the face of a production decline of 20 percent between 1950 and 1960, coal prices remained almost stable. Labor costs per ton, despite a 64 percent rise in wages, actually fell by 8 percent as increasing mechanization pushed output per miner up from 6.77 to 12.83 tons a day. Jobs, of course, fell off just as dramatically. The industry, which had employed 415,582 miners in 1950, employed 141,646 in 1963. It was a trade-off that Lewis, if not jobless miners, had always welcomed. And if final proof of the UMWA's "cooperative" stance was needed, it was forthcoming when the industry entered a cyclical downturn in

1958. The union refrained from reopening the agreement, and for the next five years wages rates remained unchanged.

At his retirement in 1960, John L. Lewis must have been well pleased by his handiwork. He had accomplished what America's miners had been struggling for ever since that effort by the Workingmen's Benevolent Association back in 1868 to push up anthracite coal prices by going on strike: that is, to master by their own collective effort the market forces that bore down so heavily on them.

But those market forces, after persisting for a century, were now about to change. Three events, all dating from about the time of John L. Lewis's departure from the scene, can serve as markers of a remarkable transformation of the American coal business.

First: In 1961–62 coal burned by the nation's electric utilities reached 50 percent of total coal consumption (compared to 18.6 percent in 1950). At that point, reversing a fifty-year trend, the coal industry began a sustained expansion, driven entirely by America's insatiable appetite for electricity. Between 1960 and 1980, coal output doubled, 80 percent of it now absorbed by the utilities. The impact on the coal market, although little noticed, was far-reaching. For one thing, the utilities, as coal consumers, had no interest in the price stabilization fostered by the BCOA-UMWA bargaining system. Hence the sudden challenge to the UMWA from the unlikeliest of places—that triumph of New Deal reform, the Tennessee Valley Authority. With its increasing reliance on steam-generating plants in the 1950s, the TVA adopted a policy of buying coal from the lowest bidders, no questions asked. The result was a proliferation of low-wage truck mines and the renewal of a nonunion threat from Kentucky and West Virginia.[78] On the other hand, the nature of utility demand very much moderated the market pressures that had called forth the BCOA-UMWA structure in the first place. For electric-power companies, fuel was a major cost item, generally over 60 percent of production expenses, and price became correspondingly important as a determinant of their coal-market behavior. Because their modern furnaces were multiple-fuel burners, moreover, the utilities could switch to coal when its price was falling. Thus, unlike major industrial consumers of the past, the demand for coal by the utilities was quite elastic and served as a counterforce to the extreme pressure on prices that had always marked a declining coal market in the past.[79]

Second: In 1961 Pennsylvania passed the Surface Mining Reclama-
tion Act. This measure, the first even modestly effective environmental
response to coal strip-mining, signaled the commercial success of a
radically different extractive process in the industry. Suited to the low-
grade requirements of steam-powered generators, surface mining took
hold in some eastern districts and then expanded dramatically in the
West. A very minor factor in Lewis's day, the Rocky Mountain and
High Plains states were producing a quarter of the nation's coal in 1980,
almost exclusively as suppliers of steam coal for the utilities. With its
giant steam shovels and dragline excavators, surface mining could
scarcely even be classified operationally in the same category as underground mining. Resistant to the UMWA (hence its support for the
1961 Pennsylvania environmental legislation), many of the surface
mines remained nonunion, or, especially in the West, were organized
by other unions. Surface mining confronted the UMWA with a different
and more formidable kind of regional threat, for while the South's
advantage had been cheaper labor, the West's was higher efficiency.[80]
And insofar as the surface-mine sector could not be accommodated
within the BCOA-UMWA structure, its uses were thereby further
eroded.

Third: In 1959 the General Dynamics Corporation purchased the
Freeman Coal Company. This marked the start of a wave of acquisitions
that in little more than a decade essentially brought to an end to the
existence of coal as an independently run industry. The need for steady,
high-volume sources of supply had already speeded the process of consolidation under way in soft coal. In the midwestern region, for example,
the four largest firms moved from 26.8 percent of total production in
1949 to 54.6 percent in 1962, and the eight largest controlled 74.2
percent by then. On top of this, the rapid depletion of the nation's cheap
oil and gas reserves now led to a re-valuation of coal as an energy
source, not only for burgeoning utility needs but also (so it was hoped)
for other uses through new liquification and gasification technologies.
Oil companies, utilities, and other resource-oriented firms moved
quickly to establish a stake in the coal business. By 1976 only three of
forty largest coal producers remained under independent management.
With the oil embargo of 1973, the energy crisis struck with a force
unanticipated even by the corporate insiders and, as it turned out, beyond
what the coal business could entirely absorb. For one thing, escalating
prices rendered oil uncompetitive with coal and, to that degree, reduced

the elasticity of demand by the utilities. For another, inflated expectations led an overexpansion of coal capacity. Over the long term, nevertheless, concentration of control by the energy conglomerates, together with the predominating utility demand, meant a coal market no longer subject to the severe downward price pressures of the past.[81]

As an economic regulator, the BCOA-UMWA structure had effectively been superceded.

Inside the underground mines, meanwhile, a workplace crisis was building. Traditionally, mining had been an autonomous labor process, with miners left largely unsupervised and pay fixed by tonnage output. In the era of hand loading, which prevailed up to the 1940s, the essential thrust of union work rules had been to regulate mine practices that cut into tonnage earnings or increased unremunerated work. The spread of coal-loading machines after 1930 changed all that, drastically reorganizing the labor process, replacing the individual miner with teams of specialists, and the tonnage-pay system with day work. Now the operator discovered that labor productivity did matter, and that supervision was a managerial function. Nor did innovation abate. In a second wave of mechanization, undercutting and loading machines began to be replaced by continuous mining equipment, which by 1970 accounted for half of all deep-mine output; in the 1980s even more sophisticated long-wall technology seemed in the offing.[82]

As workplace control disappeared, miners began to demand a different brand of work rules. Unlike the workers paid by tonnage and claiming proprietary places at the coal face, specialized day workers wanted explicit rights governing the allocation of job opportunities, hence the first inclusion of seniority rights in the 1941 and 1952 agreements. With the new division of labor, too, problems of pay equity and job classification increasingly occupied the grievance system.[83] Mine safety was likewise cast in a different light. So long as the cost had in considerable measure been borne by the contract miners (through labor they considered deadwork), the union had shied away from safety as a bargaining issue. But under the new system, health and safety became strictly management costs, and, as new machinery sped up operations, these became matters of increasing concern to the miners. So the 1941 agreement provided for mine safety committees, the first step in an agressive collective-bargaining intrusion into the realm of health and safety.[84] As mine foremen gained supervisory functions, finally, the power they wielded over workers entered union calculations—hence, among other reasons, the organizing drive directed at them by the UMWA in the 1940s.

Between the rationalizing impulses of the modern operator and the work-rule defenses of the modern miner, tensions necessarily existed, just as they did across the entire mass-production sector. In mining, however, this conflict deepened into a severe crisis. There were, first of all, the traditions of the workers' control that had to be surmounted—for operators no less than miners. The speed of technological change, too, kept things unsettled. As mining became capital intensive, moreover, operating schedules became hotly contested. Union practices going back to the hand-loading era—no Sunday work, no night shifts, vacation shutdowns—came up against insistent employer demands for continuous mine operation in order to maximize the return on expensive equipment. In the early 1970s, finally, twenty years of sustained productivity growth came to an abrupt end, evidently triggered by the Coal Mine Health and Safety Act of 1969 but then fed by widespread strife in the workplace over the next decade. From a record 15.61 tons in 1969, output per worker in underground mines plunged to 8.25 tons a day in 1978. At the opening of the 1981 negotiations, the BCOA complained bitterly about "the heavy cost burden that low productivity imposes on coal produced under the UMWA-National Agreement."[85] Whatever the real productivity advantage of the nonunion competition—for deep mines, the BCOA put it at 39 percent[86]—it was a far cry from Lewis's conception of unionized operations at the cutting edge of the industry's efficiency.

Converging over an extended period, these developments—the market impact of utility demand, the takeover of the industry by the energy conglomerates, an expanding nonunion sector, the workplace crisis—came to an altogether predictable end. The Bituminous Coal Operators' Association, with 130 members in 1980, spoke for fewer than twenty companies in the 1988 negotiations. A larger number bargained independently with the UMWA. And more bargained not at all, for by then the industry was becoming increasingly nonunion.[87] The BCOA-UMWA structure that had been the life's work of John L. Lewis served for roughly twenty-five years, and, after the early 1970s, began to weaken and then rapidly disintegrated.

Perhaps, in this postindustrial age of American capitalism, twenty-five years ought to be taken as the normal life span of any collective-bargaining system. Across the economic spectrum, from steel to trucking, postwar labor-management settlements have come apart more or less on the same schedule. But no union has handled its troubles so badly; or, between 1947 and 1985, lost so large a share of its organized territory;[88] or today seems so incapable of mounting a fresh attack on the transformed coal industry. To encapsulate the UMWA's breakdown in a single event: in 1986 this once-mighty union announced that it was ready to seek shelter in merger with a larger organization.

In some measure, the sad fate of the UMWA has to be laid at the feet of John L. Lewis. To prevail over the market forces in soft coal, he always insisted, required that the union be run as a "business proposition."[89] During the long years of struggle, that notion mostly manifested itself in Lewis's iron-fisted control over the union's affairs. But after the 1950 agreement, when the need for militancy and solidarity subsided, the UMWA experienced in full measure what it meant to be run as a "business proposition." In organizing: strong-arm tactics and money talked. On collective bargaining: a happy community of interest with the industry. Toward the rank and file: the demand only for dues, for passive loyalty, and submission to the contract's no-strike clause. Two decades of this regime were enough utterly to drain the UMWA of its vitality as a workers' organization. The history of failed leadership, rebellious rank and file, and collective-bargaining disarray that followed Lewis's departure is beyond the limits of this essay; and beyond its limits, too, is any attempt at assessing the degree to which the UMWA's own troubles contributed to the breakdown of the BCOA-UMWA structure.[90]

But there is the future to think of. It would be the crowning irony if, by virtue of his brief triumph, John L. Lewis had exhausted the chances of succeeding generations of America's miners to control their own industrial destinies.[91]

Notes

This essay was originally commissioned for a comparative study on the relations between labor, capital, and the state in the coal-mining industries of six countries (Britain, France, Germany, Belgium, Austria and the United States). Having done no previous work on miners, I approached the subject with an open mind, reading as widely as I could in the rich specialized literature and then fashioning what I hoped would be a coherent historical account of labor-capital-state relations in American coal mining. Midway through these proceedings, in July 1988, the authors from the six countries gathered in Berlin to compare notes. It was a revealing experience. Visibly, my fellow authors looked at me askance, not quite able to give credence to what I was describing, for whereas every other report placed labor relations in an historical process of cartelization, tripartism, or nationalization, mine dealt with a sustained trade-union struggle to master the market forces that made for the harsh exploitation of American miners. It is, at the moment, unfashionable to think of class relations in America as "exceptional." And admittedly, insofar as soft-coal mining was so unremittingly competitive, it was not wholly representative of American industry in the age of the large corporation. Yet I would submit that my own experience as odd-man-out corresponded to something specific to American working-class experience. In brief: no other working class has stood so exposed to the market forces of modern capitalism, or, concomittantly, been so reliant on its own collective efforts for achieving some measure of economic justice. That most certainly has been the reality driving the history of American miners over the past century. (The results of the comparative project appear in Gerald D. Feldman and Klaus Tenfelde, eds., *Workers, Owners and Politics in Coal Mining: An International Comparison of Industrial Relations* [Oxford, Eng., 1990].

1. United States Coal Commission, *Report,* 5 vols. (Washington, D.C., 1925), III, 1659 (hereafter cited as USCC). For a recent article that argues in a similar vein as this essay, but from a different theoretical perspective, see John R. Bowman, "When Workers Organize Capitalists: The Case of the Bituminous Coal Industry," *Politics and Society,* 14 (1985), 289–327.

2. A. T. Shurick, *The Coal Industry* (New York, 1924), viii.

3. Carter Goodrich, *The Miner's Freedom: A Study of Working Life in a Changing Industry* (Boston, 1925), 13 (Goodrich's italics).

4. Richard Hannah and Garth Mangum, *The Coal Industry and Its Industrial Relations* (Salt Lake City, 1985), 29–31; Barry Supple, "The Political Economy of Demoralization: The State and the Coalmining Industry in America and Britain between the Wars," *Economic History Review,* 2nd ser., 41 (November 1988), 568–69.

5. Eliot Jones, *The Anthracite Coal Combination in the United States* (Cambridge, Mass., 1914), esp. ch. 3.

6. USCC: I, 323; III, 1889.

7. William Graebner, "Great Expectations: The Search for Order in Bituminous Coal, 1890–1917," *Business History Review,* 48 (Spring 1973), 50.

8. Ibid., 52–53.

9. Keith Dix, *Work Relations in the Coal Industry: The Hand-Loading Era, 1880–1930* (Morgantown, W.Va., 1977), 37, 38; USCC, III, 1890–91, 1900.

10. See, e.g., fig. 3 in Dix, *Work Relations,* 5. On U.S. Steel's efforts to apply steel-making supervisory techniques to its mines, see Dix, *Work Relations,* 85–86.

11. USCC, III, 1918.

12. "Labor Question—'Company Stores' in the Pennsylvania Mining Districts," *The Annals,* 7 (1896), 163–64.

13. See, e.g., the analysis of grievances in Louis Bloch, *Labor Agreements in Coal Mines . . . of Illinois* (New York, 1931), pt. 2.

14. Goodrich, *Miner's Freedom,* 30–31.

15. USCC, III, 1945ff.

16. USCC, III, 1688, 1659; Dix, *Work Relations,* 721. Other explanations for Penn-

sylvania's better safety record would include a more skilled labor force, a more mature industry, and differing geological conditions.

17. The constitution is reprinted in Bloch, *Labor Agreements*, app. III.

18. See, e.g., Dix, *Work Relation*, 34–36.

19. Statistics from USCC: II, 548; III, 1112, 1422. For a strictly neoclassical analysis of the labor market in soft coal, but one taking no cognizance of the industry's product market characteristics, see Price V. Fishback, *Soft Coal, Hard Choices: The Economic Welfare of Bituminous Coal Miners, 1890–1930* (New York, 1992).

20. Charles B. Fowler, *Collective Bargaining in the Bituminous Coal Industry* (New York, 1927), 37.

21. Letter reprinted in Andrew Roy, *A History of the Coal Miners of the United States* (1905; reprint, Westport, Conn., 1970), 248–49 (my italics).

22. Arthur E. Suffern, *Conciliation and Arbitration in the Coal Industry of America* (Boston, 1915), 41.

23. Ibid., 143–44.

24. Isadore Lubin, *Miners' Wages and the Cost of Coal* (New York, 1924), 74.

25. Implementing competitive equality was, of course, a hard and always imperfect process. Precisely what concessions weaker operators needed to remain competitive was never certain. Moreover, the two main "inequalities" cut in quite different directions. In the matter of unequal transportation costs, the demand for wage concessions had a fairly straightforward basis. But when it came to unequal grades of coal deposits, the trade-offs were more complex. In less productive, so-called thin-vein mines, what operators wanted by way of concessions to remain competitive was countered by what miners demanded by way of above-standard tonnage rates to compensate for lower output relative to their effort. In this case, what the union conceded was a rate less than that needed to equalize the earnings of the disadvantaged miners in thin-vein operations. In fact, the union did aspire to getting as close to equal earning as it could, and from the first it insisted on uniform wages for inside day workers across the entire Central Competitive Field. For a full analysis, see Lubin, *Miners' Wages*, chs. 4–6; and, for district rates in the Illinois agreement, Bloch, *Labor Agreements*, 336–68.

26. The negotiating history is summarized in Suffern, *Conciliation and Arbitration*, ch. 5.

27. See the detailed analysis in Bloch, *Labor Agreements*, pt. 3. The state agreement is reprinted in app. 2.

28. John R. Commons et al., *History of Labor in the United States*, 4 vols. (Boston, 1918–35), IV, 326.

29. A. F. Hinrichs, *The United Mine Workers and the Non-Union Coal Fields* (New York, 1923), 118–19.

30. David A. Corbin, *Life, Work, and Rebellion in the Coal Fields: The Southern West Virginia Miners, 1880–1922* (Urbana, Ill. 1981), ch. 2.

31. For an analysis, see Lubin, *Miners' Wages*, ch. 9.

32. From the standpoint of northern operators, West Virginia already received unduly favorable rail rates, but, of course, the West Virginia operators had no certainty that these rates would always be in place.

33. See, e.g., Hinrichs, *United Mine Workers and the Non-Union Coal Fields*, 122–23.

34. Donald L. Miller and Richard E. Sharpless, *The Kingdom of Coal: Work, Enterprise, and Ethnic Communities in the Mine Fields* (Philadelphia, 1985), 282.

35. Lubin, *Miners' Wages,* 214.

36. For the interaction between collective bargaining and legislation, see Bloch, *Labor Agreements,* ch. 7, "Collective Bargaining in Legislation."

37. The standard work is William Graebner, *Coal-Mining Safety in the Progressive Era: The Political Economy of Reform* (Lexington, Ky. 1975).

38. Waldo E. Fisher, "Bituminous Coal," in Harry A. Millis, ed., *How Collective Bargaining Works* (New York, 1942), 250.

39. Graebner, "Great Expectations," 62.

40. Ibid., 65, 66.

41. Ibid., 63; and, on coal's relations with the FTC in 1915–16, James P. Johnson, *The Politics of Soft Coal: The Bituminous Industry from World War I through the New Deal* (Urbana, Ill., 1979), 27–31.

42. Quoting Franklin K. Lane, in Johnson, *Politics of Soft Coal,* 38.

43. Ibid., 34.

44. As it turned out, the indicted West Virginia operators were found innocent because, while they might indeed have conspired, the effect on the market had been negligible: prices had risen above three dollars before their agreement had gone into effect! (Ibid., 47–48). My treatment of these events relies on Johnson's trenchant analysis.

45. Ellis W. Hawley, "Secretary Hoover and the Bituminous Coal Problem, 1921–1928," *Business History Review,* 42 (Autumn 1968), 252.

46. Melvyn Dubofsky and Warren Van Tine, *John L. Lewis: A Biography* (New York, 1977), ch. 3.

47. Lubin, *Miners' Wages,* 209 ff.

48. Ibid., 215.

49. For a detailed analysis, see ibid., ch. 3.

50. Morton S. Baratz, *The Union and the Coal Industry* (New Haven, 1955), 60.

51. Carrie Glasser, "Union Wage Policy in Bituminous Coal," *Industrial and Labor Relations Review,* I (July 1948), 608.

52. Section I, Joint Interstate Agreement, February 19, 1924, reprinted in Bloch, *Labor Agreements,* 360–61.

53. John L. Lewis *The Miners' Fight for America Standards* (Indianapolis, 1925), 15, 186.

54. Hawley, "Secretary Hoover and the Bituminous Coal Problem," 250; Dubofsky and Van Tine, *John L. Lewis,* 107–8; Robert Zieger, *Republicans and Labor, 1919–1929* (Lexington, Ky., 1969), 229–31.

55. John Brophy, "Elements of a Progressive Union Policy," in J. B. S. Hardman, ed., *American Labor Dynamics* (New York, 1928), 186–91.

56. On this episode, see Zieger, *Republicans and Labor,* 239 ff.

57. Waldo E. Fisher and Charles M. James, *Minimum Price Fixing in the Bituminous Coal Industry* (Princeton, N.J., 1955), 18.

58. Johnson, *Politics of Soft Coal,* 131.

59. Ibid., ch. 5; Glen L. Parker, *The Coal Industry: A Study in Social Control* (Washington, D.C., 1940), ch. 6.

60. Johnson, *Politics of Soft Coal,* 153, 163.

61. Gerald G. Somers, *Experience under National Wage Agreements: The Bituminous Coal and Flint Glass Industries of West Virginia* (Morgantown, W.Va., 1953), 22–27; Keith Dix, *What's a Coal Miner to Do? The Mechanization of Coal Mining* (Pittsburgh, 1988).

62. Schedule A, Appalachian Agreement, June 19, 1941.

63. Fisher and James, *Minimum Price Fixing,* passim.

64. Ibid., 7, 17. For an economic analysis of UMWA gains, see Waldo E. Fisher, *Economic Consequences of the Seven-Hour Day and Wage Changes in the Bituminous Coal Industry* (Philadelphia, 1939).

65. Dubofsky and Van Tine, *John L. Lewis,* 390, 416.

66. Colstone E. Warne, "Coal—The First Major Test of the Little Steel Formula," in Warne, ed., *Yearbook of American Labor: War Labor Policies* (New York, 1945), 282–83; Dubofsky and Van Tine, *John L. Lewis,* 417.

67. Warne, "Coal—The First Major Test," 291.

68. For an explanation, see ibid., 297–98.

69. Dubofsky and Van Tine, *John L. Lewis,* 465.

70. Colston E. Warne, "Industrial Relations in Coal," in Warne, ed., *Labor in Postwar America* (Brooklyn, N.Y., 1949), 377. The union fine was subsequently reduced to $700,000.

71. In 1953, Lewis testified in favor of the repeal of the Wagner Act, whose federal protections of the rights of workers to organize and bargain collectively he had so desperately desired in the early 1930s. Dubofsky and Van Tine, *John L. Lewis,* 476.

72. John L. Blackman, *Presidential Seizure in Labor Disputes* (Cambridge, Mass., 1967), 177.

73. I am relying here on Dubofsky and Van Tine, *John L. Lewis,* ch. 20, and 494–97.

74. For a description, see Charles R. Perry, *Collective Bargaining and the Decline of the United Mine Workers* (Philadelphia, 1984), 188–95.

75. Albert Rees, *The Economics of Trade Unions* (Chicago, 1977), 73.

76. C. L. Christenson, *Economic Redevelopment in Bituminous Coal* (Cambridge, Mass., 1962), 268–69.

77. *Pennington v. UMWA* (1965), in Perry, *Collective Bargaining,* 80–82.

78. Christenson, *Economic Redevelopment,* 257–68.

79. I am following the economic analysis in Reed Moyer, *Competition in the Midwestern Coal Industry* (Cambridge, Mass., 1964), chs. 3, 4, 6.

80. Richard H. E. Vietor, *Environmental Politics and the Coal Coalition* (College Station, Texas, 1980), ch. 3, and app. A; Perry, *Collective Bargaining,* 36–38, 65–72; and for regional and surface–deep mining shifts, table 5, Curtis Seltzer, *Fire in the Hole: Miners and Managers in the American Coal Industry* (Lexington, Ky., 1985), 212.

81. Vietor, *Environmental Politics,* ch. 2; Robert Stobaugh and Daniel Yergin, eds., *Energy Future: Report of the Energy Project at the Harvard Business School* (New York, 1979); table 19, Moyer, *Competition in Midwestern Coal,* 68.

82. Perry, *Collective Bargaining,* 26.

83. For a detailed treatment of seniority and job classification issues, see Gerald G. Somers, *Grievance Settlement in Coal Mining* (Morgantown, W. Va., 1956), chs. 4, 5.

84. Perry, *Collective Bargaining,* 29–36.

85. Ibid., 29.

86. Ibid., 231.

87. *New York Times,* January 31, 1988.

88. Leo Troy, "The Rise and Fall of American Trade Unions," in Seymour M. Lipset, ed., *Unions in Transition: Entering the Second Century,* table 7 (San Francisco, 1987), 87.

89. Dubofsky and Van Tine, *John L. Lewis,* 384, 385.

90. In addition to Perry, *Collective Bargaining,* passim, see, e.g., Peter Navarro, "Union Bargaining Power in the Coal Industry, 1945–1981," *Industrial and Labor Relations Review,* 36 (January 1983), 214–19; William H. Miernyk, "Coal," in Gerald G. Somers, ed., *Collective Bargaining: Contemporary American Experience* (Madison, Wis., 1980), 1–48; and, on the internal union history, Brit Hume, *Death and the Mines: Rebellion and Murder in the United Mine Workers* (New York, 1971); Joseph E. Finley, *The Corrupt Kingdom: The Rise and Fall of the United Mine Workers* (New York, 1972); Paul F. Clark, *The Miners' Fight for Democracy: Arnold Miller and the Reform of the United Mine Workers* (Ithaca, N.Y., 1981).

91. For a highly favorable assessment of current UMWA President Richard L. Trumka, however, see, e.g., *Business Week* (February 15, 1988), 65–66.

5

The New Deal, Labor, and World War II

In 1948 Bruce Catton published an angry book about the American war effort. *The War Lords of Washington,* written with an insider's perspective by a newsman (and later famed Civil War historian) who had served as information chief for the War Production Board, took as its central theme the wasted opportunities of World War II. Not that Catton denied the magnitude of the military achievement. On the contrary: "In terms of sheer physical effort, America did the greatest job in the history of the human race."[1] War production multiplied four times in the first year of war and outdistanced the combined output of America's enemies. At the peak in 1944, the country was producing for the military effort alone at a rate nearly as high as the gross national product in 1929. The economy turned out a total of three hundred thousand aircraft, one hundred thousand tanks, seventy thousand landing craft, and the atomic bomb. The accomplishment was all the sweeter because it confounded the initial pessimism about the country's vitality. After the fall of France, from all sides, from Charles Lindbergh on the right to Dwight Macdonald on the left, came dire warnings that American capitalism could never hope to match the dread efficiency of the Nazi war machine.[2] In fact, the American war effort, though slow to start and hardly lacking in mistakes, far surpassed either Germany's or Japan's in the efficient

From John Braeman et al., *The New Deal: The National Level* (Columbus, Ohio: Ohio State University Press, 1975), 267–309. Reprinted with permission.

175

use of national resources for making war.[3] All this Catton granted. But he had another standard for measuring the American performance:

> Do we try to pick up all of our peacetime affairs, after the war, exactly where we were before, in exactly the same old way, as if nothing at all had been changed?
>
> Or do we, on the contrary, accept both change and the need for change, and use this tremendous effort which the people have made in such a way that the nation can adjust itself to the new world which is coming in out of the mist and the smoke?[4]

It was a fair question. For war possessed immense potential as an agent for social reform. The Civil War had led to the freeing of the slaves, had opened the way to the Fourteenth and Fifteenth amendments and Radical Reconstruction, and had, as David Montgomery has demonstrated, generated a potent labor reform movement. World War I— a more pertinent example, perhaps—had given rise to much talk of "industrial democracy" and "reconstruction"; and the domestic war programs had been seen not merely as emergency measures but as experiments containing the seeds of permanent change. True, these high expectations were swiftly punctured by the postwar reaction. But, as William Leuchtenburg and others have pointed out, the war experience was recalled and actively utilized during the Great Depression, both as a precedent for massive government action in a national emergency and as a guideline for New Deal programs in agriculture, labor, industrial recovery, and other fields.[5] For our purposes, however, the more important fact is that World War I did generate a reform impulse: in an explicit way, Americans perceived of the war crisis as an opportunity for building a better society.

In Great Britain during World War II, this connection resulted in a profound change in social policy. From Dunkirk onward, English war leaders began to plan for postwar reconstruction. The official British history of World War II draws this conclusion.

> There existed, so to speak, an implied contract between Government and people; the people refused none of the sacrifices that the Government demanded from them for the winning of the war; in return, they expected that the Government should show imagination and seriousness in preparing for the restoration and improvement of the nation's well-being when the war had been won. The plans for reconstruction were, therefore, a real part of the war effort.

Even before Labour's victory in 1945 and the consequent move toward socialism, a bipartisan commitment had been made for basic reforms in housing, education, health, and social insurance that added up to the welfare state. Reflecting on these events and turning to the evidence of earlier wars (Plutarch's account of the evacuation of Athens during the Persian invasion in 480 B.C. especially influenced him), the eminent historian of British social policy during World War II, Richard M. Titmuss, later arrived at this generalization: that the impact of war on social policy was substantially determined "by how far the co-operation of the masses is essential to the successful prosecution of war."[6]

In World War II nothing like the magnitude of British reform occurred in the United States, nor even, indeed, the kind of abortive movements that had excited both Britain and America during World War I. This is not to deny the powerful impact of the second war on American life. Race relations, internal migration, the status of women, family life—all underwent profound and permanent changes.[7] The character of government also was altered in important ways. The authority and administrative structure of the office of the presidency expanded tremendously, and the "military-industrial complex" took its modern shape. Nor did the war fail to bring about consequential, long-term changes in some areas of public policy, such as the federal financing of scientific research, in the modern tax structure, and in the G.I. Bill of Rights. But all of these had been conceived as war measures, not as vehicles for domestic reform, even where, as in the case of the G.I. Bill, profound social changes did result. In fact, efforts to link veterans' benefits to a broad program of social legislation had made no headway.[8]

What was absent was any momentum to turn the war crisis to reform purposes. On the contrary, the prevailing tendency was to draw a sharp line between the war emergency—and the progressive measures it engendered—and normal times. "Why are the good things a part of war; why can't we have them in peacetime as well?" Philip Murray asked angrily at the moment of victory in 1945.

> Are we concerned about the health and care of mothers and children only when the husband and father is being killed or mutilated? Are we willing to provide housing on the basis of people's needs for it only when soldiers in foxholes have no home or place to lay their head? Are we agreeable to feeding people more adequately when they are making or using the engines of destruction but care nothing about nourishment of the same people when war is done?

"Our citizens are not foolish persons: they will ask all these and a multitude of similar questions." It was the negative side of Murray's outburst that was significant. The beneficial programs of wartime—child care, maternity benefits for servicemen's wives, housing, and much else—had been strictly temporary responses to an emergency situation. And, in 1945, the American people had not yet begun to demand "that the fruit of victory [be] something better than we have ever had before."[9] As for Bruce Catton, he answered his own question: "We never let ourselves build a war effort that would bring us into the peace with a dynamic, this-is-democracy-in-action program."[10]

The burden of this essay is to explore Catton's proposition. He was, in fact, drawing too bleak a conclusion. For the war did make a positive contribution to American reform as a consolidating force for the New Deal. But it did not generate a new thrust forward.[11] On this main score, Catton was indubitably correct. The reasons for that failure are, of course, exceedingly complex; but it is possible, for purposes of analysis, to map out the three operative factors: first, Roosevelt's wartime administration; second, the organized groups or coherent interests capable of using the war to promote reform. The third variable—the impact of war in America—can perhaps best be treated, not separately, but in interaction with the first two.

The Roosevelt administration chose early and probably almost by reflex: it drew a sharp line between the tasks of making war and its commitment to domestic reform. When President Roosevelt spoke jocularly of Dr. New Deal and Dr. Win-the-War at his press conference in December 1943, he was in fact acknowledging the key distinction governing his wartime domestic strategy. Dr. New Deal, who had treated the patient for a grave internal disorder since 1933, "didn't know nothing" about broken bones and so turned the poor fellow, when he suffered a terrible accident on December 7, 1941, over to the orthopedic surgeon Dr. Win-the-War. President Roosevelt had occasion to express this idea in soberer terms. Rejecting as "premature" a proposal in early 1942 for a commission to advise him on ways to improve race relations, Roosevelt responded that "we must start winning the war . . . before we do much general planning for the future." He intended to avoid projects that lead away from "the realities of war. I am not convinced that we can be realists about the war and planners for the future at this critical time."[12] Harry Hopkins, Eleanor Roosevelt wrote, "put the running of the war ahead of everything else. As far as he was concerned, war needs were paramount. My husband felt similarly." Mrs. Roosevelt thought they were wrong. She "could not help feeling that it was the New Deal social objectives that had fostered the spirit that would make it possible for us to fight the war, and I believed it was vastly important to give the people the feeling that in fighting the war we were still really fighting for those same objectives. I felt it was essential both to the prosecution of the war and to the period after the war that the fight for the rights of minorities should continue. . . . I thought the groundwork should be laid for a wide health program after the war."[13]

Why did Roosevelt and Hopkins not share this perception of the connection between war and reform? The nature of the New Deal itself must serve as the starting point. Lacking a comprehensive blueprint for change, lacking even any clear vision of the new society, the New Deal was essentially *reactive* in character; the Great Depression had given it direction and momentum. The outbreak of war in Europe rapidly deprived the New Deal of the crucial stimulus for action. As unemployment shrank during 1940–41 and virtually disappeared by 1943, as farmer purchasing power zoomed by 1943 to almost double the level of 1939, as industrial production rose to record heights by 1943, the urgency vital to Roosevelt's brand of reformism departed. Indeed, the crisis mode of thinking that had shaped the New Deal now worked counter to reform; war posed the great emergency now, and Roosevelt, temperamentally inclined as he was to deal with the immediate and the concrete, would not turn his attention from the war effort.

Nor did he easily accept his wife's conviction that a reform appeal would advance the prosecution of the war. In part, this too was a matter of temperament. He was not inclined to elevate wartime emotions into a domestic crusade, as Woodrow Wilson had done during World War I. Characteristically, when a strike during the summer of 1941 was forcing the government to take over a vital shipyard at Kearny, New Jersey, Roosevelt prompted the head of the National Defense Mediation Board to appeal (unofficially) to the selfish interests of both sides: saying to the company that government compensation for seizure would be less than it anticipated; to the union that the navy would give it an inferior contract.[14] This matter-of-fact approach, characteristic of Roosevelt's wartime leadership, hardly left room for the heady promises of "reconstruction" made by Wilson and the Committee on Public Information during World War I.

More than temperament was at work here. Accommodation was the essential mode of New Deal operation. Roosevelt always sought—with declining success in later years, to be sure—to win the approval and cooperation of the groups affected by his programs. This remained preeminently his method in meeting the military crisis. When the War Resources Board in 1939 put forward its Industrial Mobilization Plan concentrating extraordinary wartime powers in the hands of a military-industrial agency, labor, agriculture, and liberals generally raised furious objections. Roosevelt hastily dismissed the board and shelved the plan. Likewise, Roosevelt opposed punitive measures against labor when strikes seriously impeded the defense effort in 1941.[15] But the primary test of the accommodating strategy was posed by the peacetime opponents of the New Deal. Could Roosevelt secure the total support of American industry? This seemed absolutely crucial to the president, and from the first he worked assiduously to carry businessmen fully with him into war mobilization. On one point they were peculiarly sensitive: a *Fortune* survey in November 1941 revealed that three-quarters of American businessmen feared that Roosevelt would use the war crisis for reform purposes.[16] This suspicion, easily aroused and ever present, severely circumscribed Roosevelt's sense of what might be done during the war.

So did congressional politics. Roosevelt's troubles here antedated the war, of course. The presidential party (as James MacGregor Burns would put it) had begun to lose ground on Capitol Hill almost as soon as Roosevelt had won his great victory of 1936. Sharp Republican gains in 1938, plus the emergence of the southern Democratic–Republican coalition, solidified the conservative grip on Congress. Roosevelt's own successes in 1940 and 1944 did not translate into appreciably greater power in Congress. And New Dealers suffered heavy losses in the crucial mid-war congressional elections in November 1942. The Republicans captured forty-four additional seats in the House (thirteen short of a majority), nine in the Senate (nine short of a majority). Democratic losses in the North, moreover, increased the relative power of the southern Democrats, and their sense of independence was further enhanced by wartime prosperity in the South and by suspicion of the administration's intentions on race relations. The conservative coalition reached the apex of its effectiveness in 1943–44.[17]

The Seventy-eighth Congress was remarkable for its fierce hostility to the New Deal. Roosevelt himself came to regard it as a Republican Congress, as well he might in view of the succession of defeats he suffered on Capitol Hill. The conservative coalition emasculated the Farm Security Administration and ended the Works Progress Administration, the National Youth Administration, and the Civilian Conservation Corps. Such New Deal agencies, asserted Congressman John Taber, "should be dropped, not only for the duration of the war, but forever."[18] The Seventy-eighth Congress overrode a presidential veto of the 1944 tax bill that Roosevelt decried for "providing relief not for the needy but for the greedy." This was the first major revenue bill in history to become law over a veto.[19] In 1944 the Senate rejected the Murray-Kilgore bill strengthening unemployment insurance coverage of war workers during reconversion and extending federal responsibility on employment matters; the more modest George bill on this subject went down to defeat in the House after passing the Senate.

In 1942 one Republican House leader vowed to "win the war from the New Deal." If conservatives could not manage that, they could at least be sure to prevent the war from advancing the New Deal. When the Department of Labor requested an appropriation to investigate absenteeism in war work, objections were raised that Frances Perkins seemed "more concerned about social gains than in winning the war."[20] This kind of mistrust actually went back to well before the Seventy-eighth Congress. In 1940 a Defense Housing Act was passed to meet critical housing shortages in defense plant areas. At House insistence, the measure prohibited any conversion of defense housing to public-housing use after the emergency without specific congressional authorization. "The New Dealers are determined to make the country over under the cover of war if they can," warned Senator Robert Taft in January 1942.[21]

Severe congressional opposition would, at any time, have blunted Roosevelt's reform impulse. The New Deal was intensely *political* in its orientation, depending always on a close calculation of congressional prospects. Roosevelt was never inclined to take up a legislative battle that could not be won (or at least pay dividends at the polls): hence the virtual abandonment of New Deal expansion after the legislative and election setbacks of 1937–38. The paralyzing effect of Roosevelt's political realism was compounded by another kind of realism arising from the war crisis. The essential support that he needed from Congress, Roosevelt felt, was for his military program and for his internationalist diplomacy. And he was entirely willing to accept a trade-off on domestic issues. This is, in fact, what transpired. Congressional relations with the White House developed a remarkable schizophrenia—partisan and negative on matters of domestic policy, bipartisan and supportive in carrying on the war and making the peace. The president seemed satisfied. He was, of course, saddened at the loss of so ancient an ally as George Norris, whose defeat summed up the conservative mood of the country in November 1942. But, on the whole, he viewed with evident equanimity the outcome of that election.[22] Only on a few rare occasions was he roused to make a fighting issue of congressional conservatism, for he was getting what he really deemed essential from Capitol Hill.

Nor was Roosevelt inclined even to follow the initiative of congressional liberals when they took up the battle in June 1943. The Wagner-Murray-Dingell bill, which drew among other sources from the recommendations of FDR's own planners, proposed a comprehensive revamping of the nation's social security system: nationalizing those parts under state control; improving the benefits and expanding the coverage of existing programs; adding compulsory health insurance; and providing benefits for veterans. Roosevelt saw the omnibus measure only after it was drafted. He wished Senator Wagner "good luck with it," but lent it little or no administration support, notwithstanding that, as Wagner's biographer notes, the bill "quickly became the focal point of New Dealers' hopes for the postwar future."[23] The president was careful, in fact, not to put a reform stamp on measures he did actively support. When Frances Perkins was preparing a speech for social security changes, he asked her to emphasize "that this is not, what some people call, a New Deal measure."[24] And he was willing to trade the scheduled increase in social security contributions for Senator Vandenberg's support in foreign policy.[25]

The natural bent of the Roosevelt administration to abandon reform during a war crisis was, finally, deeply exaggerated by the way war actually came to America. For more than two years after the German invasion of Poland, the United States stayed formally at peace. Roosevelt led a country still largely isolationist in sentiment and unwilling to go on a war footing. Always far ahead of the country on the need for American intervention, yet never daring to call the country to arms, Roosevelt had to follow a tortuous course that, as events permitted, involved the country by slow steps in the Allied cause and that brought about a sadly incomplete form of mobilization. The logic against reform operated with peculiar force during the defense period, when Roosevelt was bending every effort to carry his domestic opposition (as well as much of the New Deal support) with him in the deepening world crisis. The defense experience in turn helped shape an accommodating pattern that would apply throughout the war. Once Pearl Harbor plunged the nation into war, division was replaced by unity, irresolution by a national determination to go all out in the war effort. This dramatic reversal, ironically, also worked counter to war reform. After December 7, 1941, Roosevelt never had to worry about justifying American involvement in the war. He did not need to generate war enthusiasm by grand promises of "reconstruction," as Woodrow Wilson had felt compelled to do during World War I. (Confidence in national unity, in fact, goes a long way toward explaining why World War II did not generate the kind of evangelism—repressive as well as progressive—that marked World War I.)

On the other hand, the urgency of the war emergency tended to strengthen Roosevelt's inclination to concentrate on the immediate and the critical, and hence to divorce the war effort from matters of domestic policy.

So, if World War II was to bring reform the effort would have to come not from Washington but from the private sector. Black protest suggested the possibilities. Outraged at being shut out of the defense industries in 1940–41, African Americans began to demand effective government action against discriminatory hiring, as well as an end to segregation in the armed forces. The founder of the March on Washington Movement, A. Philip Randolph, concluded from a meeting with Roosevelt that talk would not bring justice. He came away from the White House, a subordinate later recalled, "understanding that the government was not going to give you anything unless you made them. . . . The President . . . was not going to take the leadership . . . unless he had to." He seemed, in fact, to invite Randolph to put pressure on him.[26] So black leaders rejected Roosevelt's plea to call off the march on Washington. And then the president, responding characteristically to political realities, issued on June 25, 1941, the historic Executive Order 8802 that prohibited job discrimination in federal government and in defense industry and set up the Fair Employment Practices Committee as the policing agency.

Countering pressures from the South and from industry and labor placed severe limits on the concrete achievements of the March on Washington Movement. Roosevelt actually conceded a good deal less than the MOWM had demanded.[27] And Executive Order 8802 was only weakly enforced, starved as FEPC was for funds by a hostile Congress and housed as it was in a war administration anxious to keep the lid on the race issue. The crucial weakness was the dependence on moral suasion; not once was a war contract withdrawn for failure to comply with an FEPC order. Obviously, in the final calculation production needs outweighed racial justice. Manpower shortages actually played the more important part in breaking down discrimination in employment and segregation in the military services.

Executive Order 8802 nevertheless marked a major advance, not only for the immediate accomplishments of the FEPC, but as the first step in making public policy an instrument against racial discrimination. Thus, during 1943 the War Labor Board prohibited wage differentials based on race, the U.S. Employment Service began to refuse to process requests that specified the race of applicants, and the National Labor Relations Board ruled that it would not certify unions that excluded minorities. (This went some way toward satisfying an original MOWM demand for a change in the Wagner Act to deny coverage to unions barring blacks from membership.) And the precedent had been established for more effective and far-reaching use of public policy against discrimination in the postwar period, first at the state level and then increasingly by the federal government.

For purposes of this discussion, in any case, the significance of FEPC is as a demonstration of the mechanics of wartime reform. The Roosevelt administration continued to rely on broker politics, shaping policy by a close calculation of the relative power of claimant groups. And the war emergency altered the prevailing balance; disadvantaged groups now were in a more strategic position to press their claims for reform. The March on Washington Movement could hardly have posed so potent a threat before 1941. But would the opportunity be seized? On this crucial point, African Americans were in fact quite exceptional. For them, war generated militancy, in part because of bitter memories of World War I, in part because of the discrepancy between war ideals and realities at home, and, probably most important, because of the frustration at seeing opportunities open up and be foreclosed to them because of discrimination (and, in fact, black protest did tend to subside as the bars to employment and military service fell later in the war). With its emphasis on economic issues, on exclusively black partici- pation, and on mass action, the March on Washington Movement pi- oneered a new pattern of black protest. It was during World War II, as Richard Dalfiume has stressed, that the modern civil rights movement got its start.

But for other Americans the war led not toward militancy but toward conservatism. This result occurred in two discernible ways. Most im- portant, of course, war brought good times. Unemployment dropped from roughly nine million in July 1940 to an irreducible minimum of under eight hundred thousand in September 1943. Tenant farmers and migratory laborers moved in large numbers to defense centers—the sad odyssey of John Steinbeck's Joad family doubtless ended on time-and- a-half in some aircraft plant in southern California. Weekly earnings in manufacturing industries went up by 80 percent between January 1941 and January 1945, partly due to an eight-hour increase in the work week, partly to the advance of hourly earnings by nearly 60 percent. Since consumer prices rose by only 30 percent during this period, industrial workers experienced a very substantial increase in real in- come. And for many families, this was augmented by the entry of five million women into the labor force, as well as of large numbers of teenagers. The upward-levelling effect of the war was most dramatically expressed in the shrinkage of the share of national income from 23.7 to 16.8 percent going to the top 5 percent of Americans between 1939 and 1944.

The political consequences struck home in the congressional elections of 1942. The Republican gains came not so much from any notable shift of voters as from the failure of Democrats to turn out at the polls. Comparing the 1938 and 1942 congressional elections, the public- opinion expert John Harding concluded *"that the main source of the Republican gains was the almost total disappearance of the WPA."*[28] (The Democrats also disproportionately suffered from the loss of votes of young men in the army and of workers on the move.) Insofar as economic hardship had rendered voters and interest groups reform minded, that factor was essentially neutralized by the war boom.

There was a second reason why key interest groups who might have done so did not think of the war in terms of reform. The New Deal had done its work too well, for it had already created the basic mechanisms through which both agriculture and labor could advance their interests in wartime. Organized agriculture was entirely content to function within the system of price supports written into the second Agricultural Adjustment Act of 1938. Although designed to deal with the problem of surplus, the parity system could also be put to profitable use in a time of war shortage. The key was to peg the basic commodities at a high parity level. Prodded by farm spokesmen, Congress set the minimum for commodity loan rates at 85 percent of parity in May 1941, then raised it to 110 percent in January 1942. Given greater shortages of some nonbasic crops, these levels created an abnormally high floor from which incentives would then have to be generated to encourage shifts in production from less critical basic crops such as short staple cotton. This was hardly the best system for bringing agricultural production in line with war needs, or for advancing Roosevelt's campaign for price stabilization.

The American Farm Bureau Federation won some of the ensuing battles with the administration and lost a few. The Economic Stabilization Act of October 1942 forced the parity level down to 90 percent; but agriculture got important concessions in return: first, the inclusion of labor costs in the parity formula, and, second, the provision that the price supports would continue for two years after the war as insurance against the price collapse that had befallen American agriculture after World War I. The results were likewise mixed on the struggle over the use of subsidy methods. The Farm Bureau Federation and its allies preferred price increases (beyond parity levels, of course) and were able to defeat an administration move in 1943 to use incentive payments to help shift agricultural production to meet essential war needs. On the other hand, subsidies came into wide use—at the rate of $1.6 billion a year in 1945—as a means of holding the line on consumer food prices.

On the whole, American farmers fared very well during the war: net income per person in agriculture in 1945 was three times the 1935–39 level, whereas annual income for industrial workers only doubled during the period. But the crucial point, for purposes of this discussion, was the way farmers sought to rely on existing mechanisms to advance their interests. Far from opening up new possibilities, the war reinforced adherence to the system of farm price supports gained during the New Deal. "Farm groups, with the exception of the Farmers Union, have no positive program for additional basic legislation,'' remarked a Wisconsin farm expert in 1947.[29]

Organized labor went through a comparable experience. The National Labor Relations Act of 1935 had already granted what trade unionists deemed essential, namely, effective protection of the right to organize and to engage in collective bargaining. Their impulse was to exploit the defense crisis, not to seek reform but rather to make better use of the existing framework, particularly since they had discovered that depression conditions limited the benefits to be derived from the Wagner Act. John L. Lewis gave the most striking demonstration of labor's aims. In early 1940, Lewis began to press President Roosevelt to repay political debts to labor: the CIO president wanted defense contracts withheld from any firm that was not complying with the Wagner Act. (Roosevelt's refusal partly explained Lewis's break with FDR during the presidential campaign.)[30] Lewis's extremism was perhaps exceptional, but not his eagerness to use the war emergency to advance conventional trade-union interests. All through the defense period and the war itself, the union movement carried on assiduous organizing work, exploiting labor's strategic advantages and making full use of the mechanisms of the National Labor Relations Board. The result was phenomenal growth: membership went up from nine to fifteen million between 1939 and 1945.

No less important than numbers was the union stability gained during the war. Here, too, John L. Lewis was the bellwether. The defense emergency gave him the opportunity to launch a campaign for the union shop in the captive mines during the fall of 1941. In the face of unyielding steel companies, a storm of popular disapproval, and an adverse decision from the National Defense Mediation Board, Lewis pressed his advantage—three times he called his miners out on brief strikes—and forced the deeply resentful Roosevelt to undercut the NDMB, create a special arbitration board to decide the issue, and, by this stratagem, give to Lewis the union shop in the captive mines. On the whole, the rest of organized labor took a more moderate line (and disavowed, in fact, Lewis's strong-arm methods, especially after the war began), but it too strove for union security. The result was a quite favorable compromise—maintenance of membership, that is, the requirement that made membership compulsory during the life of a contract for those already in a union—which the National War Labor Board employed to resolve the thorny issue of union security. By the end of 1945, this formula covered 29 percent of all workers under union contracts, and, especially in the traditionally open-shop industries, played a crucial role in putting trade unionism on a stable basis.[31]

Labor's organizational gains during the war, though deriving at least as much from emergency conditions as from the role of the NLRB, nevertheless were an extension of the growth process started by the Wagner Act and, more important, held labor's mind very much within the frame of reference under which that law had been adopted. The war was no time to fool with new ideas.

A negative part of labor's war experience reinforced that conclusion. To a markedly greater degree than for agriculture, labor had to accept a departure from normal practice in its affairs. Free collective bargaining, which the Wagner Act had been designed to foster, could not in fact be permitted to prevail during wartime. Labor leaders gave a voluntary no-strike pledge immediately after Pearl Harbor. On January 12, 1942, President Roosevelt created the National War Labor Board with the authority to settle "labor disputes which might interrupt work which contributes to the effective prosecution of the war." By common consent and by the use of presidential war powers, therefore, the right to strike came to an end (although violations of the rule, both actual and threatened, kept the strike issue inflamed throughout the war). The need to control inflation soon eliminated what remained of normal collective bargaining, namely, the freedom to make contractual agreements that did not involve labor disputes. With the passage of the Economic Stabilization Act of October 1942, government control over voluntary wage increases began, using as a guideline the Little Steel Formula that pegged wage stabilization at the level of real wages as of January 1, 1941. The application of this rule became very stringent once the president issued his "hold the line" executive order of April 8, 1943.

Compulsion of this kind, even admitting its necessity, would have been hard for American labor to accept under the best of circumstances. And, as it happened, circumstances seemed far from best to union leaders. They unceasingly charged the administration with unfairness: government statistics underestimated price increases; actual economic needs of workers received too little consideration; and, worst of all, salaries, profits, and prices lacked the stringent controls placed on wages. Wage earners were making "a disproportionate sacrifice relative to other groups."[32] At least, the unions had equal representation with management on the National War Labor Board. But, as the stabilization policy tightened, control over wage regulation shifted to James F. Byrnes's Office of Economic Stabilization, where labor had no effective voice and little influence.

Labor's wariness was fostered, finally, by the visible hardening of public opinion against the union movement during the war. President Roosevelt, for example, received in June 1943 a confidential survey that asked leading people to estimate opinion in their congressional districts: 81 percent believed the local feeling was that the administration had "bungled" on labor; asked to select the major local criticism of the administration from a list, 49 percent chose "Labor Policies too Soft. Should Stop Strikes." This hostile sentiment, brought to white heat by John L. Lewis and his miners' strikes, resulted in the passage of the punitive Smith-Connally War Labor Disputes Act, which gave to President Roosevelt more power over strikes than he wanted (the measure passed over his veto) and, additionally, restricted the use of union funds for political activity. No wonder, then, that organized labor thought no further than of a return to the status quo after the war. Most unionists applauded the lifting of controls over wages and strikes and ignored President Truman's request that they continue the no-strike pledge during the reconversion period.[33]

For both agriculture and labor, therefore, World War II provided an experience of a quite different order than had World War I. In 1917, neither had yet found ways to counterbalance its structural weaknesses in the economic order. World War I had produced answers: price supports for farmers, protection of organizing rights for workers. From these starting points, effective public mechanisms had been perfected during the New Deal. The second war experience acted wholly to reinforce the adherence of both agriculture and labor to the existing framework.

So the cause of reform lacked either of the kinds of champion capable of promoting significant change through the American political system. Neither from the public sector nor from the private sector did there arise a compelling initiative to seize on the war crisis for reform purposes. The blunting of that possibility can perhaps best be studied in the handling of industrial mobilization—first, because this offered the central opportunity, and, second, because it did evoke one genuine proposal for basic change.

Late in 1940, Walter Reuther, then a youthful vice president of the United Automobile Workers of America in charge of the union's General Motors division, came forward with an imaginative plan for speeding up the lagging program for aircraft production. At the time, the official program called for the construction of new facilities specifically designed for the manufacture of war planes. The projected plants would not be fully operative until late in 1942. Meanwhile, Britain was battling for her life, and the United States was drawing ever closer to war. Why not make use of idle capacity in the automobile industry? Himself an old tool-and-die man, Reuther had been studying the problem for months. Having gathered data on available plant facilities and skilled labor and having conferred at length with design engineers and skilled machinists, he concluded that automobile plants could be readily converted to aircraft manufacture. The second part of Reuther's plan involved the pooling of the industry's technical resources and idle production facilities for this massive project. Plants of the various companies would be assigned the manufacture of plane parts, and assembly would take place at a few central points. (Reuther had in mind the idle Hupmobile plant in Detroit as the central motor assembly plant.) "We propose to transform the entire unused capacity of the automotive industry into one huge plane production unit," asserted Reuther. His dramatic plan advanced a third idea: an aviation production board, drawn equally from government, management, and labor, and with "full authority to organize and supervise the mass production of airplanes in the automobile and automotive parts industry."[34]

The Reuther plan was actually the foremost expression of a broader CIO approach to defense. The Roosevelt administration was obviously groping toward centralized direction of industrial mobilization, first in a very halting way with the revival of National Defense Advisory Commission in May 1940 (based on statutory powers going back to World War I), then somewhat more vigorously in the formation of the Office of Production Management in January 1941. On December 18, 1940, Philip Murray urged President Roosevelt instead to turn the defense effort over to industrial councils (such as the proposed aviation production board). The CIO chief wanted control to be housed in each industry, not in a Washington agency whose efforts were clearly "unwieldy, inefficient and unfunctional." A national defense board would retain supervisory functions, but not direct administrative authority over industrial activity. The ineffectiveness of the Office of Production Management quickly gave point to Murray's argument on this score. Finally, full labor participation both on the national board and in the industrial councils capped the CIO scheme. To achieve industrial peace, and the fullest effort from American workers, Roosevelt would have to give labor "a voice in matters of [industrial] policy and administration."[35] In the following months, CIO unions developed specific plans for steel, aluminum, farm equipment, and nonferrous metals, but it was the Reuther scheme that evoked the greatest interest. At a time when the nation's most pressing need was for aircraft production, no rallying cry could have been more arresting than Reuther's call for five hundred planes a day within six months.

The CIO proposals stressed immediate problems. "Emergency requires short-cut solutions," said Reuther. "This plan is labor's answer to a crisis."[36] But it also laid the basis for far-reaching reform of the economic order. The struggle to organize the mass-production industries had generated an authentic thrust that went beyond pure-and-simple unionism. From among old labor progressive types such as John Brophy and Powers Hapgood who had rallied to the industrial-union cause, from young leaders such as the Reuther brothers and James Carey who had sprung from the rank-and-file, came a keen sense that the CIO was destined for more than business unionism.[37] If the reform impulse proved short-lived, if John L. Lewis and Sidney Hillman too quickly became fallen idols, if factional battles with the Communists consumed too much of the initial idealism, if the day-to-day practice of collective bargaining swiftly diverted energies into the conventional trade-union mold, CIO progressivism was nevertheless briefly a genuine phenomenon, and one still much alive when war broke out in Europe. The industrial-council notion sprang from these labor progressives, who saw in labor's participation in the management of defense industry the prospect of permanent economic reform.

"The heart of the Murray plan is the proposal for Industrial Councils," John Brophy explained.

> This matter of production cannot be handled by issuing orders at Washington. It can only be handled by men who are intimately familiar with the peculiar production problems of their own industries. . . . The participation of labor is particularly important in order to guarantee that profits are not placed above the national interest in this emergency. It is essential likewise to the full protection of civil and industrial rights of the American people.

The council plan would serve "as a valuable method for the post-war world." Observers saw the implications as well. The Reuther proposal, remarked Walter Lippmann, was "of such historic importance" because it represented "the first great plan which organized labor had offered in its status not of a hired man but of the responsible partner." The radical journalist I. F. Stone perceived in the Murray plan "the beginnings of a kind of industrial democracy far better suited to the spirit of the American people than either control by a few men through monopoly or control by a few men through a Socialist bureaucracy. . . . If our businessmen, our workers, our engineers, learn to work in harness together in the job of defending America, they will learn how to reconstruct America . . . in the flexible framework of a co-operative industrial democracy."[38]

The history of the CIO plan reveals in a concrete way the interplay of forces that blunted the reform potential of World War II. The fate of Reuther's conversion scheme tells part of the story. Anxious to speed up aircraft production, President Roosevelt liked the conversion idea and issued orders that it be given full consideration. Others in his administration, both liberal advisers and defense officials, were enthusiastic. But the automobile companies objected. They denied the technical feasibility of conversion to aircraft production: plant floor space was too small, machine tools not easily altered and in any case not up to the low tolerance requirements for plane engines, and massproduction techniques not applicable to the complex problems of aircraft manufacture. Underlying this was a denial that national needs called for so drastic a departure from business-as-usual. The auto makers gladly undertook large contracts for building new aircraft facilities, but they wanted their business in the civilian car market left undisturbed. Ironically, the defense program boomed domestic demand: cars were rolling off the assembly lines at an annual rate of five million by the spring of 1941, and the year would ultimately prove to be the second largest in the industry's history. The Reuther proposal actually did not call for any cutbacks in civilian production (one of the practical motives behind the plan was to create jobs for idle auto workers); but it did contemplate such far-reaching departures from normal industry practice as postponement of new models, leveling production over the whole year, and pooling of equipment and technical data. Moreover, the way would have been opened for readily shifting from civilian production as defense needs required it. The administrative arrangements that Roosevelt had set up to run the defense program virtually foreclosed the possibility of overriding the industry's resistance to conversion. The Office of Production Management was manned by executives drawn from business; and, as it happened, the head was William Knudsen, formerly president of General Motors. Knudsen and his associates took the same negative view of conversion as did the industry, and thereby assured the rejection of the idea.[39]

As 1941 passed, pressure built up on the auto industry for conversion from a different direction. Shortages of strategic materials raised demands from within the War and Navy departments for the curtailment of civilian output. Moving haltingly, the OPM in mid-April announced a 20 percent cut in auto production effective August 1, 1941. It was, ironically, the agency charged with civilian problems, Leon Henderson's Office of Price Administration and Civilian Supply, that forced the issue by ordering a 50 percent reduction in car output on July 20. Prodded into action, Knudsen gave the auto industry a quota of 51.4 percent of 1941 production for the year beginning August 1, 1941. But the curtailment was to be gradual, rising from only a 6.5 percent cut in the first quarter to 62 percent in the last. Nor did the administration have any substantial success in its intensifying efforts to bring about conversion in the auto industry (which was one of the aims of curtailment). Knudsen held back, and Roosevelt, despite his increasing restiveness, was unwilling to take the auto makers on directly. Until Pearl Harbor, they had their way; auto production went on essentially unabated almost up to the outbreak of war. Nothing told more about Roosevelt's accommodating strategy during the defense period than his failure to extract a greater contribution from Detroit.[40]

Pearl Harbor at last brought decisive action. The government quickly ordered a complete halt to car production and announced that it was prepared to place five billion dollars worth of military contracts with the industry. Spurred by these moves and by the crisis itself, the car makers proceeded to convert their plants rapidly to war production—not, to be sure, to the manufacture of complete aircraft, as Reuther had proposed, but to aircraft parts, tanks, machine guns, and so on. By June 1942, the industry was using 66 percent of its machine tools on military goods. Late in the war, the president of Chrysler boasted that his company had converted 89 percent of its automotive capacity to war work.[41] This order of productive achievement, reproduced throughout American industry, signified the country's willingness and ability to take extreme measures in the war crisis. After Pearl Harbor, it was agreed on all sides that the situation demanded a radical departure from business-as-usual—the more so, ironically, because so much had been left undone in the defense period.

But the barriers to reform did not come down: radical measures there would have to be, but not such as would threaten the status quo. The other side of the Reuther plan—the industrial council idea—provides us with a starting point. Industry was, of course, unalterably opposed to any notion of labor participation in management. In fact, sensitivity on this score evidently had something to do with the refusal to give the technical aspects of the scheme a trial. "They wanted to come into the shop as a union committee and try to design fixtures for the present machinery," Knudsen remarked in March 1941. "We had to stall on that one and say that it couldn't be handled." When Reuther renewed his demand for labor participation in industrial direction after the United States entered the war, General Motors President Charles E. Wilson answered sharply that "to divide the responsibility of management would be to destroy the very foundations upon which America's unparalleled record of accomplishment is built." If Reuther wanted a place in management, General Motors would be glad to hire him. (Reuther declined.)[42]

Throughout the war, business displayed intense hostility to any intrusion on managerial prerogatives. Even the War Production Board's modest program for plant joint committees ran into rough going and required repeated assurances that the sole objective was more production. Hence, for example, this statement by four national labor and business leaders a year after the campaign had been launched in 1942:

> The labor-management committee program . . . , endorsed by us, is not designed to increase the power or position of any union. It does not interfere with any bargaining machinery or undertake its functions. It is not designed to conform to any scheme that contemplates a measure of control of management by labor or labor by management. . . . It is the War Production Drive Plan to increase production by increasing efficiency through greater management and labor cooperation.

"This is probably the most completely negative bit of sales talk in the history of salesmanship," remarked Bruce Catton.[43] At the president's National Labor-Management Conferences in 1945, business placed managerial inviolability at the center of its program for postwar labor relations.[44] Given Roosevelt's accommodating strategy toward business, its objections would have doubtless constituted a veto of labor participation in any case.

But, as it happened, countering pressure from the labor movement, which might have made some difference, was largely absent. The AFL expressed indifference; it preferred adequate labor representation on government agencies. William Green himself was puzzled: Why should labor be interested in a managerial role? When war came, the federation called for a truce in which neither labor nor management would exploit wartime controls "to prosecute either's advantage at the expense of the other." Within the CIO, too, conventional union elements were cool to the idea, and the left was hotly opposed from start to finish. Before June 22, 1941, the Communists branded the Murray plan as a form of warmongering and a scheme for labor speed-up. Afterward, they regarded it as a vexatious impediment to fullest cooperation for maximum war production. When the United Electrical Workers (UE) urged its locals to set up joint plant committees, it stressed one point: "The authority to run the plant is in the hands of management." To reassure employers who feared a loss of authority, Julius Emspak explained, "We made it perfectly and unmistakably clear that we are not interested in 'taking over' a plant; we have but one interest, and that is increasing the plant's production."[45] The industrial-council idea, in fact, drew its support almost wholly from the liberal wing of the CIO, especially from those elements identified with the Association of Catholic Trade Unionists. Philip Murray, a devout Catholic, said that his plan "follow[ed] . . . almost completely" Pius XI's social encyclical of 1931. Nor did most of its advocates give the industrial-council proposal more than ritual support after the American entry into the war. Although the CIO actively revived the idea in 1944 as "one of the surest methods" for solving the problems of reconversion, no real attempt was made to formulate the plan into a workable program, and in the postwar years it served primarily to establish the progressive credentials of the anti-Communist left within the CIO. Only Walter Reuther made a fight for labor's right to participate in management after the war: that was the point, for example, of his unsuccessful battle to force General Motors to open its books for inspection as a condition for raising prices to meet UAW wage demands.[46]

On March 28, 1945, both the AFL and CIO had signed with the U.S. Chamber of Commerce a New Charter for Labor and Management that, while proclaiming full employment, high wages, and labor's right to organize, also proclaimed a free-enterprise system with managerial prerogatives protected and a minimum of governmental interference.[47] Labor's treatment of the industrial-council proposal reveals the larger point: that it was a "satisfied" movement, quite incapable during World War II of seeking in the war crisis an opportunity to bring about reform.

With industry rigidly opposed and labor at heart apathetic, the Roosevelt administration would hardly do otherwise than turn down the industrial-council plan. It was left to labor's own man in the defense administration, Sidney Hillman, to administer the final blow when, in mid-December 1941, he concluded that the country "cannot delegate to any combination of private interests final decision on matters of basic policy."[48] How, then, would industrial mobilization take place? It was part of Roosevelt's genius as a war leader to devise an answer that resolved the dilemma: to take radical action but not to threaten the status quo.

There were three components to Roosevelt's answer. The primary one was an extraordinary centralization of control over the war effort. On January 16, 1942, the president created the War Production Board and lodged in it all his constitutional war powers (as supplemented by Congress) as these bore on industrial mobilization. Executive Order 9024 directed the WPB chairman to "exercise general direction over the war procurement and production program . . . including conversion, requisitioning, plant expansion, and the financing thereof . . . and his decisions shall be final." Nor was this immense power to be delegated out to industry committees, as the War Industries Board had done during World War I. All powers of decision would remain in the hands of WPB personnel. One of Chairman Donald Nelson's first actions was to appoint a WPB official to take charge of the conversion of the auto industry and to dissolve the meeting of management and labor representatives considering this problem. Labor and industry committees would be strictly limited to advisory roles, Nelson said at the first meeting of the War Production Board. Overall direction of industrial conversion and production went to a Division of Industry Operations, with industry branches in charge of each manufacturing industry.[49]

But if this centralization of power was unprecedented in its completeness, it was also emphatically temporary and narrowly confined to the specific task of war-making. This was among the reasons, Robert Sherwood has suggested, that Roosevelt deliberately separated the war agencies from the regular federal bureaucracy.[50] The War Production Board, moreover, carefully limited its decisions to matters touching the war effort. The board, for example, ordered that production be concentrated in full-operation facilities in such industries as sugar refining that were functioning below capacity. Should the owners of the idled plants be compensated for their resulting losses, either by government subsidy or by pooling the industry's income? The WPB turned down the idea because, as its general counsel remarked, "compensation involves policy questions with respect to social planning which should be determined by higher authority."[51]

This strategy expressed itself, finally, in the refusal to set aside the antitrust laws. By the time the defense crisis began in 1938–39, New Freedom proponents such as Robert Jackson and Thurman Arnold had gained the upper hand within the Roosevelt administration; and, with the appointment of John Lord O'Brian as general counsel of the Office of Production Management (and then WPB), they succeeded in committing the administration to operating within the framework of existing antitrust legislation for the duration. This did not mean that the normal rules of competition would continue to apply, but rather that the anticipated departures would be at the direction of government agencies, not of private industry as during 1917–18. Industry committees could only be advisory, the members would be selected not by trade associations but by the government, and recommendations would require the approval of the Department of Justice before WPB industry branches could act on them. To regularize the procedure for authorizing the necessary violations of antitrust laws, the WPB chairman was empowered in June 1942 to grant Certificates of Immunity, after consultation with the attorney general, for firms so operating at WPB request.[52]

By centralizing economic control in the government and by drawing a sharp division between the war program and permanent public policy, the Roosevelt administration devised a radical form of industrial mobilization that contained no seeds of reform. Government control over industry hardly seemed a desired blueprint for peacetime. And any thinking in this direction would be cut short by the emphasis on the strictly temporary character of the war program. There was a third component to the administration's strategy. The war program had to be so implemented as to give no alarm to the nation's industrial interests.

The starting point was the selection of a chairman for the War Production Board. Secretary of War Henry Stimson admonished the president not to pick anyone with an antibusiness reputation. Roosevelt had initially preferred Supreme Court Justice William Douglas (against whom Stimson was especially warning him), but he finally chose Donald Nelson, whose credentials could hardly have been better for meeting the conflicting requirements for a production czar. A former Sears, Roebuck executive, he was identified neither with Wall Street nor with big business; he was held in high regard in New Deal circles; and, as executive director of the Supplies Priorities and Allocations Board, he stood out as an energetic all-outer during the irresolute defense effort.[53] But Nelson was also a safe man from the standpoint of those who would be subject to his sweeping powers. He was, for one thing, not personally inclined to use those powers unreservedly. Conciliatory and patient by temperament, Nelson sought to get "action in the democratic way without dictatorial tactics." Deeply imbued with the virtues of the American productive system, moreover, Nelson did not believe it was up to him "to *tell* industry how to do its job; it was our function to *show* industry what had to be done, and then to do everything in our power to enable industry to do it, placing our chief reliance on the limitless energy and skill of American manufacturers. . . . What we did was to establish a set of rules under which the game could be played the way industry said it had to play it."[54]

Business was quickly reassured by Nelson's manner of administration. Not only was the WPB staffed by people drawn from business, but key posts—over eight hundred by 1943—were held by dollar-a-year men on loan from their companies. Nelson defended the latter policy from persistent criticism by the Truman committee on grounds of expediency; essential high-level people would not come on low government salaries. Nor was WPB policy against heading industry branches with executives associated with those industries regularly followed. Aside from the branch chief, in any case, staff tended to be recruited from the same industries. So the control emanating from Washington was a good deal more comfortable in practice than it might have seemed in theory. And the industry advisory committees, specifically excluded as they were from making or carrying out policy, in fact collaborated very closely with the WPB branches and exerted substantial influence over the decisions affecting their industries.

Labor received, by contrast, a quite different welcome on the WPB. Largely indifferent to the Murray plan as it was, the labor movement from the first did press for a major part in governmental direction of industrial mobilization. In a formal way, trade unionism came closest to that goal during the defense period when Sidney Hillman served as associate director general of the Office of Production Management. As it happened, Hillman's participation hardly satisfied organized labor: the AFL considered him a CIO man; the CIO had not chosen him; and Hillman, in any event, soon demonstrated by his performance that he was Roosevelt's lieutenant, not labor's. After the drastic administrative reorganization in early 1942, Hillman was bypassed and edged out of power. When he resigned in April, no labor leader replaced him on the War Production Board. Donald Nelson, who prided himself as a friend of trade unionism, did favor labor's participation on the WPB, but in a subordinate, advisory role except on specifically labor matters. The director of the WPB Labor Production Division was selected in consultation with the AFL and CIO, and the two associate directors came directly from the two labor federations. But, since manpower responsibilities had been carved out of the WPB in April 1942 and transferred to the War Manpower Commission, the Labor Production Division was little more than an advisory and liaison agency. No success met the efforts to increase its authority, especially by giving it charge of the War Production Drive that was fostering labor-management plant committees. The touchy issue had to be kept free of even a hint of partisanship, Nelson felt.[55] Finally, in June 1943, Nelson created two new offices—vice chairman for manpower requirements and vice chairman for labor production—and appointed to them CIO man Clinton Golden and AFL man Joseph Keenan (thus satisfying the rival labor federations, if not the administrative need for a single unified office). Nelson also advanced the policy of appointing labor assistants to the industry branches. Ever since mid-1941, too, labor advisory boards had served as counterparts to the industry advisory boards.

But these concessions in practice fell far short of labor's ambitions. For one thing, strong resistance developed within the WPB. The Tolan committee reported in October 1942 that recommendations from the Labor Production Division were "ignored or shelved for long periods," and its employees "treated as outsiders and their presence resented by industry branch representatives."[56] Unlike the active industry advisory boards, the labor advisory boards quickly atrophied. They were treated, one labor man complained, as "undigested lumps in the stomachs of the management people."[57] Nor were they permitted, under Nelson's policy, to meet jointly with the industry advisory committees. Only late in the war, as business suspicions moderated and firmer guidelines came down from the WPB, did the labor advisory committees revive and the labor assistants assume real responsibilities in the industry branches. Even then, however, labor participation remained narrowly confined: only on specifically labor matters did union representatives receive policy-making powers; otherwise, with some exceptions in industry branches, they were limited to advisory roles.[58] Never did labor participation threaten the safe administration of the immense powers guiding industrial mobilization.

A more inadvertent development worked also to hold production control in a safely conservative channel. The sweeping power granted to the WPB in January 1942 gave the chairman clear supremacy over all agencies of the executive branch "in respect to war procurement and production." But Nelson favored the broad delegation of authority, and he applied this principle freely to the armed services. They continued to do their own procurement, and the Army-Navy Munitions Board soon received extensive priority powers relating to contracts let by the military services. Nelson expected, of course, that all participants would view "the war supply organizations . . . as a single integrated system operating under the general direction of the Chairman of the War Production Board in a unified effort to win the war and not as a group of autonomous or semi-autonomous organizations acting in mere liaison with one another."[59] The military people, however, held quite other ideas. All their mobilization planning of the interwar years had rested on the notion of military control. When President Roosevelt rejected their M-Plan in 1939, the army and navy chose the next best alternative: to carve out the widest scope and greatest degree of independence that civilian control would permit. General Brehon Somervell proved to be singularly aggressive in his pursuit of that goal for his Army Services of Supply at the expense of WPB authority. And the Army-Navy Munitions Board managed to maneuver President Roosevelt in June 1942 into granting the ANMB an independent priority over military production, and even a concurrent voice on priorities for civilian production. "ANMB now lay beyond Nelson's grasp," remarked the official historians of World War II mobilization.[60]

But the military had overreached itself. As its faulty judgments about the complex industrial economy and its own requirements threatened to reduce the war effort to chaos, Nelson moved to regain civilian control.[61] Having allowed the military to penetrate so deeply into production concerns, Nelson probably had no other means to curb the services than by incorporating their key people and functions into the WPB. This he did in September 1942 by bringing in Ferdinand Eberstadt, chairman of the Army-Navy Munitions Board, to head the new Requirements Committee that would allocate scarce materials. To handle production scheduling, Nelson appointed Charles E. Wilson of General Electric as chief of the new Production Executive Committee. Although it was composed of representatives of the armed services, Wilson was himself an outsider; and when he moved to take over scheduling functions hitherto in military hands, the War and Navy departments strenuously objected. In the struggle for internal control that followed this reorganization of the WPB, Eberstadt and his military backers almost won; but at the last moment in February 1943, Nelson moved decisively, dismissed Eberstadt, and installed Wilson as executive vice chairman of the WPB. Even so, the military had established itself as a major presence within the civilian agency controlling industrial mobilization.

This development reinforced the safe conduct of war production. For one thing, important internal shifts accompanied the battle for control of the WPB: key New Dealers such as Leon Henderson departed; Nelson placed operational control in Charles Wilson's hands and so undermined his own authority; and the industry branches, renamed industry divisions, assumed much greater powers. More crucial was the conservative perspective of the military men who would henceforth play a central role within the WPB. Nothing would have been more alien to their way of thinking than to see industrial mobilization as an opportunity for postwar reform. They were, first of all, resolutely single-minded in their advocacy of specifically military needs (sometimes, indeed, to the detriment of the overall war effort). And they tended, moreover, to share the social outlook of business. In fact, key civilian officials—such as James Forrestal and Ralph Bard of the Navy Department and Robert Patterson of the War Department—had been drawn from much the same financial and corporate circles as their strictly civilian counterparts on the WPB. Between the military and the industrial people (including Charles Wilson) there developed a durable community of interest.

The testing came over reconversion. By mid-1943, with WPB priority and scheduling procedures perfected and war production moving into high gear, planning for the return to a peacetime economy commenced. When and how should surplus capacity and material revert to the civilian economy *during* the war period? This was an interim matter, to be sure, but not one taken lightly. On November 30, 1943, Donald Nelson laid down guiding policy: as manpower, facilities, and material became available in any area, the WPB would authorize the production of additional civilian goods, "provided such production does not limit programs of higher urgency." Nelson had rejected an alternative proposal that called for full programming of reconversion. "It has been my objective from the very start to confine detailed economic planning to war-time production. . . . To start out with the policy of planning our peace-time economy in detail . . . would do irreparable injury to the free enterprise system."

With this philosophy, the business participants in the WPB were of course in hearty agreement, but not with its uncompromising application to the first phase of reconversion. The consequences seemed sure not to be random. Since the nation's major producers dominated war production—67.2 percent of the prime contracts by value up to September 1944 went to one hundred companies—small business stood to benefit most from Nelson's laissez-faire approach. To forestall "competition's getting a jump" (as Lemuel Boulware put it), the big-business interests that dominated both the industry advisory committees and the machinery of the WPB initially advocated a plan that would protect competitive patterns by assigning production quotas on a prewar basis and by precluding new competition. But Nelson opposed any such guarantees. Companies should be permitted to shift to civilian production "whenever it is possible to do so, even though the effects on competitive situations may be painful." As for prohibiting companies from moving into new fields, Nelson rejected the notion out of hand because "there would clearly be grave danger of shackling the country with a regimented economy."[62]

During the spring of 1944, the business elements on the WPB backed away from making any overt plan to protect the competitive status quo during reconversion. The same end might be attained in a quite different way. The military had at once objected to Nelson's approach: early reconversion would undermine morale on the battlefront and at home, divert manpower from essential areas, and eat up scarce material needed for war production. The military addressed itself wholly to the impact on the war effort, of course, but the economic effect happened to fall neatly in with big-business desires. The postponement of reconversion would permit all producers to shift to the civilian market at the same time. There is no way of assessing business motives here: to what extent was delayed reconversion favored because of the force of military arguments? and to what extent because of competitive consequences? What is certain is that unity on this issue swiftly developed between the military and the industrial groups. In December 1943, Charles Wilson and General Lucius Clay moved jointly to have reconversion placed in the hands of Wilson's Production Executive Committee, which was essentially beyond Nelson's control and which included none of the WPB vice chairmen who favored early reconversion. Nelson rejected the scheme. But, yielding to opposition within the WPB and himself anticipating no imminent reduction in military needs, Nelson made no move to implement the general policy that he had set forth on November 30, 1943.

Events soon forced his hand. In May 1944, the navy suddenly cut back fighter plane production at the Brewster Corporation, without any provision for utilizing the idled facilities or the nine thousand angry workers. Seizing the opportunity, the Production Executive Committee circumvented Nelson and gained unqualified control over the cancellation of munitions contracts, obviously a key determinant of the pace of reconversion.[63] But Nelson took hold of the other side of the process. On June 18, 1944, he announced a four-point program, including "spot" authorization by regional WPB offices for civilian production wherever manpower, material, and facilities were not needed for war production. A furious storm immediately blew up in Washington. The military led the attack. Nelson's reconversion orders "may necessitate [a] revision in strategic plans which could prolong the war," charged Admiral William Leahy of the Joint Chiefs of Staff.[64] Although the industrialists in the WPB remained discreetly silent in the public debate, they too opposed early action on a reconversion plan.

The alignment of forces was thus heavily one-sided. Not only were the military and industrial elements within the WPB against Nelson, but so essentially was his own superior, James F. Byrnes, director of the Office of War Mobilization, which had been created in May as a super-agency coordinating the war effort. The only solid internal support for Nelson's reconversion program came from three of the lesser WPB vice-chairmen—the two labor representatives and the redoubtable Maury Maverick, head of the Smaller War Plants Corporation, who candidly favored early reconversion because it would benefit small business and hence counterbalance the favoritism he felt had been shown big business in the granting of war contracts. Maverick, in particular, proved to be quite formidable, not within the WPB, to be sure, but in his skill at airing the controversy and gaining support in Congress. Senator Truman charged that reconversion was being delayed by "some selfish business groups that want to see their competition kept idle . . . [and] by Army and Navy representatives who want to create a surplus of manpower."[65] This kind of publicity (with the threat of senatorial investigation behind it) certainly had an impact: it led, among other things, to the angry resignation of Charles E. Wilson just as he was about to replace Nelson. But liberal criticism was more than counterbalanced by the campaign of the armed services to discredit Nelson's reconversion plan not only by a skillful patriotic appeal but also by manufacturing a production crisis that did not exist.

Within the mobilization establishment, the military-industrial coalition worked persistently to postpone and emasculate the Nelson plan. Byrnes countermanded Nelson's directive to make the four orders effective on July 1, 1944, staggering them instead and placing spot authorization last. Before it could go into effect, Byrnes on August 4 removed spot authorization from the control of the WPB regional offices and required certifications from the hostile War Manpower Commission. Then President Roosevelt, anxious to end the noisy dissension within his war administration, eased Nelson out of office on August 18 and sent him off on a mission to China. His replacement, Julius Krug, proved to be a good deal more amenable to the military-industrial viewpoint within the WPB. Spot authorization went into effect, but was so hamstrung as to hold actual reconversion to a snail's pace. When optimistic predictions for an early end to the European war proved wrong, Byrnes suspended spot authorization in many areas and then virtually eliminated it after the German counteroffensive began in late December 1944 in the Ardennes. Only with V-E Day almost upon the country did industrial reconversion resume in earnest, so late as to impose no handicaps on the big defense contractors in the scramble for civilian markets.

This tortuous battle over early reconversion was perhaps less important in itself—Maverick's high hopes for a resurgence of business competition hardly would have materialized even if he had won—than for its delineation of the locus of wartime control over the nation's industrial economy. With business interests strongly entrenched in the mobilization structure, and reinforced by their working alliance with the military, the immense economic powers concentrated in Washington held no terrors for American industry. The radical means demanded by the war crisis could hardly be diverted to reform ends.

The ultimate testimony to the success of Roosevelt's strategy came only after his death. As the war drew to an end, no other possibility existed than the swift dismantling of industrial control. There was no counterpart in 1945 to the enthusiasm felt by many business leaders in 1918 for the experiment in industrial self-government during World War I, nor for the desire to carry wartime arrangements over into peacetime instead of returning to the antitrust laws.[66] The War Production Board led to a dead end for American business: its single-minded desire was to revert to the status quo after the war. In September 1944 Julius Krug laid down detailed guidelines for the removal of WPB controls after V-E Day. Among Krug's operating assumptions, the official historians of industrial mobilization noted the following:

> The free enterprise system would remain the basis of our economic activity; should Government intervene to maintain high levels of employment, it would do so mainly by means of fiscal policy; controls would not be used to restore prewar economic relationships or to accomplish social or economic reforms; and wartime controls would be abandoned as rapidly as possible.[67]

The last point gave rise to a dispute that revealed the deep commitment to the quick restoration of the free-market economy. Important interests—the very ones, ironically, who had sought to lift controls to speed reconversion—now wanted to utilize the WPB in the transition to a peacetime economy. Within the WPB, these included the labor vice chairmen, who were concerned about employment, the vice chairman in charge of civilian requirements, and Maury Maverick, who feared that small business would lose out in the scramble for scarce raw materials. They were joined by Chester Bowles of the Office of Price Administration, who considered controls over production and resources an essential adjunct to price control to stem inflation during the reconversion period. This New Deal–oriented group stood little chance of success. Krug answered that, after Japan was defeated, he intended to "get rid of regulations and production limits as soon as possible. They automatically put ceilings on initiative, imagination and resourcefulness—the very qualities the country will need most . . . [for a] resilient and rapidly expanding economy."[68] Within the WPB, the industry divisions and the business officialdom wholeheartedly approved Krug's position. So did American business generally, even small manufacturers who stood to benefit from controlled allocation of raw materials. A government survey found little business concern about the problems of reconversion: ''Answers to questions about transitions would often begin thoughtfully but suddenly break into a flood of words about American principles.''[69] After wavering, President Truman permitted Krug to have his way. After V-J Day, the War Production Board swiftly lifted its controls and, before the end of the year, passed out of existence. The remarkable wartime undertaking ended with hardly a trace on the nation's public policy.

And yet, if World War II did not generate new departures, it did consolidate older achievements. The reform wave of the 1930s stopped at the war's edge, but did not recede. The consolidating process had been going on all along, of course. It had been a part of the New Deal genius to draw conservative interests into its orbit. The New Deal had, in fact, gained strength from the ease with which interest groups had accepted and sometimes taken over its programs. Nor had the Republican party ever dared base its national politics on reversing the gears of New Deal reform. If Thomas E. Dewey seemed to echo Roosevelt in 1944, so had Landon and Willkie before him. Still, the New Deal had not fully secured itself at the outbreak of European war. It had not yet established the legitimacy of the underlying assumption of governmental responsibility for the nation's economic well-being. Nor had it overcome business hostility, which, indeed, had deepened and grown more embittered in the middle years of the New Deal era. Both of these intractable problems yielded to the pressures of wartime. The war experience helped make possible the Employment Act of 1946 that legitimized the shift of economic responsibility to Washington.[70] In yet more decisive ways, it reconciled American business to the changes wrought by the New Deal.

The test case was New Deal collective-bargaining policy. No reform had evoked greater opposition from industry, for no other had so clearly deprived management of power and curbed its prerogatives. Opposition continued even after the Supreme Court validated the Wagner Act in April 1937. The next year, the National Association of Manufacturers, the U.S. Chamber of Commerce, and other segments of organized business launched a major campaign for a sweeping revision of the law. In the spring of 1939, both houses of Congress held lengthy hearings on the NLRB and the Wagner Act. Some hard-core employers resisted the law outright, especially by exploiting its weak spot—the requirement to engage in bona fide collective bargaining. In all the mass-production industries, there were major firms still successfully fending off unionization at the end of 1939. The majority of open-shop employers, of course, had bowed before the law of the land after 1937, but they had done so reluctantly. They continued to deal grudgingly and conditionally with the new industrial unions. Hardly anywhere in formerly open-shop territory could collective bargaining be said to be on a solid footing when war started in Europe.

The defense period swiftly broke open this uneasy stalemate. As manpower needs grew and Washington exerted influence, Ford gave in unconditionally to the UAW, the steel independents moved toward union recognition, and everywhere collective bargaining resumed for the first time since weak original contracts had been negotiated before the recession of 1937–38. Wartime carried this accommodating process much further along. Now the government could—and sometimes did—coerce recalcitrant companies into full acceptance of trade unionism. The National War Labor Board virtually wrote the contracts in such unyielding cases as that involving Wilson and Company. On the whole, however, the war influence was benign, as indeed it had to be to work a genuine change in managerial thinking about organized labor.

For one thing, the industrial unions grew strong and became internally stable. The early militancy faded, Julius Emspak remarked regretfully, as war conditions encouraged a "nice, cushy, administrative apparatus form of organization, and [unionists] got accustomed to bureaucracies and paperwork and looking for things through magic formulae."[71] The subsiding of the bitter rivalry between the AFL and CIO further answered the reservations of open-shop management. By 1945 no grounds remained to sustain hopes that unionization might be reversed, nor fears that responsible relations could not be established with the industrial unions. The war experience also worked directly to break down barriers to the full acceptance of trade unionism. Although by the fall of 1942 the National War Labor Board tightly circumscribed collective bargaining, it did not permit the function to atrophy. The NWLB would not consider a case until there had been a direct attempt at settlement; and its awards invariably left some issues open for further negotiation. In this wartime school in collective bargaining, both management and labor received training on limited problems and under controlled conditions, and precedents were set on fringe issues (which labor emphasized because of the wage freeze) that would serve as guidelines for postwar negotiation. In a broader way, too, ingrained animosities dissipated in the war setting. The union campaign for a major role in war administration may have fallen short, but it did have the effect of exposing business to representatives of the labor movement. Stereotypes could hardly survive the close contact in a common effort on government boards and agencies. The performance of union representatives, noted a government report in 1944, "would convince any sincere doubters that they had worked for the general welfare rather than any special labor interest."[72] Even on the War Production Board, the most sensitive place because it housed the control apparatus over industry, the efforts to circumvent labor participation gave way to substantial acceptance; late in the war labor had gained a measure of the effective role it had been fighting for on the WPB.

Nothing better signified the wartime change in labor relations than the abandonment of the principle of the open shop (i.e., the right to work without regard to union membership). Employers did not accept gladly the imposition of the maintenance-of-membership rule by the NWLB. They protested, as a spokesman from Swift and Company said, that unions have "not yet reached the permanency of organization to rightfully demand such security."[73] The converse was, of course, that the gradual acceptance of this modified form of union security meant recognition of unions as an established fact. The NWLB did its part here: responsible behavior was its test of whether to grant a union maintenance-of-membership. And, if the rule was imposed, it did nevertheless represent something of a consensus, for the employer members on the NWLB did accept the principle (although not its application in many cases).[74] By the war's end, the open shop had lost its force as a rallying cry against trade unionism, and that fact reflected a quite profound change of heart within American industry. The President's Labor-Management Conference of November 1945, although torn on many points, was not divided on the central issues: business signified its genuine acceptance of trade unionism and the basic national labor policy.

Progress on the labor front was part of a much broader accommodation by business to the New Deal during the war. In 1944, President Eric Johnston of the U.S. Chamber of Commerce published a thoughtful book, *America Unlimited,* that revealed new modes of thought among at least more progressive American businessmen. The book, first of all, exuded a prideful spirit. "Credit for the most astounding production job in all history must go primarily to American capitalism," boasted Johnston, to "the initiative, resourcefulness, and ability of private business." Its confidence thus restored by wartime achievement, business could appraise the New Deal free of the corroding defensiveness of the depression years. Nor could old hostilities well survive the wartime atmosphere of common effort, especially not when business played so major a role in that effort. "The war has proved to us a fact which has been true all along, but concealed from sight—that the areas of agreement transcend by far the areas of conflict . . . on which the most diverse groups in our national community can meet as friends in search of solutions and not as enemies in search of lethal weapons." Johnston's book also corroborated an acute prediction that Thurman Arnold had made in *The Folklore of Capitalism* (1937): that a war might serve to cut through the received truths that had constricted the business response to the New Deal. A war crisis would force people to act in fresh and pragmatic ways and reduce their faith in old rules. Considering the problems of demobilization, Eric Johnston warned against "doctrinaire free-enterprise theory." "In this, as in all things, we must guard against the dangers of absolutist thinking, of putting theory above fact." Finally, Johnston perceived now the immense prospects of positive, intelligent action in the common interest. War had dealt the old economic fatalism a hard blow. "What the American people have done under the impetus of a war challenge they can do again . . . for a more abundant existence for the whole nation," argued Johnston. "The upsurge of energy, inventiveness, productivity evoked by an external enemy can and must be maintained for war against internal enemies such as poverty." The time had come for American business to accept the New Deal, concluded the Chamber of Commerce president.[75]

National crisis generated the liberating forces, but the guides that led business toward reconciliation with the New Deal came from the latter's own champions. In choosing not to turn the war to reform purposes, they laid the basis for acceptance of what had already been accomplished. The chief architect was of course President Roosevelt himself. At once setting to rest industry's fears and satisfying its need for a dominant role in the war effort, Roosevelt shrewdly created the conditions by which former enemies might let go the past in the crisis of

war. Nor was this FDR's only contribution to the consolidation of the
New Deal. If he did not press it forward, neither did President Roosevelt
ever abandon the banner of reform.

In his annual message to Congress in January 1941, Roosevelt called
for a postwar world based on Four Freedoms. One of these—freedom
from want—developed into the notion of an economic bill of rights.
President Roosevelt gave the theme its fullest expression in his State
of the Union Message of January 11, 1944.

> True individual freedom cannot exist without economic security and
> independence. "Necessitous men are not free men." People who are
> hungry—people who are out of a job—are the stuff of which dictatorships
> are made.
>
> In our day these economic truths have become accepted as self-evident.
> We have accepted, so to speak, a second Bill of Rights under which a
> new basis of security and prosperity can be established for all—regardless
> of station or race or creed.
>
> Among these are:
>
> The right to a useful and remunerative job in the industries or shops
> or farms or mines of this Nation;
>
> The right to earn enough to provide adequate food and clothing and
> recreation;
>
> The right of farmers to raise and sell their products at a return which
> will give them and their families a decent living;
>
> The right of every businessman, large and small, to trade in an at-
> mosphere of freedom from unfair competition and domination from mon-
> opolies at home or abroad;
>
> The right of every family to a decent home;
>
> The right to adequate medical care and the opportunity to achieve and
> enjoy good health;
>
> The right to adequate protection from the economic fears of old age
> and sickness and accident and unemployment;
>
> And finally, the right to a good education.
>
> All of these rights spell security. And after this war is won we must be
> prepared to move forward, in the implementation of these rights, to new
> goals of human happiness and well-being.

"The most radical speech of his life," Roosevelt's biographer James
MacGregor Burns called it. "Never before had he stated so flatly and
boldly the economic rights of all Americans. And never before had he
so explicitly linked the old bill of political rights against government to
the new bill of economic rights to be achieved *through* government."[76]

President Roosevelt carried this lofty pronouncement one step toward realization. From an early point, he recognized the need to plan for the postwar period. The country had suffered after World War I from the lack of planning for peacetime, Roosevelt felt. This time around, in any case, there was no confidence in an automatic return to "normalcy." On the contrary, it was widely believed, even among economists, that the depression would resume unless the government acted. By this time, too, fairly coherent thinking had emerged about the kind of government program needed to attain full employment. Keynesian ideas had begun to penetrate White House circles in the later 1930s. The new economics received solid confirmation from the recession that followed the sharp cutback in public spending in 1937 and in the boom that began with defense spending. To some extent also, the Beveridge Report and other British social planning had some influence in Washington. All of these elements—the memory of World War I, the expectation of postwar depression, some confidence about solutions—prompted Roosevelt to initiate planning for postwar America. This job he lodged in the National Resources Planning Board as early as November 1940. The NRPB would lay plans for public works, expanded social security, and development of national resources; more broadly, it would oversee the planning activities of all agencies of the executive branch. The NRPB defined itself "as a clearing house for the plans and proposals for the avoidance of a depression after the defense period, and to open the road for economic freedom expressed in the new Economic Bill of Rights."[77]

The ambitious enterprise soon foundered. The object of deep suspicion from the outset, the National Resources Planning Board came under sharp congressional attack in early 1943. Roosevelt chose this moment to send to Capitol Hill two NRPB reports on social security expansion and on postwar planning. The resulting furor led to congressional refusal to fund the NRPB. The agency ended in August 1943, and with it went the key to the coordinated direction of postwar planning. Staking out its own claim, Congress set up special postwar policy committees dominated by conservatives; Walter George of Georgia headed the Senate committee, William F. Colmer of Mississippi the House committee. Roosevelt himself, having tended to keep the NRPB at arm's length all along, now abandoned further thought of overall planning within his administration. Much of the responsibility went to the Bureau of the Budget, whose Fiscal Division was staffed largely by Keynesian economists.[78] But the Office of War Mobilization also took over important planning functions, and when Congress reconstituted it as the Office of War Mobilization and Reconversion in October 1944 with greatly increased authority, it became the primary planner of reconversion. Confining its attention to contract termination, disposal of surplus property, and the relaxation of economic controls, the OWMR approach was more to the taste of conservatives and won their hearty approval on Capitol Hill.

Why did Roosevelt permit his design to come to this faltering end? In part, doubtless, for the reason that James MacGregor Burns has suggested: namely, FDR's genuine ambivalence and skepticism about grand planning.[79] But the failure also expressed the lack of specific purpose behind postwar planning. The aim was, of course, to implement the economic bill of rights, but Roosevelt had divorced this lofty statement of principle from any program of action. For reasons explored earlier in this essay, he had imposed a moratorium on reform legislation for the duration of the war. Not only did no initiatives emanate from the White House but no help went to congressional progressives when they took up the battle. Nor did Roosevelt even attempt to give his economic bill of rights any functional relationship to the defense effort as a rallying cry that would justify wartime sacrifice. No more than the enunciation of hopeful intent, the economic bill of rights could not sustain even the first step of planning for its implementation. There was not a shadow of the kind of detailed preparation for swift action under way in England at this time.

It may be, as Margaret Hinchey has argued, that Roosevelt intended to shift gears late in 1944.[80] The election gave him a handsome personal victory, the crucial help of the CIO's Political Action Committee strengthened labor's influence on administration policy, and the European war seemed about to end in victory. If Roosevelt had meant to act on the economic bill of rights, he was swiftly deflected. The German counterattack in the Battle of the Bulge suddenly revived FDR's sense of military urgency. His presidential messages of the new year dutifully referred to postwar concerns, but, as he told the nation on January 6, 1945, "it is obviously impossible for us to do anything which might possibly hinder the production for war at this time."[81] Not the economic bill of rights but a national service law received Roosevelt's urgent endorsement. (The "work or fight" bill never did get through; bitterly opposed by organized labor, it bogged down in Congress and died in April as manpower needs subsided.) Thus, to the last, Roosevelt adhered to his wartime strategy of compartmentalizing social reform and of keeping the door locked so long as defense needs remained paramount. By the time the final German thrust had failed, Roosevelt was off to Yalta; the problems of peacemaking absorbed him until his death in April.

Even so, by steadily holding up the banner of an economic bill of rights during the war, Roosevelt had contributed mightily to the consolidation of the New Deal. He had served notice on old enemies that they had better discard any lingering illusions and come to terms with the New Deal. The concept of economic rights went a long distance toward securing the legitimacy of the New Deal; Roosevelt had paved the way for the Employment Act of 1946. To some degree, too, Roosevelt's wartime pronouncements did lead into the future, laying down guides to fresh areas for action (such as health, education, and housing) and committing himself to renew the battle for social reform. Harry Truman so understood the economic bill of rights, and he conceived his duty to be to fulfill the legacy that FDR had left him. That sense of historic responsibility may well have made Harry Truman a more pugnacious fighter for reform than Roosevelt would have been had he lived.

The limits on American reform were, ultimately, a function of the limits of the American war experience. In England, World War II came as a hurricane: German bombings killed roughly 60,000 civilians and injured 235,000; destroyed 222,000 houses and damaged 4,698,000 others; and sent upwards of 3.5 million women and children fleeing to evacuation areas outside the bombing zones. Civilian America never felt the war in this direct, calamitous way. Quite the contrary, on the home front Americans tended to associate the war with good times—with an end to depression, with plentiful jobs, overtime, new opportunities. The shortages of consumer goods, the rationing, and the wage-and-price controls hardly counterbalanced the real economic benefits flowing to most Americans from the war. Dislocation and stress occurred, of course, in many spheres: in housing shortages, in urban conditions, in labor mobility, in family life, and in education. But these home-front problems could either be ignored as matters of public policy or handled in relatively limited and conventional ways. Not so England's evacuations, casualties, and homelessness. These demanded an extraordinary expansion and rethinking of public welfare policy. In his detailed study of this development, Richard M. Titmuss describes the results:

By the end of the Second World War the Government had . . . assumed and developed a measure of direct concern for the health and well-being of the population which, by contrast with the role of the Government in the nineteen-thirties, was little short of remarkable. . . . It was increasingly regarded as a proper function or even obligation of Government to ward off distress and strain among not only the poor but almost all classes of society. And, because the area of responsibility had so perceptibly widened, it was no longer thought sufficient to provide . . . a standard of service hitherto considered appropriate for those in receipt of poor relief. . . . The assistance provided by the Government to counter the hazards of war carried little social discrimination, and was offered to all groups in the community. . . .

The evacuation of mothers and children and the bombing of homes during 1939–40 stimulated inquiry and proposals for reform long before victory was thought possible. This was an important experience, for it meant that for five years of war the pressures for a higher standard of welfare and a deeper comprehension of social justice steadily gained strength. And during this period, despite all the handicaps of limited resources in men and materials, a big expansion took place in the responsibilities accepted by the state for those in need.

The reality of military disaster and the threat of invasion in the summer of 1940 urged on these tendencies in social policy. The mood of the people changed and, in sympathetic response, values changed as well. If dangers were to be shared, then resources should also be shared. Dunkirk, and all that name evokes . . . summoned forth a note of self-criticism, of national introspection, and it set in motion ideas and talk of principles and plans . . . to be repeatedly affirmed with the bombing of London and Coventry and many other cities. The long, dispiriting years of hard work that followed these dramatic events on the home front served only to reinforce the war-warmed impulse of people for a more generous society.[82]

Great Britain emerged from the war with the welfare state. In the United States, World War II made a more modest contribution: it finished old business so that the country could turn unencumbered to the postwar world.

Notes

1. Bruce Catton, *The War Lords of Washington* (New York, 1948), 306.
2. Robert Sherwood, *Roosevelt and Hopkins: An Intimate History* (New York, 1948),

152–53; Dwight Macdonald, "National Defense: The Case for Socialism," *Partisan Review* 7 (1940): 250–66.

3. U.S. Bureau of the Budget, *The United States at War* (Washington, 1946), chap. 16.

4. Catton, *War Lords*, 226.

5. David Montgomery, *Beyond Equality: Labor and the Radical Republicans, 1862–1872* (New York, 1967), chap. 3; William E. Leuchtenburg, "The New Deal and the Analogue of War," in John Braeman, Robert H. Bremner, and Everett Walters, eds., *Change and Continuity in Twentieth-Century America* (Columbus, Ohio, 1964), 81–143; Gerald D. Nash, "Franklin D. Roosevelt and Labor: The World War I Origins of the Early New Deal Policy," *Labor History* 1 (1960): 39–52; Tom Gibson Hall, "Cheap Bread from Dear Wheat: Herbert Hoover, the Wilson Administration, and the Management of Wheat Prices, 1916–1920" (Ph.D. diss., University of California, Davis, 1970).

6. W.K. Hancock and M. M. Gowing, *The British War Economy* (History of the Second World War: United Kingdom Civil Series, W. K. Hancock, ed.) (London, 1949), 451; Richard M. Titmuss, "War and Social Policy," in *Essays on "The Welfare State"* (London, 1958), 86. For a theoretical treatment of a hypothesis similar to Titmuss's, see the work in comparative sociology by Stanislaw Andrzejewski, *Military Organization and Society* (London, 1954). And for a critique based on the British experience in World War I, see Philip Abrams, "The Failure of Social Reform: 1918–1920," *Past and Present*, no. 24 (April 1963), 43–64.

7. See, e.g., Francis E. Merrill, *Social Problems on the Home-Front* (New York, 1944); William F. Ogburn, *American Society in Wartime* (Chicago, 1943); Robert J. Havighurst, *The Social History of a War-Boom Community* (New York, 1951); I.L. Kandel, *The Impact of War upon American Education* (Chapel Hill, N.C., 1948); Marvin W. Schlegel, *Conscripted City* (Norfolk, Va., 1951); and, for a useful guide to the literature, Jim F. Heath, "Domestic America during World War II: Research Opportunities for Historians," *Journal of American History* 58 (1971–72): 384–414.

8. Richard Polenberg, *War and Society: The United States, 1941–1945* (Philadelphia, 1972), 97.

9. U.S. Senate, Subcommittee of the Committee on Banking and Currency, *Hearings on S. 380: A Bill to Establish a National Policy and Program for Assuring Continuing Full Employment in a Free Competitive Economy*, 79th Cong., 1st sess. (1945), 223–35.

10. Catton, *War Lords*, 311.

11. We are speaking here of immediate consequences, not of later reforms that might be traced back to origins in World War II; and we are treating reform as it was expressed in public policy.

12. Quoted in Richard M. Dalfiume, "The 'Forgotten Years' of the Negro Revolution," *Journal of American History* 55 (1968–69): 105–6.

13. Eleanor Roosevelt, *This I Remember* (New York, 1949), 238–39.

14. Roosevelt to W. H. Davis, Sept. 1, 1941, OF 407B, Roosevelt Papers (Franklin D. Roosevelt Library).

15. Paul A. C. Koistinen, "The Hammer and the Sword: Labor, the Military, and Industrial Mobilization, 1920–1945" (Ph.D. diss., University of California, Berkeley, 1964), 61–71, 98 ff.

16. "Quarterly Management Poll," *Fortune,* November 1941, 200.

17. Dewey Grantham, *The Democratic South* (Athens, Ga., 1963), 69–75; John R. Moore, "The Conservative Coalition in the United States Senate, 1942–1945," *Journal of Southern History* 33 (1967): 368–76; James T. Patterson, *Congressional Conservatism and the New Deal: The Growth of the Conservative Coalition in Congress, 1933–1939* (Lexington, Ky., 1967); Donald R. McCoy, "Republican Opposition during Wartime, 1941–1945," *Mid-America* 49 (1967): 174–89.

18. Polenberg, *War and Society,* 80.

19. James M. Burns, *Roosevelt, Soldier of Freedom* (New York, 1970), 434, 436.

20. Roland Young, *Congressional Politics during World War II* (New York, 1956), 23, 62.

21. Polenberg, *War and Society,* 185.

22. Burns, *Roosevelt, Soldier of Freedom,* 277–81.

23. J. Joseph Huthmacher, *Senator Robert F. Wagner and the Rise of Urban Liberalism* (New York, 1968), 292–93.

24. Polenberg, *War and Society,* 87.

25. Margaret Hinchey, "The Frustration of the New Deal Revival, 1944–46," (Ph.D. diss., University of Missouri, 1965), 51–52.

26. Benjamin McLaurin Memoir (1960), 64, 296, Oral History Collection (Columbia University Library).

27. Richard M. Dalfiume, *Desegregation of the U.S. Armed Forces: Fighting on Two Fronts, 1939–1953* (Columbia, Mo., 1969), 116–22.

28. John Harding, "The 1942 Congressional Elections," *American Political Science Review* 38 (1944):56.

29. Walter W. Wilcox, *The Farmer in the Second World War* (Ames, Iowa, 1947), 387; see also chaps. 9 and 15.

30. Lauchlin Currie to Roosevelt, Memorandum, March 6 1940, Roosevelt to Currie, Memorandum, April 1, 1940, OF 2546, Sidney Hillman to John L. Lewis, July 30, 1940, OF 522, Roosevelt Papers; Allen Haywood to August Scholle, Oct. 31, 1940, John Brophy Papers (Catholic University).

31. James M. Burns, "Maintenance of Membership: A Study in Administrative States-manship," *Journal of Politics* 101 (1948): 114–16.

32. Joel Seidman, *American Labor from Defense to Reconversion* (Chicago, 1953), 118, and passim, chap. 7; also, e.g., Philip Murray to Roosevelt, July 18, 1942, PPF 6988, William Green to Roosevelt, Dec. 18, 1943, PPF 3189, Roosevelt Papers.

33. Oscar Ewing to Roosevelt, Memorandum, June 16, 1943, PPF 471, Roosevelt Papers; Seidman, *American Labor,* 217ff. For the claim that some CIO leaders, including Philip Murray, would have preferred to have the wartime stabilization system carried over into the reconversion period, see Nelson Lichtenstein, "Industrial Unionism under the No-Strike Pledge" (Ph. D. diss., University of California, Berkeley, 1974), 684–86.

34. *New York Times,* Dec 23, 1940.

35. Murray to Roosevelt, Dec. 18, 1940, Mar. 11, 1941, OF 2546, Roosevelt Papers; Philip Murray, *The CIO Defense Plan,* CIO Publication No. 51 (1941); Philip Murray, *Planning for Democratic Defense,* CIO Publication No. 59 (1941).

36. Henry M. Christman, ed., *Walter Reuther: Selected Papers* (New York, 1961), 2.

37. E.g., the editor of the *CIO News:* "The CIO offered everything I had worked and

hoped for—an ambitious, practical, crusading movement to organize American working people for the betterment of their immediate conditions without setting limits to the aspirations which a well-organized, militant, intelligently led working class should have for the eventual transformation of society.'' Len De Caux Memoir (1961), 4–5, UAW Oral History Collection, Wayne State University; also Len De Caux, *Labor Radical* (Boston, 1970).

38. John Brophy to CIO Industrial Union Councils, Feb. 17, 1941, Jay Franklin, ''We, the People,'' typescript, May 1941, Brophy Papers; I. F. Stone, *Business as Usual: The First Year of Defense* (New York, 1941), 238, 264, 266; Morton W. Ertell, ''The CIO Industry Council Plan—Its Background and Implications'' (Ph.D. diss., University of Chicago, 1955), chaps. 1 and 2.

39. On the vicissitudes of Reuther's conversion idea in 1941, see George R. Clark, ''The Strange Story of the Reuther Plan,'' *Harper's Magazine* 184 (1941–42): 643–54; Eliot Janeway, *The Struggle for Survival: A Chronicle of Economic Mobilization in World War II* (New Haven, Conn., 1951), 220 ff., 253 ff.; Catton, *War Lords*, chaps. 8, 9.

40. Barton J. Bernstein, ''The Automobile Industry and the Coming of the Second World War,'' *Southwestern Social Science Quarterly* 47 (1966–67): 22–23; Roosevelt to H. L. Stimson, July 9, 1941, in Elliott Roosevelt, ed., *F.D.R.: His Personal Letters, 1928–1945*, 2 vols. (New York, 1950), 2:1183.

41. Koistinen, ''The Hammer and the Sword,'' 695; Colston E. Warner et al., eds., *Yearbook of American Labor* (New York, 1945), 476.

42. Clark, ''Reuther Plan,'' 650, 653; *Minutes of the War Production Board* (Washington, 1946), 237–38, 290–91 (hereafter cited as *WPB Minutes*); Stone, *Business as Usual*, 239–41.

43. Catton, *War Lords*, 149.

44. *President's National Labor-Management Conference. Official Conference Documents* (Washington, 1945), 44, 47.

45. Seidman, *American Labor*, 78; Philip Taft, *The A.F. of L. from the Death of Gompers to the Merger* (New York, 1959), 210–11; Julius Emspak, ''Labor-Management War Production Councils,'' *Science and Society* 7 (1943): 91, 95; Joel Seidman, ''Labor Policy of the Communist Party during World War II,'' *Industrial and Labor Relations Review* 4 (1950–51): 55–69; Irving Howe and Lewis Coser, *The American Communist Party: A Critical History* (Boston, 1957), 409–12.

46. Ertell, ''The CIO Industry Council Plan,'' chap. 1; CIO, *Proceedings* (1944), 89, 261; ibid. (1951), 2.

47. Koistinen, ''The Hammer and the Sword,'' 754; Irving Howe and B. J. Widick, *The UAW and Walter Reuther* (New York, 1949), 107–8; Julie Meyer, ''Trade Union Plans for Postwar Reconstruction in the United States,'' *Social Research* 11 (1944): 491–505.

48. Quoted in Koistinen, ''The Hammer and the Sword,'' 613.

49. U.S. Civilian Production Administration, *Industrial Mobilization for War: History of the War Production Board. . . . Program and Administration* (Washington, 1947), 208; Donald M. Nelson, *Arsenal of Democracy: The Story of American War Production* (New York, 1946), 195–96; *WPB Minutes*, 2; Koistinen, ''The Hammer and the Sword,'' 613–14.

50. Sherwood, *Roosevelt and Hopkins*, 158.

51. *WPB Minutes,* 168–69.

52. Richard Polenberg has pointed out the lax enforcement of the antitrust laws during the war, and the administration's hamstringing of Thurman Arnold's efforts (Polenberg, *War and Society,* 77–78). This was wholly in keeping with the third phase of FDR's strategy, described in the next paragraphs. The significant point here is the determination not to suspend the laws nor to set aside permanent policy during the crisis.

53. Koistinen, "The Hammer and the Sword," 631; Janeway, *Struggle for Survival,* 285ff.

54. CPA, *Industrial Mobilization,* 209; Nelson, *Arsenal of Democracy,* 208–9.

55. CPA, *Industrial Mobilization,* 247.

56. Ibid., 265.

57. Koistinen, "The Hammer and the Sword," 676.

58. CPA, *Industrial Mobilization,* 749–50; Bruno Stein, "Labor's Role in Government Agencies during World War II," *Journal of Economic History* 17 (1957): 389–408.

59. CPA, *Industrial Mobilization,* 213.

60. Ibid., 221.

61. The crystallizing event was the feasibility controversy, in which Nelson asserted his right to set maximum production limits and cut back projected military requirements for 1943 from ninety-three to eighty billion dollars.

62. Nelson, *Arsenal of Democracy,* 392, 398–99; Koistinen, "The Hammer and the Sword," 704–5; U.S. Smaller War Plants Corporation, *Economic Concentration and World War II* (Washington, 1946), 30–31; Barton J. Bernstein, "The Debate on Industrial Reconversion: The Protection of Oligopoly and Military Control of the Economy," *American Journal of Economics and Sociology* 26 (1967): 164.

63. Koistinen, "The Hammer and the Sword," 709–10.

64. Ibid., 714.

65. Quoted in Bernstein, "The Debate on Industrial Reconversion," 167.

66. Robert F. Himmelberg, "The War Industries Board and the Anti-Trust Question in November 1918," *Journal of American History* 52 (1965): 59–74; Melvin I. Urofsky, *Big Steel and the Wilson Administration: A Study in Business-Government Relations* (Columbus, Ohio, 1969), chaps. 5, 6, 8.

67. CPA, *Industrial Mobilization,* 818.

68. Barton J. Bernstein, "The Removal of War Production Board Controls on Business, 1944–1946," *Business History Review* 39 (1965): 248.

69. Ibid., 249; CPA, *Industrial Mobilization,* 814ff.

70. For a helpful brief survey of assessments of the Employment Act, see Barton J. Bernstein, "Economic Policies," in Richard S. Kirkendall, ed., *The Truman Period as a Research Field* (Columbia, Mo., 1967), 98–99.

71. Julius Emspak Memoir (1960), 319, Oral History Collection (Columbia University Library). For a detailed account of the imposition of discipline on rank-and-file militancy by the CIO leadership, aided by the War Labor Board, see Lichtenstein, "Industrial Unionism under the No-Strike Pledge." [In the years since my essay first appeared in 1975, the argument Lichtenstein advanced in his dissertation has loomed large in twentieth-century labor history. For the most recent assessments, see the contributions by Lichtenstein and James Atleson in Nelson Lichtenstein and Howell Harris, eds., *Industrial Democracy in America: The Ambiguous Promise* (New York, 1993), chaps. 5 and 6.]

72. Quoted in Koistinen, "The Hammer and the Sword," 675.

73. Quoted in David Brody, *The Butcher Workmen: A Study of Unionization* (Cambridge, Mass., 1964), 210, and passim, chap. 10.

74. Burns, "Maintenance of Membership"; Seidman, *American Labor*, chap. 6.

75. Eric Johnston, *America Unlimited* (New York, 1944), 29, 107, 116, 138. It was not much of a jump from these ideas to acceptance of the Employment Act of 1946; and some progressive businessmen—those represented by the Committee on Economic Development, for instance—gave support to the original and more radical Full Employment bill of 1945. See, e.g., the testimony of Ralph Flanders, Subcommittee of the Committee on Banking and Currency, *Hearings on S. 380*, 356–69.

76. Burns, *Roosevelt, Soldier of Freedom*, 425–26.

77. Hinchey, "Frustration of the New Deal Revival," 3, 4, and passim, chap. 1; W. S. Woytinsky, "What Was Wrong in Forecasts of Postwar Depression?" *Journal of Political Economy* 55 (1947): 142–51; Alonzo L. Hamby, "Sixty Million Jobs and the People's Revolution: The Liberals, the New Deal, and World War II," *Historian* 30 (1968–69): 585–87.

78. The division's White Paper on Full Employment provided the basis for F.D.R.'s major campaign statement on domestic policy, the Chicago speech of October 28, 1944, that held out the goal of "close to 60 million jobs" (Hinchey, "Frustration of the New Deal Revival," 13–18).

79. Burns, *Roosevelt, Soldier of Freedom*, 353.

80. Hinchey, "Frustration of the New Deal Revival," 48–49.

81. Samuel I. Rosenman, ed., *The Public Papers and Addresses of Franklin D. Roosevelt*, 13 vols. (New York, 1938–50), 13:516.

82. Richard M. Titmuss, *Problems of Social Policy* (History of the Second World War: United Kingdom Civil Series, W. K. Hancock, ed.) (London, 1950), 506–8.

6

Workplace Contractualism:
A Historical/Comparative Analysis

Out of the struggle for industrial unionism that began in the New Deal era there emerged a distinctive and strongly rooted system of workplace representation. There is no argument about the essential characteristics of that system: first, that the shop-floor rights of industrial workers would be specified rather then be left undefined; second, that specification of those rights would occur through the process of collective bargaining and take contractual form; and, finally, that the contractual rights of workers so achieved would be enforced through a formal grievance procedure (itself specified in the contract) with arbitration by a neutral third party normally as the final and binding step. The historical boundaries of this regime, which I will call *workplace constractualism,* are likewise clearly marked. First, workplace contractualism lasted as a relatively unchallenged system from roughly the late 1940s to the late 1960s. Second, its locus was the mass-production sector where, despite a certain amount of variation between industries and among companies within industries, workplace contractualism can be said to have been experienced in essentially the same way.

Every generation of scholars defines afresh what it considers worthy of study. For this generation of labor scholars, the shop floor occupies a

Reprinted with permission from *Industrial Democracy in America: The Ambiguous Promise,* edited by Nelson Lichtenstein and Howell John Harris, published by the Woodrow Wilson Center Press and Cambridge University Press. Copyright © 1992 by the Woodrow Wilson International Center for Scholars.

special place. The initiating work, Harry Braverman's *Labor and Monopoly Capital: The Degradation of Work in the Twentieth Century,* appeared in 1974. In its wake, there followed a stream of notable books and articles in economics, sociology, critical legal studies, and history in what might be called the rank-and-file school of labor scholarship.[1] Braverman himself drew on Marx's concept of work alienation in capitalist production, while many younger scholars were inspired by New Left visions of participatory democracy, in which, as the critical legal scholar Karl Klare has put it, "[T]he struggle [is] to make the workplace a realm of free self-activity and expression."[2]

Why the workplace should be treated as a central subject has perhaps been most cogently stated by Charles F. Sabel. His book *Work and Politics* (1982) is about justice. Industrial workers in all societies, says Sabel, hold notions of what is right and honorable at the workplace. Rooted in diverse "worldviews" that they bring into the factory, and, as between craftsmen, semiskilled operatives, and peasant workers, linked to specific interests within the occupational structure, their sense of workplace justice can manifest itself in submerged and even divisive ways. But whatever its guises, the notion of justice is always at the core of how workers understand the treatment they receive at the hands of managers. What happens on the shop floor is not a secondary affair in the lives of working people. On the contrary, it engages their innermost sense of self-worth and honor.

In times of crisis, the division of labor (and the sectional notions of industrial justice it engenders) can suddenly be surmounted and new, unifying conceptions of workplace justice can be forged. It is these transformative moments that occupy Sabel's attention. The paradigmatic event for him is the *autunno caldo* of 1969, when peasant migrants from the southern provinces and seasoned craft workers rose up together and imposed an extraordinary degree of workers' control over Italy's factories. For America, the 1930s are to Sabel a comparable experience. During the unionizing struggle of that era, the division of labor in mass-production industry was surmounted, and workers began to demand industrial unionism, notwithstanding past ethnoracial divisiveness, contrary traditions of craft exclusiveness, and the unyielding opposition of the American Federation of Labor. Indeed, the meaning of industrial unionism seems to me much better understood in Sabel's terms of rank-and-file transformation than as a trade-union dispute over the appropriate jurisdictional response to the mass-production sector. Industrial unionism won out not because it offered a more efficient way of dealing with General Motors or U.S. Steel but because it expressed the solidarity of the mobilized industrial workers. In the course of that struggle, too, unilateral control by corporate employers over the workplace dissolved, and for the first time a measure of power passed into the hands of industrial workers.

And how was the promise of that "transformative moment" fulfilled? The emergent system of workplace contractualism, writes Nelson Lichtenstein, was "one in which the effort to introduce certain democratic norms was subordinated to the seemingly more pressing effort to find social mechanisms that could maintain industrial discipline and resolve economic conflict between the big unions and their management adversaries." Workplace contractualism "defined industrial democracy in process terms—outcomes or fairness are irrelevant," writes the legal scholar James Atleson. "Collective action or self-help in the resolution of labor disputes" is constrained, making "it difficult for employees to assert their individual contract rights when they seek to challenge an employer's action which the union fails to challenge or where the arbitration process is tainted in some way." For the rank and file, industrial justice has not been won. On the contrary, as Katherine Van Wezel Stone has argued in probably the most influential critique, workplace contractualism (or, more precisely in her argument, the ideology of "industrial pluralism" underlying it) "serves as a vehicle for the manipulation of employee discontent and for the legitimation of existing inequalities of power in the workplace."[3]

From this tragic disjuncture between promise and fulfillment, a compelling logic of historical causation follows. In Stone's analysis, workplace contractualism is the work of an identifiable group of actors. Without George W. Taylor, Harry Shulman, and other strategically placed industrial pluralists, the future could have been different. In parallel fashion, Lichtenstein assigns to wartime labor administration the responsibility for "creat[ing] the institutional framework for the kind of collective bargaining that evolved in the decade or so after the war." The National War Labor Board, in particular, "was a powerful force in nationalizing a conception of routine and bureaucratic industrial relations," which included "fixing a system of industrial relations on the shop floor."[4] What Stone and Lichtenstein share is a sense of historical *contingency:* that is, a tendency to explain the outcome they are describing by the intervention of specific actors or events.

If the transformative moment is seen as genuinely open, and in particular if the actual outcome outrages the historian's own sense of values, then he or she is powerfully impelled toward a logic of contingent explanation: it could have been otherwise.

Yet there is strong empirical evidence to the contrary. Signs of workplace contractualism can be found before the Congress of Industrial Organizations (CIO), before the Wagner Act, before the first contracts. In Flint, for example, workers were already demanding seniority based on length of service and an impartial grievance procedure in March 1934. "People were longing for some kind of security in their work," one Buick rank-and-file leader recalled. "We had seen so much discrimination . . . people who had a lot of service and had been laid off and friends and relatives kept on. It was easy to organize people." And expectations were clearly rising during the NRA period. In 1935 fear of layoffs kept workers on the truck assembly line at the Chevrolet St. Louis plant quiet, remembered another rank-and-file leader. "I mean we were supposed to have seniority but they did not recognize it when it came to layoffs." From the very start of collective bargaining in 1936 and 1937, seniority was high on labor's agenda.[5] Everywhere at the local level a major preoccupation after recognition was the renegotiation of individual wage rates to conform to some standard of equity within the job-classification structure. The first contracts with U.S. Steel and Jones and Laughlin called for the elimination of inequalities in pay rates, and, since this turned on the comparability of jobs, quickly led to demands for the negotiation of rationalized job-classification systems.[6]

Inherent in seniority and pay equity was a notion of a workplace rule of law whose corollary was an adjudicative approach to grievance settlement. The very first contracts established formal grievance procedures. Final-step arbitration soon followed, initially only with the consent of both parties, but increasingly as the required final step in the process. When General Motors accepted a permanent umpire in 1940, the model of the grievance-resolution structure was virtually complete.[7]

This adjudicative development in turn magnified the contractual responsibilities of the union. By 1941 agreements commonly contained clauses formally obligating the union to enforce compliance on its members. By specifying the numbers, duties, and rights of the shop stewards, moreover, the early agreements incorporated shop-floor representation into the contractual relationship between union and company. That shop-floor relations fell within their orbit was a claim enunciated by every industrial union, although it took a highly centralized and well-financed union such as the Steel Workers Organizing Committee (CIO) to put that claim fully into effect. The steel union made itself signatory to every agreement, specified plant grievance committees "designated by the Union," required the entry of national SWOC representatives at the fourth step, and dealt sternly with rebellious shop stewards and local unions. Altogether, conclude two industrial-relations scholars after surveying four hundred contracts of the 1935–42 period, the contractual pattern was fixed very early. "Many 'modern' provisions in fact existed in the prewar period. . . . It is clear that the parties did not require the civilizing influence of the NWLB to invent these features."[8]

If the evidence marshaled here seems strong, however, it by no means makes an ironclad empirical case for the necessity of workplace contractualism. "In the later 1930s and early 1940s," Nelson Lichtenstein has written, "the institution of collective bargaining was but one of several elements that defined the relationship between workers and their employers. At the shop-floor level, day-to-day conflict over production standards and workplace discipline permeated the work structure and authority in the factory. . . . Shop–floor assemblies, slowdowns, and stoppages proliferated after the sit-down strikes of 1936 and 1937. . . . Direct shop-floor activity legitimized the union's presence for thousands of previously hesitant workers who now poured into the union ranks, and such job actions established a pattern of union influence and authority unrecognized in the early, sketchily written contracts."[9] Granting Lichtenstein's authority on these matters, there would seem to be as much empirical evidence to justify his sense of unforeclosed possibilities as for the rival conception of a contractualist outcome already determined even in the heat of the shop-floor struggles of the New Deal era.

Which is the correct assessment? The conundrum of contingency versus necessity does not seem to me susceptible to empirical resolution. Much remains to be learned about the shop-floor history of the industrial-union period, of course, but a deeper reservoir of information will surely not flow in only one direction. And if we know that the war had an important impact, or that (as with Sidney Hillman's role in the installation of an

impartial umpire at GM) identifiable people of industrial-pluralist per-
suasion played a part, we have no empirical test of the determinative
power of either the war or of key individuals. To settle the fundamental
issue of causation, we need to shift the discussion to a different level
of inquiry and ask whether or not a larger logic existed calling forth
those choices that made for workplace contractualism.

To that end, I propose to engage in a certain amount of opportunistic
comparative analysis. The difficulties inherent in the comparative
method are always formidable, but in this instance they seem manageable. For one thing, workplace relations are a well-bounded topic.
Moreover, we can be reasonably confident of holding things constant,
since the period under review was a time of notable stability within the
industrial relations systems of all the principal industrialized countries.
This perhaps bears emphasis: the comparisons I am making relate strictly
to the postwar quarter century before the onset of a new cycle of change
in the late 1960s. For this stable period, finally, there is a rich and
accessible descriptive literature on which to draw, thanks to the flourishing industrial relations scholarship of that era.[10]

In 1966 the International Labor Organization (ILO) took up an agenda
item entitled "Examination of Grievances and Communications within
the Undertaking." Under ILO procedures, the secretariat prepares a
working document, which is circulated for comment to the member
countries. Their replies to the questionnaire on grievances make instructive reading.[11] Consider the following demurrers from the American
responses to the ILO preliminary document. On the formal procedures
strongly favored by the United States: not in the Netherlands, where
collective agreements or works regulations generally made no provision
for grievance mechanisms. Instead, the Dutch relied on "the natural
facilities offered by the organization of the undertaking," with the
opportunity always available to appeal to an outside public authority.
"In the Netherlands there is no need to draw up formal procedures at
the level of the undertaking." On the question of granting a major role
for trade unions in the grievance process: not in West Germany, where
this would have been illegal under the Works Constitution Act (1952).
The representation of workers within plants was by law the function of
the works councils.

What about the distinction that U.S. and Canadian unions draw between grievances and "general claims," that is, in American parlance,
between "rights" and "interests"? French unions rejected the rights/

interests distinction because they did not rely on rights-creating works agreements or differentiate between grievances and collective claims. Workplace regulation in France, in fact, fell much more to a multiplicity of public agencies than within the realm of collective bargaining. Likewise, Australia's compulsory arbitration system rendered the rights/interests distinction inoperable. On matters covered by arbitration awards, the tribunals adjudicated all disputes, making no distinction between individual grievances and general claims. What the awards did not cover, which included almost everything touching the workplace, was left to informal resolution within the plants. As the Australian response delicately put it: "The formulation of an international instrument dealing exclusively and specifically with grievances, however defined, may therefore introduce unreal, in local terms, or inappropriate conceptual distinctions into the industrial relations systems of some countries."[12]

On the mechanisms for securing the grievance rights of workers, the ILO listed works regulations, collective agreements, arbitration awards, national laws or regulations, "or in such other manner consistent with national practice as may be appropriate under national conditions." No one could take exception to so ecumenical an approach, of course, but the United Kingdom did put a word in for informality and diversity, as indeed it consistently did in its responses. What this reflected was the ambiguous nature of the concept of a grievance system in contemporary British industrial relations. Industrywide agreements did specify dispute-settlement procedures, but within the plants these were rendered essentially inoperable by the shop steward system, which relied on unwritten "custom and practice" enforced through an ongoing process of informal shop-floor negotiation and shop action. As the Donovan Commission concluded two years later, collective bargaining had "become increasingly empty, while the practices of the informal system have come to exert an ever greater influence on the conduct of industrial relations . . . and . . . cannot be forced to comply with the formal system."[13]

The Japanese, although always assenting, were discreetly unresponsive to the ILO proposals. Their formal grievance systems, as in England, had little correspondence to the realities of Japanese industrial relations. For one thing, the distinction between labor and management was blurred. At Hitachi, for example, it was the foremen who routinely protested too-high standards set by rate fixers, while union officials wore company overalls and considered themselves part of the company team.[14] Collective-bargaining agreements were drawn in terms so general and ambiguous as sometimes to be ruled by the courts as technically impossible to adjudicate. The formal dispute procedures were, in any case, rarely used. "Japanese industrial relations are not concerned with the exact definition of the rights of parties in a dispute," remarked the labor law scholar Tadashi Hanami, but turn rather on "a kinship type relationship within the enterprise-family" in which harmony is expected to prevail and differences resolved through "emotional understanding." "Subordinates are not supposed to express disagreement or to state their grievances openly; they are expected to endure hardships in anticipation of the benevolent consideration of the superior."[15]

Given the remarkable diversity of workplace regimes thus revealed, it becomes hard to think of the American arrangements as in any sense "normal." That is surely the first step toward useful comparative analysis. The second is to identify the influences that best account for the significant variations among workplace regimes.

In the case of workplace contractualism, the most salient influences derive from the technical and structural characteristics of the American mass-production sector. To get our bearings here, we start with the enlightening historical analysis of mass production in Michael Piore's and Charles Sabel's *The Second Industrial Divide* (1984). Piore and Sabel insist, first of all, on the historically contingent nature of technological development. At the first industrial "divide" in the nineteenth century, mass production emerged as the dominant system, but it was neither the only possibility nor the inevitable victor. Other real alternatives existed, in particular, what Piore and Sabel call "flexible specialization," which relied on skilled workers using sophisticated general-purpose machinery capable of turning out constantly changing products on demand—this in contrast, of course, to rigid mass-production techniques based on special-purpose machinery making standardized products for extensive, stable markets. From this, Piore and Sabel derive a second key point—namely, a persisting technological diversity within the twentieth-century industrial order. Although perceived worldwide as the paradigmatic model, mass production actually took relatively complete hold only in the United States. In varying degrees and ways, craft production persisted in the manufacturing industries of Germany, Italy, France, Japan, and England. And it is within the resulting diversity of productive systems—with the United States as the baseline case of mass production—that the diversity of their shop-floor regimes flourished.[16]

British metal fabricating affords the most instructive comparison for our purposes. Spurred in the 1890s by intensifying foreign competition and by access to advanced American machine tools, British engineering firms formed a strong trade association and moved to break the hold of craft regulation over production. In the great lockout of 1897–98, the Amalgamated Society of Engineers was decisively defeated. In the United States a remarkably similar struggle occurred at almost the same time, with very much the same outcome. But in England this did not lead to a major reorganization of the workshop. Instead, the victorious British employers chose to exert their power *within* the existing system of craft production. Payment by results was the key to their strategy, enabling them to contain labor costs and intensify effort norms without having to incur the heavy capital investment and accept the managerial responsibilities that were the preconditions for asserting direct control over the labor process. Following Frederick W. Taylor, of course, American metal-trades employers also favored piecework,[17] but where they treated it merely as an incentive mechanism within a larger scheme of managerial control, British engineering employers saw piecework as a solution in itself. In the American metal trades, industrial warfare developed into a life-and-death struggle over control of the shop floor;[18] in England it took the form of endless skirmishing over the price of work. What became the very heart of the informal shop steward system—individual bargaining over piece rates—had started as an employer demand during the crisis of the 1890s.

Initially, the Anglo-American divergence remained somewhat masked because in the engineering trades, notwithstanding the claims of Taylor's disciples, there were very considerable technical constraints on managerial control of the labor process. But in automobile manufacturing, Henry Ford's assembly-line innovations effectively removed those constraints. British manufactures were of course keenly aware of what was happening in Detroit. After a certain amount of experimentation, as Wayne Lewchuk demonstrates in his important recent study, British car firms adopted much of the technology but opted against the flow methods and managerial control structures that characterized American-style mass production.[19]

Only after the almost simultaneous resurgence of union organization among auto workers on both sides of the Atlantic from the mid-1930s onward did the shop-floor consequences of this technical divergence fully emerge. In their spontaneous beginnings, their bent for direct action, and their reliance on rank-and-file support, the shop steward structures that sprang up in Coventry and Detroit seem on their face to have been much alike. But over the longer term, after the heady seizure of power, fundamental differences surface. The work groups operating on collective piecework at the Coventry firms expelled the "gangers"— the foremen who shared in the collective wage—and elected their own gang leaders who, in Jonathan Zeitlin's words, "became in practice shop stewards negotiating collective piece rates with management."[20] No structural change occurred; the basis for independent action was already in place; and, so Lewchuk concluded, as soon as labor conditions turned favorable, "this independence was formalised in the rise of shop stewards and shop stewards' committees."[21]

In American automobile plants, there was no such supervisory vacuum. At the outermost limits, shop stewards might achieve what Nelson Lichtenstein has described at the Ford River Rouge complex as "dual power."[22] But without being rooted in a technically determined and self-sustaining workplace autonomy, even this degree of seized authority could not be carried beyond the enabling periods of militant organizing or wartime advantage. Afterward, management moved to regain the initiative, to restore the weakened supervisory structures, and to deny to the shop stewards any shop-floor basis for autonomous authority. That campaign never wholly succeeded, of course. Informal work groups persisted. Even in automobile plants, not more than 20 percent of the labor force was on assembly-line work, and elsewhere, in rubber and electrical manufacturing, machine-paced control was much less a factor. And where management relied heavily on piece-rate systems, as at International Harvester, shop-floor resistance was likely to be especially strong.[23] But the redesign of work and machinery was unrelenting, and, what was perhaps more important, so was the supervisory oversight that confined the power of informal work groups to marginal and covert forms.[24] The American shop steward system was ultimately sustained, not as in England by the organization of work on the shop floor but by its validation as a useful representational mechanism within the larger contractual relationship between managements and unions.

How workers perceived shop-floor justice was likewise expressive of differing factory regimes. Where tasks were subdivided and precisely defined, as they were in American mass production, the notion of job classification could not be far behind. The Ford Motor Company was designing such a scheme even before it introduced the five-dollar day in 1914.[25] Within the large manufacturing firms, the hallmarks of an internal labor market began to emerge—personnel departments, internal job ladders, promotion from within, welfare and training programs, and some consideration of seniority in layoffs and job assignments. So that, if pay equity and seniority rights were immediate union demands, they were demands arising out of the logic of the mass-production enterprise itself.

Ironically, these became fighting issues because corporate employers themselves proved only imperfectly committed to their own creation. As the wartime labor crisis subsided in the 1920s, in fact, there was considerable backsliding from earlier movements for personnel reform, including a relaxation of efforts to rein in the foremen.[26] Even in progressive firms such as General Electric and Westinghouse, Ronald Schatz has remarked, workers "lived in a half-way house between arbitrary rule and systematic policy."[27] And with the Great Depression, the worker's stake in predictable, rule-bound treatment grew enormously. Favoritism and capriciousness came to seem so peculiarly reprehensible because such acts violated the very precepts of bureaucratic order by which the corporate enterprise itself lived. When the Chevrolet management in St. Louis fired two union men in 1934 for violating Factory Rule #23 (prohibiting solicitation of workers on company premises), the AFL local charged that the action was "plainly discriminatory" because that rule and others had been "promiscuously broken" by foremen and company-union men. The two unionists were not reinstated, but the management did announce that Rule #23 would henceforth be strictly and uniformly enforced.[28] In these ways, a quite precise meaning of industrial justice emerged from the factory environment.

Prior to the New Deal, the workplace was a realm mostly beyond the direct reach of the state. Certain industries, it was true, had experienced some degree of public intrusion as, for example, coal, where state mining laws not only regulated safety conditions but mandated checkweighmen, licensed miners, and in other ways influenced workplace relations. From the Erdman Act (1898) onward, too, the mediation of disputes and adjustment of grievances on the railroads became matters of federal provenance. And there were a number of specific public interventions in workplace relations—prohibiting the use of Taylorist methods in federal arsenals, for example, or granting workers the right to shop committees during World War I. But, on the whole, the direct impact of the state was essentially negative, serving mainly to underwrite and legitimate the unilateral rights of management at the workplace. In what was surely the emblematic event, the *Hitchman* decision (1917) upheld the yellow-dog contract as a "lawful agreement" issuing from "the constitutional rights of personal liberty and private property." With the Norris–La Guardia Act (1932), the balance began to shift. Congress repudiated that fictitious contractual equality between employers and individual workers and curbed the antiunion powers of the federal courts. Only when the New Deal granted workers' rights to organize and engage in collective bargaining, however, did the state begin to bear down in a direct way on American shop-floor relations.

Section 7a of the National Industrial Recovery Act (1933) set in motion a remarkable process of experimentation and controversy. Corporate employers denied that, as written, section 7a required them to recognize or contract with trade unions. The antidote was the employee representation plan (ERP), which had gained some currency among the welfare capitalists of the New Era but was in 1933 seized on wholesale by open-shop employers. According to the National Industrial Conference Board's guiding definition, employee representation was "a form of industrial organization under which the employees of an industrial establishment, through representatives by and from among themselves, share collectively in the adjustment of employment conditions in that establishment."[29] The ERPs were systems of workplace representation; they were, by design, not collective-bargaining agencies. The NRA battles over labor policy are best understood, in fact, as a competition between two rival conceptions of labor organization. And if we look at that competition for what it tells us about the development of workplace contractualism, events of very considerable magnitude suddenly come into focus.

First of all, the institutional structure of workplace contractualism began to take shape at this time. Even at their most pliant, the employee representation plans mark a kind of beginning for a grievance system. After seven months of operation, for example, the AC [Sparkplug] Employes' Association reported 148 "requests" to management, mostly involving lighting, ventilation, and toilets, to be sure, but also a scattering of issues—complaints about job classification, layoffs, speed-up, scheduling—destined to be the main business of union grievance processing. Employee representation, moreover, could provide a framework for more aggressive activity. At the Dodge Main plant in Detroit, where an independent union led by Richard Frankensteen gained control of the works council by participating in proportional representation elections under the Automobile Labor Board, the plan became an increasingly robust advocate of the Dodge workers.[30]

The AFL unions themselves strenuously resisted the ERP system, rightly viewing it as a stratagem for denying them genuine collective bargaining. But, given their impotence, they had little choice but to channel their energies into workplace organization. Failing to gain bargaining rights, they concentrated on representing their members within the plant. How far this might lead was evident in the settlement of the bitter strike at the Chevrolet Toledo plant in April 1935: no signed agreement or wage increase, but a shop committee of five selected by and representing union members in the plant. The committeemen were authorized to present grievances and, if not resolved with the shop foremen, to carry them to a higher company official. Discharged or suspended workers could appeal to the superintendent through the shop committee or personally and, if they appealed within twenty-four hours, could expect a decision in their cases within three days.[31]

The sense of formal process inherent in these emerging workplace structures was fostered as well by the NRA's halting efforts at adjudicating violations of section 7a. In appealing to the Automobile Labor Board or the regional labor boards, for example, local unionists were instructed to pay attention to board procedures, clear cases through the AFL Detroit office, and check "as best they can upon cases to be certain that only legitimate cases are presented for hearing. . . . "[32]

Consider next how seniority emerged as a formal issue. The right to organize under section 7a implied the existence of a standard by which employer discrimination could be tested. The insidious power of this logic is best observed in the industry most strongly situated to resist section 7a. In negotiating the auto code, industry spokesmen insisted on a clause reserving the "right to select, retain or advance employees on the basis of individual merit, without regard to their membership or nonmembership in any organization." The idea was to defend the open shop, but in fact the industry was conceding something quite fundamental—namely, that layoff and rehire of workers was not absolutely a management prerogative but subject to some objective test. Merit was not much of a standard, to be sure, but a standard it was, and from it came a remarkable provision in the president's auto settlement of March 25, 1934: in layoff and rehire, "such human relationships as married men with families shall come first and then seniority, individual skill and efficient service," and within these categories "no greater proportion of outside union employees similarly situated" were to be laid off than "other employees." The Automobile Labor Board, created by the terms of the settlement, then promulgated specific rules—among them, seniority—governing layoff and rehire in the industry. Invoked as a corollary of section 7a rights, seniority almost at once took on a broader meaning. At Fisher Body in St. Louis in November 1934, for example, the AFL union was protesting "the laying off of men out of turn in the Receiving Department." Neither the Labor Board nor the industry in fact limited seniority claims to discrimination cases. From March 1934 onward, the documentary record fills up with talk of seniority, or, more precisely, with complaints about the weakness of the ALB provisions and/or about company violations.[33]

Within the framework of state regulation stemming from section 7a there thus sprung up conceptions of workplace rights and organization that might well be characterized as proto-workplace contractualism.

In the competition with collective bargaining, workplace representation initially had the edge. By putting the ERPs swiftly into place, corporate industry seized the field, and for a time defined the terms of debate. The power balance was likewise in industry's favor. The AFL was never capable of mustering enough power on its own to impose collective bargaining on the major corporate employers. Nor was any basic challenge likely to come from within the New Deal, so long at least as it needed business cooperation for the industrial-recovery program. President Roosevelt was in fact sympathetic to the concept of workplace representation. This was the basis on which he had engineered the auto settlement of March 1934, from which he hoped might develop "a kind of works council in industry in which all groups of employees, whatever may be their choice of organization or form of representation, may participate in joint conferences with their employers."[34]

Had this line of thinking prevailed, some variant of the European works-council system (a notion not entirely discounted by sophisticated employers)[35] might well have issued from the competition between employee representation and collective bargaining of the early New Deal era. When the ALB sponsored representation elections under its own supervision, auto unionists charged that a form of "government" unionism was being imposed on the workers. The AFL boycott of the elections underscored the real nature of the challenge. But then open-shop industry lost the initiative, and there followed a reversal of fortunes that was at once stunning and utterly decisive. With the National Labor Relations [Wagner] Act of 1935, the impact of the state on American workplace relations enters a second phase.

The Wagner Act signaled the triumph of collective bargaining over employee representation as the goal of New Deal labor policy. The law aimed, by its own blunt assertion (section 1), at the promotion of "actual liberty of contract" and the remedying of the "inequality of bargaining power" between employers and employees. Everything in the law's provisions was keyed to promoting collective bargaining: majority rule in the selection of bargaining agents; exclusive representation by such certified agents; the obligation of good-faith bargaining imposed on employers; their interference in any way with the independence of labor organizations prohibited; labor's right to strike specifically assured; and, of course, the right to organize protected by a powerful, quasi-judicial National Labor Relations Board. But, massively intrusive as it was in these ways, the reach of the law was quite precisely circumscribed. It would set collective bargaining in motion and leave the process itself within the realm of contractual freedom. "The law does not compel agreements between employers and employees," asserted the landmark *Jones and Laughlin* decision (1937). "It does not compel any agreement whatever."

Where did this leave the workplace rights of workers? Excepting to be free of employer coercion in the exercise of their associational rights (and to be free as individuals to confer with and present grievances to employers [section 8 (2), section 9 (a)]), the law conferred no workplace rights. As the Supreme Court pointedly remarked in *Jones and Laughlin,* "the Act does not interfere with the normal exercise of the right of the employer to select its employees or to discharge them." Only by means of collective bargaining could the employer's power over employment be limited. And this held as well for the mechanisms for enforcing job rights. Nothing in the law demanded either a shop steward system or a formal grievance procedure. Workplace representation had become, so far as the state was concerned, the creature of collective bargaining.

Even so, the substance of what went into the first collective-bargaining agreements came directly out of the ERP period. In settling the Flint sit-down strike, for example, General Motors was bent on showing that it had not abandoned its established labor policy. The starting point in negotiating seniority was the ALB rules that the corporation claimed it had been observing since 1934. Similarly, the company considered the new grievance procedure "in principle a revision of the procedure" already in place except that, as William Knudsen said, "it is more specific now. The steps are perfectly definite from top to bottom now."[36] And likewise on the question of shop-floor representation. General Motors refused to recognize the shop-steward system that had sprung up during the strike; in fact, supplementary agreements explicitly denied to this structure any role in the grievance procedure. Instead, the contract lodged this function in committeemen, specified as to numbers and rights, along the lines of what GM had granted to AFL unions prior to 1936.

In one fundamental way, however, the corporation's claims to continuity were profoundly wrong. By signing a union contract, even one not conceding exclusive bargaining rights, GM undercut the very foundations of the employee representation system it had been fostering since 1933. In that sense, the 1937 settlement conformed to what New Deal labor policy would henceforth require: that workplace representation be the product of collective bargaining.

After the auto settlement, a wave of wildcat strikes and slowdowns hit GM's plants. The corporation's response revealed the watershed change: the grievance procedure was a matter of contract, and the UAW, as signatory, was obliged to enforce it or, so GM warned more than once, forfeit its contractual standing. The UAW's answer was no less telling: it agreed with GM's basic contention. The union accepted, indeed (in Walter Reuther's words), "contends staunchly that a disciplined and responsible organization must be maintained" and that "the Union is to be held responsible for its contractual responsibilities. . . ."[37] The ensuing history is entangled in the union's factional fights, in the machinations of a still unreconstructed corporation, and in endemic warfare on the shop floor. But the outcome is altogether clear, and altogether assertive of the contractualist character of workplace representation. And, once the constitutionality of the Wagner Act was settled, this was what the law itself demanded. The paramount duty, as the Supreme Court said in the decisive *Sands* case (1939), was to abide by the contract: workers who did otherwise forfeited the protections of the Wagner Act.[38]

State influence on workplace contractualism thus occurred in two stages. In the formative NRA period, key internal characteristics emerged; and then, with the Wagner Act, this workplace regime became the creature of the labor contract. There next followed a third stage in which, as it tried to define its own responsibilities, the state conferred on workplace contractualism the imprimatur of legitimacy.

What was the legal standing of the labor agreement under the Wagner Act? Did contracts achieved under its provisions acquire a binding force not hitherto attached to collective bargaining agreements? The Wagner Act was silent on that score, but the affirmative drift of court decisions was at once evident.[39] The postwar labor crisis brought the issue to a head. Under the punitive atmosphere prevailing at the time, the Republican Congress moved to make the unions more "responsible." Section 301 of the Taft-Hartley Act made "suits for violation of contracts between an employer and a labor organization" actionable and granted jurisdiction to the federal district courts. The provision remained effectively a dead letter[40] until, in *Lincoln Mills* (1957), the Supreme Court directed the lower courts "to fashion a body of federal law for the enforcement of these collective bargaining agreements."

Faced by this formidable task, the courts did a remarkable thing. They shifted the responsibility to the privately created grievance and arbitration machinery. The logic turned on the linkage the courts found between the arbitration and no-strike clauses in labor agreements. Insofar as they abandoned the resort to force over disputed rights, the parties in effect accepted as binding and *legally enforceable* the processes of the grievance and arbitration machinery they had established. It was the function of the courts, the Supreme Court ruled in the *Steelworkers' Trilogy* (1960), only to enforce the contractual obligation to arbitrate and without review of (save where it was "apparent" that an award did not derive from the terms of the agreement) the decision of the arbitrator.

Thus the law swung behind this private arrangement of dispute settlement, elevating it to quasi-legal status, and, moreover, legitimating the larger system of workplace representation within which it rested. The collective agreement, pronounced the Supreme Court, is "more than a contract." It is "an effort to erect a system of industrial self-government" and calls into being "a new common law—the common law of the particular industry or a particular shop." Within this industrial order, arbitration is "the means of solving the unforeseeable by molding a system of private law."[41]

And what of the rights of the individual worker? If he or she was denied access to tort law, then a particularly heavy "duty of fair representation" fell to the unions. Under *Vaca* v. *Sipes* (1967), they became liable for how they handled the grievances of their members. The sight of dissatisfied workers suing their unions for mishandling or rejecting their grievances must surely have struck foreign trade unionists as one of the more arresting oddities of the American labor scene.

From a comparative perspective, the legal configuration whose evolution I have described would seem just as specific to the United States as were the characteristics of the American mass-production regime. On the enforcement of the rights of workers, for example, it appears that no other country established precisely the public/private balance enunciated in the *Trilogy* doctrine, not even Canada. In the United States arbitration in the grievance procedure was contractually determined, and only to the extent that the parties agreed to it—most contracts reserved some issues from final arbitration—did they invoke the enforcement powers of the courts. Canadian law, on the other hand, required labor agreements to contain no-strike, binding arbitration clauses. Elsewhere, especially in countries with works-council legislation, labor courts enforced the rights of workers, while, at the other extreme, in England no legal standing was accorded to labor agreements. Australia offered a still different mix of state-enforced arbitration awards and informally determined workplace rights.[42] So it is not any wonder that the ILO encountered so much difficulty in fashioning a policy on worker grievances that would be acceptable to all the signatory countries.

"The proposed instrument should not be too detailed, but should leave a large measure of freedom to the practices and customs of the various countries." So went the Swiss response. "Regulations must take national peculiarities into account," said the West Germans.[43] And so on. The very concreteness of grievance handling as an issue prevented the usual evasions and brought forth these acknowledgments of national diversity. In its particularities, so the ILO episode implies, the law of workplace relations must ultimately be linked to characteristics embedded in the larger political environment.

Consider, for example, the fate of American labor law in Japan. In the course of the democratization process of the postwar occupation, the Japanese accepted as their model the National Labor Relations Act.

"Thus," observes William B. Gould in his illuminating comparative study, "to an extent unknown in the case of any two other industrialized countries in the world, a similar legal framework provides us with the opportunity to see how institutions offer different answers to the same legal questions in dissimilar cultural settings."[44]

The concept of the unfair labor practice, which is at the heart of the Wagner Act, underwent a transmutation in Japan. The term, literally translated in the 1945 law, made no sense as applied to labor-management relations. "It seems that the Japanese language lacks an appropriate word to express the concept of fairness or unfairness in personal relations," remarks Hanami.[45] The Trade Union Act of 1949 retranslated the term to mean "improper" labor practices. In patron-client relations, however, impropriety can characterize the acts only of the authority figure. So that, in a variety of ways, Japanese law and the courts took a much more permissive attitude toward the behavior of unions and workers than toward employers. Likewise, although the Taft-Hartley Act had just made American unions subject to unfair labor practices, such a step seemed inadmissible in Japan. And since impropriety was something to be assuaged and mitigated, the functions of the Labor Relations Commission—the counterpart of the NLRB—became more nearly mediatory than adjudicative in nature.

Given Japan as borrower, Gould's comparative legal analysis naturally throws its light on the peculiarities of the Japanese. But the process can be reversed so as to suggest what was American about the law from which the Japanese were borrowing. Our instance is the representation election. This was never adopted in Japan, partly because it had been overtaken by events. Japanese workers unionized before the right to organize went into effect, thereby rendering irrelevant the central premise of the American law, namely, that without state coercion the antiunion power of management could not be overcome. Moreover, representation elections might have disturbed an emergent trade-union structure with which the Japanese authorities did not want to tamper. But the representation election was not only a matter of expediency, either in Japan or the United States.

The point can perhaps be more fruitfully exploited by shifting the comparison to Australia. As in the United States since 1935, access to certain state mechanisms is crucial to Australian unions. They cannot function within the arbitration system without being *registered,* any more than can American unions engage in collective bargaining within the terms of the National Labor Relations Act without being *certified*. Certification is what a union gains when it wins a representation election under the rules of the NLRB. Registration under the Commonwealth Conciliation and Arbitration Act, comparably important for Australian unions, is likewise closely regulated, with internal union rules and jurisdictional lines closely scrutinized. But there is no provision for determining whether or not workers within that jurisdiction want to be so represented.[46]

That the Wagner Act should turn on *the right to choose* of course touches basic assumptions about the American working class. What is generally unarguable in other advanced industrial societies—that workers do act as a class and that trade unions are their natural representatives—are in the United States open questions. The Wagner Act is not about the rights of unions but about the rights of workers. And insofar as they choose to exercise those rights, the representatives they select as bargaining agents are defined not as trade unions—a term absent from the law—but as "labor organizations" in a broadly inclusive sense (section 2[5]). The new law in fact contradicted historic premises of American trade unionism, a truth brought painfully into focus by the rise of the CIO. No longer was the Federation's authority to assign union jurisdictions paramount, nor were its affiliates absolutely free to enter agreements with employers. When it realized that these fundamentals of trade-union voluntarism had been lost, the AFL moved to have the law amended. But the AFL did not challenge what had caused this legal crisis, namely, the assertion of the workers' right to choose. Nor, despite its insistent demands for labor law reform, does the AFL-CIO do so today. So compelling is the notion of free choice that, at least in this respect, there is no going back to the *status quo ante* 1935. Thus the recent settlement of the AFL-CIO boycott of Coors beer: the NLRB is to be excluded, but a representation election there would be, under the auspices of the American Arbitration Association.[47]

Insofar as it embodies the larger political culture, the law can give shape to the rank-and-file conceptions of industrial justice that animate shop-floor struggle. For most of the nineteenth century, the American labor movement had drawn its inspiration from the Declaration of Independence and the American Revolution. Artisan republicanism celebrated personal independence, citizenship, and equal rights. These principles oriented the labor movement toward fundamental, even radical, questions—over what the Preamble of the Knights of Labor took to be "an inevitable and irresistible conflict between the wage-system of labor and the republican system of government"—but they also defined industrial justice at the workplace and translated readily, for example, into the ethical code that David Montgomery finds in nineteenth-century craft-controlled machine production.[48]

In the mass-production regime of the twentieth century, workers found a more appropriate political analogue in the legal-constitutional order. That was, indeed, what Sumner H. Slichter perceived in his pioneering survey of collective bargaining as practiced in the 1930s. *Union Policies and Industrial Management* (1941) took as its central theme what Slichter called "industrial jurisprudence," which he defined as "a method of introducing civil rights into industry, that is, of requiring that management be conducted by rule rather than by arbitrary decision." The rules, as Slichter was at great pains to demonstrate, varied enormously from union to union. For example: in coal mining, union agreements did not regulate layoffs; in the needle trades, work sharing prevailed; in printing and on the railroads, it was seniority; a few unions gave job preferences to members; and elsewhere various combinations existed. This diversity, Slichter remarked, most of all reflected "differences in conditions within industries." And he did not doubt—indeed, his book already demonstrated as much—that in the newly organized mass-production sector workplace representation would develop its own distinctive character, but also embodying the tradition of industrial jurisprudence, because all modern American workers "expect management to be conducted in accordance with rules . . . and to have an opportunity to appeal to a proper person when, in their judgment, the rule has not been observed."[49]

Nothing better reveals this rights consciousness than the booklet handed out by UAW Local 7 to new hires at the Chrysler Jefferson-Kercheval plants in Detroit in 1949: "If you think that justice is not being done you . . . see your steward about it. . . . The grievance structure functions like a court of appeals—an agency to which the worker can appeal his case when he feels an injustice has been done him." Among the submerged histories yet to be charted is how a diverse, largely immigrant labor force moved to a conception of industrial justice that subordinated ethnic networks and personal connections to equal treatment by workplace rule[50]—from a world in which "the fair-haired boys . . . [in some cases] blood kin to the foremen, such as nephews and brothers-in-law . . . got all the breaks" to a world in which "if you had the seniority you stayed on the job.'' Some opposition certainly came, so the Buick-Flint activist Norm Bully believed, from those who "thought they could do better or had been doing better by being friends with the boss or relatives to supervision." But once in place, the contractual system overwhelmed, or at least forced underground, that kind of thinking. UAW Local 174 emblazoned this message on its application card: "The other fellow is only interested in helping you protect your job if you help protect his. PLAY FAIR—DO YOUR SHARE." A quasi-legal idiom—"to substitute civil procedure for civil war in this industry"—suffused official UAW doctrine and reached down to the local unions. Thus the concluding words of Local 7's booklet for new hires: *"Remember! Your union is your best friend. It is that wonderful defense lawyer, at the point of production, that every worker needs and desires."*[51]

To return to our original question: Ought workplace contractualism to be explained as a historically contingent event? In the setting within which it arose from the mid-1930s onward, surely not. The proximate causes as I have explored them compel us to see workplace contractualism as determined by the contemporary mass-production and legal-political regimes.

Our difficulty in accepting that conclusion arises in some degree, certainly, from a failure of historical imagination. Nearly twenty years after celebrating the industrial jurisprudence of American union-management relations, Sumner H. Slichter and two colleagues published a massive sequel to *Union Policies and Industrial Management*. The second book, *The Impact of Collective Bargaining on Management* (1960), bears witness to the centrality of workplace contractualism in the industrial relations system of the Eisenhower era. Procedure has become of commanding importance. In the 1941 book, dispute-resolution machinery received only passing attention and, as Slichter (or his coauthors) notes sheepishly, arbitration is not even in that book's index.[52] In the 1960 book, however, the grievance procedure consumes over a hundred closely packed pages. And the dominating topics— seniority, a minor topic in 1941, and job classification issues, entirely absent from the 1941 book—are likewise treated essentially as complex procedural problems.

This was not perhaps what Slichter had hoped for. Labor-management cooperation, a major enthusiasm of his in 1941, can be of little account (and receives scant attention) in a book that takes General Motors as the model industrial enterprise. The central question of the first book—was it possible to square labor's quest for justice with management's quest for efficiency?—has become much more problematic in the second. And if "the American workman is more richly endowed with self-determined rights than the workman of any other country," labor's quest for justice has perhaps succeeded too well.[53] Slichter's own perspective has grown overtly managerial, and his message is that employers must defend their prerogatives.

It is the Slichter of 1960, not of 1941, who resonates in our own day. As the manufacturing sector has fallen on hard times, Slichter's misgivings have blown up into a generalized repudiation of workplace contractualism. "The American system of organizing and managing work is obsolete," says John P. Hoerr in his account of the collapse of American steel in the 1980s. "The problem [is] rooted in forty years of poor management of people and a misdirected union-management relationship. . . . Those decades of adversary relations on the shop floor . . . created an atmosphere of suspicion and hostility."[54] A wider-ranging analysis by three leading scholars in the field posits a systemic shift of historic proportions in American industrial relations: "Over the course of the past half century union and nonunion systems traded positions as the innovative force in industrial relations. . . . An alternative human resources management system . . . gradually overtook collective bargaining and emerged as the pacesetter by emphasizing high employee involvement and commitment and flexibility in the utilization of individual employees."[55] The force of this assault on workplace contractualism has converted even some within the labor movement to the cause of "employee involvement," "commitment," and "flexibility in the utilization of individual employees."

Criticism of workplace contractualism from the left has today been joined—odd bedfellows—by denunciation from the right and center.[56] It would probably be fair to say that workplace contractualism has nearly exhausted the official legitimacy it once enjoyed. The historian must therefore search doubly hard for a vantage point that recaptures what Slichter had seen in 1941, that is, an emerging system congruent with past experience and congruent, too, with the New Deal environment.

So let me conclude by invoking the name of Nick DiGaetano. One of the first at the Chrysler Jefferson plant in Detroit to join the UAW-CIO in 1937, DiGaetano was afterward elected a chief shop steward and, except for one term out of office, he served continuously from 1940 as a committeeman and then as chief steward of the OK assembly line until he retired in 1958. A few months later, still fresh from the shop, he recorded his experiences. In his oral history, there is an authentic voice about workplace contractualism as the embodiment of industrial justice for the mass-production workers of his generation.

DiGaetano was no innocent at shop-floor representation. He was a skilled metal polisher—"I was pretty good at the wheel, not to brag about it"—and before going to Chrysler he had worked in a contract shop where every polisher and buffer had belonged to Local #1 of the Metal Polishers' International Union. The jobs were strictly piecework, and while the company did not recognize the union—"[W]e had our own recognition," says DiGaetano—the foreman was in practice obliged to bargain over the rate for each new job. For this purpose, the metal polishers elected two committeemen. From 1925 to 1928 DiGaetano was one of the two. Informal bargaining continued after he and most of the others followed the foreman over to Chrysler, but now they bargained over production standards, since Chrysler paid on a group incentive basis, not a straight piece rate. "Among ourselves we said, 'Well, this is what we want, demand so much time on this job.' . . . We had the time-study men and . . . we argued about it, and we came to an agreement that so many pieces per hour, eight hours, were enough. That was all there was to it." What DiGaetano was describing was a system of informal bargaining not unlike that in British auto plants at the time, and, although little is known about it, probably widely practiced by an elite of American craft workers in many presumably open-shop industries.[57]

The possibility of holding to that informal system seems not have crossed his mind. But DiGaetano did weigh the old against the new. With the UAW, first of all, "we had the bargaining structure in the contract to follow." Informal bargaining had always been rushed, a few minutes snatched from the wheel, since, as pieceworkers, the committeemen were losing money every time they talked to the foreman. As a shop steward, DiGaetano was on company time, and he took as long as necessary—maybe longer!—to handle a grievance.[58] Then there was the question of access. In the informal system, the foreman was the end of it. But the stewards could get to the top labor-relations man, "the whole cheese to transact the business of labor. . . . He had to talk with the Shop Committee, and he had to talk to the shop steward when it came down to it.'' And much more was on the table than the piece rate: ''When we talked to the foreman, we talked to the foreman on an equal basis: 'This work is too hard; this man can do the job; this man's got seniority; this man does not get enough pay for his classification; this man got a pay shortage.' '' But what was gained went beyond this. ''We did not have to stand up like the Italian boys,'' DiGaetano digresses at one point. ''They tell me in Italy when they they go to speak with management about conditions . . . they stand up with their hat in their hand.'' What DiGaetano meant becomes clear his parting words: ''I tell you this: the workers of my generation from the early days up to now had what you might call a labor insurrection in changing from a plain, humble, submissive creature into a man. The union made a man out of him. . . . I am not talking about the benefits. . . . I am talking about the working conditions and how they affected the men in the plant . . . Before they were submissive. Today they are men.''

Anyone who characterizes workplace contractualism ''as a vehicle for the manipulation of employee discontent and for the legitimation of existing inequalities of power'' will have to reckon with Nick Di-Gaetano. And lest he be too readily dismissed as just another victim of false consciousness, one further biographical fact might be entered into the record: DiGaetano was a veteran Wobbly. He had joined the IWW back in 1912 at the time of the Lawrence strike, he had participated in the Italian-language Propaganda League, he knew Ettor, Giovannetti, and Big Bill Haywood, and he remained an IWW member until 1938. DiGaetano considered his small circle to be ''the cream of the crop'' of the working class, not like the mass of auto workers who ''did not have any ideology.''[59] If anyone understood that the class struggle took place at the point of production, it was Nick DiGaetano. And he likewise understood that workplace contractualism was, in its origins, a product of that struggle.

Notes

For critical readings of earlier versions of this essay, I would like to thank (in chronological order, since each reading forced a further revision) George Strauss, Jonathan Zeitlin, Gary Gerstle, and Sandra Van Burkleo.

   1. Key early works are: Michael Burawoy, *Manufacturing Consent: Changes in the Labor Process* (Chicago, 1979); Richard Edwards, *Contested Terrain: The Transformation of the Workplace in the Twentieth Century* (New York, 1979); Karl E. Klare, ''Judicial

Deradicalization of the Wagner Act and the Origins of Modern Legal Consciousness, 1937–1941," *Minnesota Law Review* 62 (March 1978): 265–339; David Montgomery, *Workers' Control in America* (New York, 1979). And for an early survey of works in the rank-and-file vein: Jeremy Brecher, "Uncovering the Hidden History of the American Workplace," *Review of Radical Political Economics* 10 (Winter 1978):1–23.

2. Klare, "Judicial Deradicalization," 338–39.

3. Nelson Lichtensteim and Howell Harris, eds., *Industrial Democracy in America: The Ambiguous Promise* (New York, 1993), 115, 149; Katherine Van Wezel Stone, "The Post-War Paradigm in American Labor Law," *Yale Law Journal* 90 (June 1981): 1517.

4. Nelson Lichtenstein, "Industrial Democracy, Contract Unionism, and the National War Labor Board," *Labor Law Journal* 33 (August 1982): 524.

5. Ronald Edsforth, *Class Conflict and Cultural Consensus: The Making of a Mass Consumer Society in Flint, Michigan* (New Brunswick, N.J., 1987), 158–59, 166; James F. Doherty Interview, Oral History Collection, Walter Reuther Archives of Labor and Urban Affairs, Detroit, 18; Carl Gersuny, "Origins of Seniority Provisions in Collective Bargaining," *Labor Law Journal* 33 (August 1982): 518–24; Gersuny, "Seniority and the Moral Economy of U.S. Automobile Workers, 1934–1936," *Journal of Social History* 18 (Spring 1985): 463–75.

6. Frederick H. Harbison, "Steel," in Harry A. Millis, ed., *How Collective Bargaining Works* (New York, 1942), 553; *SWOC Handbook* (Pittsburgh, 1937), 15. For early UAW concern with job classification systems, see Press Release, September 16, 1937 [re demands at GM], and *Chrysler Demands* [March 1937], box 11, Henry Kraus Collection, Reuther Archives. The centrality of pay equity as a local bargaining issue at General Motors during 1939–41 is very apparent in the correspondence in box 1, series 1, UAW General Motors Department Collection, Reuther Archives.

7. On Reuther's successful efforts at negotiating for an impartial umpire, see Reuther to GM locals, June 2, 18, 1940, box 1, series 1, UAW-GM Department Collection. As early as mid-1938, the GM Department was already advocating an impartial umpire. Homer Martin and William E. Dowell to GM locals, June 15, 1938, op. cit.

8. David Brody, "The Origins of Modern Steel Unionism: The SWOC Era," in Peter F. Clark et al., eds., *Forging A Union of Steel* (Ithaca, N.Y. 1987), ch. 2; Sanford Jacoby and Daniel J. B. Mitchell, "Origins of the Union Contract," *Labor Law Journal* 33 (August 1982): 512–18.

9. Lichtenstein, "Industrial Democracy," 525.

10. Useful entry points are Walter Galenson, ed., *Comparative Labor Movements* (New York, 1952); Adolf Sturmthal, *Workers Councils* (Cambridge, Mass., 1964); and, for a sustained effort at comparative analysis, John T. Dunlop, *Industrial Relations Systems* (New York, 1958). For specific countries, see, e.g., George S. Bain, ed., *Industrial Relations in Britain* (Oxford, Eng., 1981); Robert E. Cole, *Japanese Blue Color* (Berkeley, CA, 1971); Andrew Gordon, *The Evolution of Labor Relations in Japan: Heavy Industry, 1853–1955* (Cambridge, Mass., 1985); Val R. Lorwin, *The French Labor Movement* (Cambridge, Mass., 1954); Wolfgang Streeck, *Industrial Relations in West Germany: A Case Study of the Car Industry* (New York, 1984); Kenneth F. Walker, *Australian Industrial Relations Systems* (Cambridge, Mass., 1970). Especially rewarding among journals for its comparative coverage is *The British Journal of Industrial Relations* (1962-).

11. The responses are in International Labor Organization, *Examination of Grievances and Communications within the Undertaking* [Report 7] (Geneva, 1966), vol. 2.

12. Ibid., 12, 28, 31, 42, 96.

13. Quoted in Bain, *Industrial Relations in Britain*, 139.

14. Ronald Dore, *British Factory-Japanese Factory: The Origins of National Diversity in Industrial Relations* (Berkeley, Calif., 1973), 169–70.

15. Tadashi Hanami, *Labor Relations in Japan Today* (Tokyo, 1979), 54, 57.

16. It need hardly be added, of course, that diversity could be found in the United States as well. For a detailed study of flexible specialization in the Philadelphia textile industry, see Philip Scranton, *Proprietary Capitalism: The Textile Manufacture at Philadelphia, 1800–1885* (New York, 1983).

17. In 1928, 53 percent of all manufacturing workers were on piecework (Sanford Jacoby, *Employing Bureaucracy: Managers, Workers, and the Transformation of Work in American Industry, 1900–1945* [New York, 1985], 195).

18. David Montgomery, *The Fall of the House of Labor* (New York, 1987), chs. 4–6.

19. Wayne Lewchuk, *American Technology and the British Vehicle Industry* (Cambridge, Eng., 1987), 113 and passim; Jonathan Zeitlin, "The Labour Strategies of British Engineering Employers, 1890–1920," and Wayne Lewchuk, "Fordism and British Motor Car Employees, 1896–1932," both in Howard F. Gospel and Craig R. Littler, eds., *Managerial Strategies and Industrial Relations: An Historical and Comparative Study* (London, 1983), 25–54, 82–110.

20. Jonathan Zeitlin, "The Emergence of Shop Steward Organization and Job Control in the British Car Industry: A Review Essay," *History Workshop Journal 5* (Autumn 1980), 123.

21. Wayne Lewchuk, "The Motor Vehicle Industry: Roots of Decline," in Bernard Elbaum and William Lazonick, eds., *The Decline of the British Economy* (New York, 1986), 140.

22. Nelson Lichtenstein, "Life at the Rouge: A Cycle of Workers' Control," in Charles Stephenson and Robert Asher, eds., *Life and Labor: Dimensions of American Working-Class History* (Albany, N.Y., 1986), 243.

23. Nelson Lichtenstein, "Auto Worker Militancy and the Structure of Factory Life, 1937–1955," *Journal of American History* 67 (September 1980): 335–53; Daniel Nelson, "Origins of the Sit-Down Era: Worker Militancy and Innovation in the Rubber Industry," *Labor History* 23 (Spring 1982): 198–225; Ronald W. Schatz, *The Electrical Workers: A History of Labor at General Electric and Westinghouse, 1923–1960* (Urbana, Ill., 1983); Stephen Meyer, "Technology at the Workplace: Skilled and Production Workers at Allis-Chalmers, 1900–1941," *Technology and Culture* 29 (October 1988): 839–64. On the influence of union ideology, see Toni Gilpin, "The FE-UAW Conflict: The Ideological Content of Collective Bargaining in Postwar America," and Mark McCulloch, "The Shop Floor Dimension: The Case of Westinghouse" (papers delivered at the North American Labor History Conference, October 20–22, 1988).

24. See especially James W. Kuhn, *Bargaining in Grievance Settlement: The Power of Industrial Groups* (New York, 1961). For an argument that seeks to minimize Anglo-American shop-floor differences, see Steven Tolliday and Jonathan Zeitlin, "Shop-floor Bargaining, Contract Unionism and Job Control: An Anglo-American Comparison," in

Tolliday and Zeitlin, eds., *The Automobile Industry and its Workers: Between Fordism and Flexibility* (Oxford, Eng., 1986), 99–120.

25. Stephen Meyer, *The Five-Dollar Day: Labor, Management and Social Control in the Ford Motor Company, 1908–1921* (Albany, N.Y., 1981), ch. 4; David Gartman, *Auto Slavery: The Labor Process in the American Automobile Industry, 1897–1950* (New Brunswick, N.J., 1986), 213.

26. Jacoby, *Employing Bureaucracy*, ch. 6.

27. Quoted in ibid., 193.

28. George S. Danner, FLU #18386, to P. E. Baugh, plant manager, November 14, 1934, box 1, Homer Martin Collection, Reuther Archives. See also, e.g., David M. Gordon, Richard Edwards, and Michael Reich, *Segmented Work, Divided Workers: The Historical Transformation of Labor in the United States* (New York, 1982), ch. 6, which views industrial unionism as the "consolidation" of an earlier phase of corporate labor policy.

29. Quoted in Session 1, GM Executive Training Program: Section G—Employee Relations (1933), box 16, Kraus Collection, Reuther Archives.

30. AC Employes' Association, *A Report of Activities (From September 1933 to March 1934),* box 16, Kraus Collection; "Automotive Industrial Workers' Association Members: We Swept the Primary Election for the Union!" box 16, Kraus Collection; Dodge Main Works Council Minutes, 1935–1937, passim, box 17, Kraus Collection

31. Proposed Agreement, FLU #18384, May 11, 1935; To the Officers and Members of UAW FLUs—F. J. Dillon, May 17, 1935; clipping, *Toledo Blade,* May 14, 1935, all in box 2, Martin Collection.

32. "Duties of Union Officers," n.d., box 2, Martin Collection.

33. Sidney Fine, *The Automobile under the Blue Eagle* (Ann Arbor, Mich., 1963), 68, 212, 251; Blanche Bernstein, "Hiring Policies in the Auto Industry," WPA Research Project (1937), box 1, W. Ellison Chalmers Collection, Reuther Archives; Joseph R. Wood to Homer Martin, November 14, 1934, box 1, Martin Collection.

34. Fine, *Blue Eagle,* 223–24.

35. See, e.g., Session 1—GM Executive Training Program (1933), box 16, Kraus Collection; Arthur H. Young, "Lessons to Be Drawn from Industrial Relations Experience Abroad," Sept. 20, 1933, A. H. Young Collection, California Institute of Technology.

36. *Flint Journal,* February 17, March 13, 1937, clippings, box 2, Flint Labor Collection, Reuther Archives; Sidney Fine, *Sitdown: The General Motors Strike of 1936–1937* (Ann Arbor, Mich., 1969), 306.

37. "Review of the Situation in General Motors," [n.d., 1939], 4, folder 12, box 4, Reuther Collection.

38. For a treatment of the key cases, see Klare, "Judicial Deradicalization," 293–325.

39. Phillip Selznick, *Law, Society, and Industrial Justice* (New York, 1969), ch. 4. On the earlier legal history of the labor contract, see Christopher H. Tomlins, *The State and the Unions: Labor Relations, Law, and the Organized Labor Movement in America, 1880–1960* (New York, 1985), chs. 2–3.

40. Except for its influence on collective bargaining: in exchange for release from legal liability, many unions accepted tough management rights clauses and greater responsibility for policing the contract.

41. David E. Feller, "A General Theory of the Collective Bargaining Agreement," *California Law Review* 61 (May 1973): 686–90, 700–707; Robin W. Fleming, *The Labor Arbitration Process* (Urbana, Ill., 1965), ch. 1.

42. For an extended consideration of the relationship between the legal system and the private rule of law in which the unionized workplace of the 1960s is offered as an important paradigm, see Selznick, *Law, Society and Industrial Justice.* For a convenient survey, see Roger Lanpain, ed., *Comparative Labour Law and Industrial Relations* (Deventer, Holland, 1982).

43. ILO, *Examination of Grievances,* 2: 85, 94.

44. William B. Gould, *Japan's Reshaping of American Labor Law* (Cambridge, Mass., 1984), 19.

45. Hanami, *Labor Relations in Japan,* 81. For an astute historical analysis of the patron/client basis for Japanese labor relations, see Thomas C. Smith, "The Right to Benevolence: Dignity and Japanese Workers, 1890–1920," *Comparative Studies in History and Sociology* 26 (October 1984): 587–613.

46. Walker, *Australian Industrial Relations Systems,* ch. 1. Other countries, especially in the Caribbean and in Southeast Asia, have followed the U.S. model of representation elections, but only in response to the problem of union competition, which was of course not an issue for the original Wagner Act. For a survey, see Alan Gladstone and Muneto Ozaki, "Trade Union Recognition for Collective Bargaining Purposes," *International Labour Review* (August–September 1985): 163–89. I am grateful to E. M. Kassalow for calling this article to my attention.

47. *New York Times Magazine,* January 31, 1988, 19ff.

48. Montgomery, *Workers' Control,* ch. 1. On the transition from a republican to a constitutional orientation, see Leon Fink, "Labor, Liberty and the Law: Trade Unionism and the Problem of the American Constitutional Order," *Journal of American History* 74 (December 1987): 904–25.

49. Sumner H. Slichter, *Union Policies and Industrial Management* (Washington, D.C., 1941), 1–3, and, on layoffs, ch. 4, especially tables, 105–7. Given the jurispru-dential tradition described by Slichter, it was entirely predictable that the new industrial unions would draw on the experience of established trade unions. Richard Frankensteen, for example, claimed as his model for seniority the Brotherhood of Railway Trainmen ("whose seniority is reputedly and by application the best") in negotiating the first contract with Chrysler in April 1937; and Walter Reuther, when he became interested in revising the grievance system at General Motors, turned to Sidney Hillman for advice about how the garment trades had used impartial umpires. *UAW-Chrysler Agreement with Intro-duction* (April 1937), 6, file 2, box 3, Reuther Collection; Reuther to the Officers and Members of [GM] Locals, October 3, 1939, box 1, series 1, UAW-GM Department Collection, Reuther Archives.

50. For an instance capturing this shift of consciousness in one textile town, see Gary Gerstle, *Working-Class Americanism: The Politics of Labor in a Textile City, 1914–1960* (New York, 1989), ch. 4.

51. J. A. Beni Interview (1963), 4–5, Norm Bully Interview (1961), 2, both in Reuther Archives; Local 174 application card [n.d., 1938?], file 46, box 1, Reuther Collection; "Welcome, Fellow Workers" [UAW Local 7, January 1949], 14–15, box 3, Nick DiGaetano Collection, Reuther Archives.

52. Sumner H. Slichter, James J. Healy, and E. Robert Livernash, *The Impact of Collective Bargaining on Management* (Washington, D.C., 1960), 739, n. 2. It was a puzzling omission, explained by the authors by the lack of surveys "undoubtedly . . . due to the infrequent use of the process." But in fact arbitration was the established practice in coal, printing, the railroads, and all the clothing industries (i.e., in a substantial part of the older unionized sector). In 1941 the U.S. Conciliation Service reported arbitration clauses in 62 percent of the 1,200 contracts in its files. Fleming, *Labor Arbitration Process,* 13.

53. Slichter, Healy and Livernash, *Impact of Collective Bargaining,* 3

54. John P. Hoerr, *And the Wolf Finally Came: The Decline of the American Steel Industry* (Pittsburgh, Penn., 1988), 14, 20.

55. Thomas Kochan, Harry Katz, and Robert McKersie, *The Transformation of American Industrial Relations* (New York, 1986), 226–27.

56. It may be worth noting that critics from the right/center also seem inclined toward contingent historical explanations for workplace contractualism, as, for example, the theme of "the road not taken" in Hoerr, *And the Wolf Finally Came,* ch. 24.

57. For a highly revealing account of noncontractual bargaining in one industry, see Philip Scranton, *Figured Tapestry: Production, Markets and Power in Philadelphia, 1885–1941* (New York, 1989); and for its existence under militantly open-shop conditions, Howell Harris, "Employers' Collective Action in the Open-Shop Era: The Metal Manufacturers' Association of Philadelphia, ca. 1903–1933," in Steven Tolliday and Jonathan Zeitlin, eds., *The Power to Manage? Employer and Industrial Relations in Comparative-Historical Perspective* (London, 1991), 117–46.

58. The local's executive board minutes for 1940–41, in fact, contain regular notations of company letters complaining of too much time away from work by stewards. UAW Local 7 Collection, box 1, Reuther Archives. The GM agreement, on the other hand, limited shop committeemen to four hours of paid grievance time per day and then down to two hours in 1938 agreement.

59. Nick DiGaetano Interview (1959), Oral History Collection, Reuther Archives, quotations from pp. 14, 22–23, 48, 71–72, 73, 74. DiGaetano's grievance books as chief steward are in his own collection, box 1, in the Reuther Archives.